YORK NOTES

HAMLET

WILLIAM SHAKESPEARE

Notes by Jeff Wood

Longman
is an imprint of

PEARSON

YORK
PRESS

The right of Jeff Wood to be identified as the Author of this Work has been asserted
by him in accordance with the Copyright, Designs and Patents Act 1988

YORK PRESS
322 Old Brompton Road, London SW5 9JH

PEARSON EDUCATION LIMITED
Edinburgh Gate, Harlow,
Essex CM20 2JE, United Kingdom

Associated companies, branches and representatives throughout the world

First published 1998
This new and fully revised edition 2013

10 9 8 7

ISBN 978–1–4479–4887–2

Illustration on p. 9 by Neil Gower
Phototypeset by Chat Noir Design, France
Printed in Great Britain by Ashford Colour Press Ltd.

Photo credits:

© INTERFOTO/Alamy for page 6 / Garysa/Shutterstock.com for page 7 top / Minerva Studio/Shutterstock.com for page 7 bottom
/ © maximimages.com/Alamy for page 8 / sharpner/Shutterstock.com for page 11 / Tomasz Bidermann/Shutterstock.com for page
12 / kstudija/Shutterstock.com for page 13 / bg_knight/Shutterstock.com for page 14 / Anneka/Shutterstock.com for page 15 /
Zack C/Shutterstock.com for page 16 / Nejron Photo/Shutterstock.com for page 17 / Sashkin/Shutterstock.com for page 18 top /
wongwean/Shutterstock.com for page 18 bottom / Ekaterina Pokrovskaya/Shutterstock.com for page 19 / KA Photography
KEVM111/Shutterstock.com for page 20 / mangojuicy/Shutterstock.com for page 21 / LilKar/Shutterstock.com for page 22 /
ritarita/Shutterstock.com for page 23 / Jaroslaw Grudzinski/Shutterstock.com for page 24 / Netfalls - Remy
Musser/Shutterstock.com for page 25 top / Igor Kovalchuk/Shutterstock.com for page 25 bottom / Eric Isselee/Shutterstock.com
for page 26 / Alex Staroseltsev/Shutterstock.com for page 27 / Sergio Martinez/Shutterstock.com for page 28 /
David Hughes/Shutterstock.com for page 30 / MillaF/Shutterstock.com for page 31 middle / szpeti/Shutterstock.com for page 31
bottom / Brian A Jackson/Shutterstock.com for page 32 top / Serg Zastavkin/Shutterstock.com for page 32 bottom /
©iStockphoto.com/Thomas_EyeDesign for page 33 / Eric Isselee/Shutterstock.com for page 34 top / Gwoeii/Shutterstock.com for
page 34 bottom / Senol Yaman/Shutterstock.com for page 35 top / Anneka/Shutterstock.com for page 35 middle / Andrea
Danti/Shutterstock.com for page 36 / Maxx-Studio/Shutterstock.com for page 37 / solarseven/Shutterstock.com for page 39 /
Fotofermer/Shutterstock.com for page 40 / Nejron Photo/Shutterstock.com for page 41 / ©iStockphoto.com/irabell for page 42 /
St. Nick/Shutterstock.com for page 45 / Monika Wisniewska/Shutterstock.com for page 46 top/ Eric Isselee/Shutterstock.com for
page 46 bottom / Krivosheev Vitaly/Shutterstock.com for page 47 / nahariyani/Shutterstock.com for page 48 top /
bg_knightShutterstock.com for page 48 bottom / Shebeko/Shutterstock.com for page 49 / Robyn Mackenzie/Shutterstock.com for
page 50 / HomeStudio/Shutterstock.com for page 51 / konstantynov/Shutterstock.com for page 52 /
Elena Elisseeva/Shutterstock.com for page 53 / kovtynfoto/Shutterstock.com for page 54 / Pukhov Konstantin/Shutterstock.com
for page 56 / Michael Drager/Shutterstock.com for page 57 / Matt Gibson/Shutterstock.com for page 58 /
Dirk Ercken/Shutterstock.com for page 59 / Piotr Krzeslak/Shutterstock.com for page 60 / Dan Kosmayer/Shutterstock.com for
page 61 / Dragana Gerasimoski/Shutterstock.com for page 61 / De Mango/Shutterstock.com for page 62 /
ER_09/Shutterstock.com for page 63 / bg_knight/Shutterstock.com for page 64 / Pablo H Caridad/Shutterstock.com for page 65 /
Nejron Photo/Shutterstock.com for page 66 / ABIES/Shutterstock.com for page 67 / bg_knight/Shutterstock.com for page 68 /
Elnur/Shutterstock.com for page 69 / konstantynov/Shutterstock.com for page 70 / Catmando/Shutterstock.com for page 71 /
Ekaterina Pokrovskaya/Shutterstock.com for page 72 / ©iStockphoto.com/lenta for page 73 / George Muresan/Shutterstock.com
for page 74 / IgorGolovniov/Shutterstock.com for page 75 / ©iStockphoto.com/duncan1890 for page 76 top /
unkreativ/Shutterstock.com for page 76 bottom / rui vale souse/Shutterstock.com for page 77 top / © Universal Images Group
Limited/Alamy for page 77 bottom / Jeff Banke/Shutterstock.com for page 78 top / Simon Bratt/Shutterstock.com for page 78
middle / kanvag/Shutterstock.com for page 79 / koya979/Shutterstock.com for page 80 / Nejron Photo/Shutterstock.com for page
81 top / Sergej Razvodovskij/Shutterstock.com for page 81 bottom / Anna Omelchenko/Shutterstock.com for page 82 middle /
Syda Productions/Shutterstock.com for page 82 bottom / ULKASTUDIO/Shutterstock.com for page 83 / gillmar/Shutterstock.com
for page 84 / Gwoeii/Shutterstock.com for page 85 / Kachalkina Veronika/Shutterstock.com for page 86 /
©iStockphoto.com/ultramarinfoto for page 87 / Roman Dementyev/Shutterstock.com for page 88 / kuleczka/Shutterstock.com for
page 89 / Valentina Photos/Shutterstock.com for page 90 top / Lightspring/Shutterstock.com for page 91 / Dimedrol68/
Shutterstock.com for page 92 / © The Print Collector/Alamy for page 93 / © Eye Ubiquitous/Alamy for page 94 / © North Wind
Picture Archives/Alamy for page 95 / Neftali/Shutterstock.com for page 96 top / © Mary Evans Picture Library/Alamy for page 96
bottom / ollyy/Shutterstock.com for page 97 / Maxx-Studio/Shutterstock.com for page 98 / Sebastian Kaulitzki/Shutterstock.com
for page 99 / Sergey Nivens/Shutterstock.com for page 100 top / STILLFX/Shutterstock.com for page 100 middle

CONTENTS

PART ONE: INTRODUCING *HAMLET*

PART TWO: STUDYING *HAMLET*

PART THREE: CHARACTERS AND THEMES

PART FOUR: STRUCTURE, FORM AND LANGUAGE

PART FIVE: CONTEXTS AND CRITICAL DEBATES

PART SIX: GRADE BOOSTER

ESSENTIAL STUDY TOOLS

HOW TO STUDY *HAMLET*

These Notes can be used to help you explore, study and (where relevant) revise *Hamlet* for your examation or assessment.

READING THE PLAY

Read through the play fairly quickly. This will give you some idea of the shape of the drama, the key moments, the pace, style and sequence of events. You may like to ask yourself:

● How does each character change or develop? How do my responses to him/her alter as the action unfolds?

● How does Shakespeare allow the audience to see into the minds and motives of the characters? Does he use asides, **soliloquies** or other dramatic devices, for example?

● What sort of language do different characters use? Does Shakespeare use **imagery**, or recurring motifs or symbols?

● What impression does the setting – Elsinore – make on my reading and response to the play?

● How could the play be presented on the stage in different ways? How could different types of performance affect the audience's interpretation of the play?

On further readings, make notes around these bullet points, bearing in mind the Assessment Objectives, such as the importance of form, language, structure (AO2); links and connections to other texts (AO3) and the context/background for the play (AO4). The ojectives may seem daunting at first but these Notes will suggest particular details to explore.

INTERPRETING OR CRITIQUING THE PLAY

Although it's not helpful to think in terms of the play being 'good' or 'bad', you should consider the different ways the play can be read. How have critics responded to it? Do their views match yours – or do you take a different viewpoint? Are there different ways you can interpret specific events, characters or settings? This is a key aspect in AO3, and it can be helpful to keep a log of your responses and the various perspectives which are expressed both by established critics, but also by classmates, your teacher, or other readers.

REFERENCES AND SOURCES

You will be expected to draw on critics' or reviewers' comments, and refer to relevant literary or historical sources that might have influenced Shakespeare or his contemporaries. Make sure you make accurate, clear notes of writers or sources you have used, for example noting down titles of works, authors' names, website addresses, dates, etc. You may not have to reference all of these when you respond to a text, but knowing the source of your information will allow you to go back to it, if need be – and to check its accuracy and relevance.

REVISING FOR AND RESPONDING TO AN ASSESSED TASK OR EXAM QUESTION

The structure and the contents of these Notes are designed to help to give you the relevant information or ideas you need to answer tasks you have been set. First, work out the key words or ideas from the task (for example, 'form', 'Act I', 'Ophelia', etc.), then read the relevant parts of the Notes that relate to these terms or words, selecting what is useful for revision or written response. Then, turn to **Part Six: Grade Booster** for help in formulating your response.

> **GRADE BOOSTER** AO2
>
> An enjoyable and effective way to study *Hamlet* is to listen to an audio recordings. There are many audiobooks of *Hamlet*, including excellent performances by Derek Jacobi and Kenneth Branagh in the title role.

HAMLET IN CONTEXT

SHAKESPEARE'S LIFE AND TIMES

1564	Shakespeare born in Stratford-upon-Avon
1570	Pope excommunicates Queen Elizabeth
1587	Mary Queen of Scots implicated in plot against Queen Elizabeth and executed
1588	Defeat of the Spanish Armada
c.1588	Early play of *Hamlet*, probably by Thomas Kyd
c.1590–2	Shakespeare writing for Pembroke's Men. Plays include the popular bloody **Revenge Tragedy**, *Titus Andronicus*
1594	Formation of The Lord Chamberlain's Men, including Kempe, Burbage and Shakespeare as shareholders
1594	*Romeo and Juliet*
1599	*Henry V, Julius Caesar, As You Like It.* The Lord Chamberlain's Men open the Globe Theatre; Kempe leaves the company
1600	Children's companies acting at St Paul's and Blackfriars. *Hamlet* probably first performed: it is immediately popular
1601	Essex's rebellion and execution
1603	Death of Queen Elizabeth; accession of King James I

HAMLET: ARTISTRY AND POPULARITY

Hamlet was written by Shakespeare around the turn of the seventeenth century. Elizabethan London was a cauldron of intellectual and artistic debate. The atmosphere was politically turbulent and dangerous. But above all the artistic debate was lively and experimental. And Shakespeare's art was at the stage where, having brought his poetic technique and his stagecraft to a degree of mastery which aroused both the envy and admiration of his contemporaries, he was beginning to attempt radical new ways of engaging his audiences. The **soliloquies** of Brutus in *Julius Caesar*, for example, dramatised the **protagonist's** inner life and his characteristic ways of thinking, and the development of Shakespeare's **imagery** created new possibilities for generating atmosphere and exploring themes.

One reason for *Hamlet's* enduring popularity is its artistic exuberance. There is no other play which offers such a rich and varied diet of incident, **characterisation**, subject matter and language. To explore the variety of poetic styles Shakespeare employs in this work would take a sizeable volume. We have magnificent bombastic **pastiche** when the First Player narrates a riveting episode from the Trojan War. There are Ophelia's pretty, plaintive-bawdy songs and the gravedigger's humorously unsettling one. The Ghost and his widow are given **narrative set pieces** of great power, Gertrude's having generated numerous representations. Claudius has some of the most accomplished **rhetoric** of any Shakespearean villain, poised on a razor's edge between engaging plausibility and evident hypocrisy. There is Hamlet's moving declaration of love for Horatio and his friend's tender farewell. And as **foils** to all this eloquence, we have the verbal absurdities of Polonius, Laertes and Osric, Hamlet's biting **satire**, and the confused wanderings of Rosencrantz and Guildenstern. And then, of course, there are the soliloquies of Hamlet and Claudius.

STUDY FOCUS: *HAMLET*'S SOLILOQUIES A02

These speeches, above all, give *Hamlet* its distinction and account for much of its absorbing interest. Shakespeare is engaged in the most complex task: to give an audience the illusion that they are listening to two very different people (Hamlet and Claudius) trying to think clearly about fundamental human problems. Although Shakespeare is writing a play, listening to the soliloquies in *Hamlet* is almost like reading a novel. We are at the edge of what is artistically achievable: presenting genuinely complex, apparently dynamic states of mind in a clear and intelligible manner. Deciding

whether these speeches achieve what they attempt to achieve is genuinely problematic. In exploring them we find ourselves asking fundamental questions about human psychology, epistemology (the theory of knowledge) and the nature of language. The soliloquies also make us think about about the nature of texts and audiences, and the challenge posed to Shakespeare, the artist, in creating them.

CRITICAL VIEWPOINT A03

'It may seem a **paradox**, but I cannot help being of the opinion that the plays of Shakespeare are less calculated for performance on stage than those of almost any other dramatist whatsoever. ... There is so much in them, which comes not under the province of acting ...' Charles Lamb, *The Tragedies of Shakespeare* (1818).

HAMLET: PRINCE OF DENMARK

Hamlet is never a dry read. It is universally popular because the central character is somebody to whom few people can feel indifferent. For every playgoer or reader who finds Hamlet a puritan, a coward or a bully, there are a dozen who earnestly identify with him as a kind of spokesman for their own experience of the bewildering human condition.

It is of little consequence what view we take of Hamlet on first acquaintance; he fascinates us, frustrates any attempt to reduce him to a tidy analysis and demands that we sit through and share his trials again and again. He is fascinating partly because he is so passionately interested in things himself. Like us, he cares about the theatre. He is excited and tested by language and irritated by its misuse. He is by turns full of energy, originating ideas more quickly than others can keep up with, and then dejected and forlorn at his isolation, disgust and impotence.

As we develop as readers or audience-members, Hamlet and his interesting problems develop with us. At one point in the play he says: 'for there is nothing either good or bad but thinking makes it so' (II.2.239–40). That sentence has many different meanings, several of which operate simultaneously at that moment in the drama. But one thing the words underline is the necessity and the excitement of thinking.

STUDY FOCUS: KEY ISSUES IN *HAMLET* A03

Hamlet urges us to think about so many things. It is a family drama. Brother and sister, brother and brother, father and son, father and daughter, mother and son, son and stepfather: these are the dynamics which generate so much of the play's electricity. Then we have friendship and friendships betrayed; the nature of duty: to one's country, to those in power, to oneself, to God, to truth. There is the enduringly absorbing debate about sexuality and sexual morality, central to any reading of this play. And there is the question of power – of seizing and losing control; the powerlessness of individuals in a world which marginalises them. As society continues to change, the nature of these debates shifts.

And there, perhaps, is the reason why a four-hundred-years-worn text in Elizabethan English continues to engage people from so many different cultures and **ideological** positions. In this play Shakespeare identifies and dramatises, in colourful, memorable and provocative ways, issues central to everyone's critical self. The question of who we are and why; where we come from, where we have got to and where we will go next. And the degree to which it is possible for any individual to share these investigations with others. The focus shifts continually between appreciating the sureness of Shakespeare's craft and responding to the complex, serious and beautiful game he has set in motion between a text and an ever-renewing audience.

We enjoy *Hamlet* as we enjoy watching somebody doing his best to do something all but impossible and, by a whisker, achieving it.

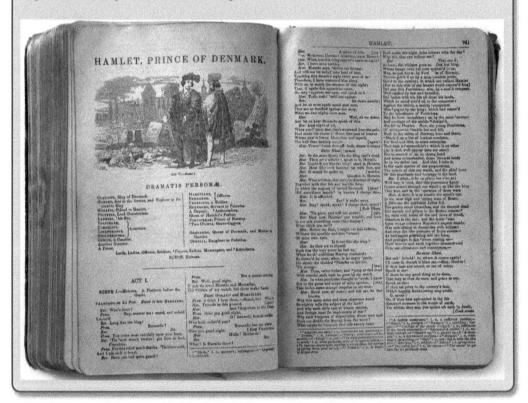

CHARACTERS IN *HAMLET*

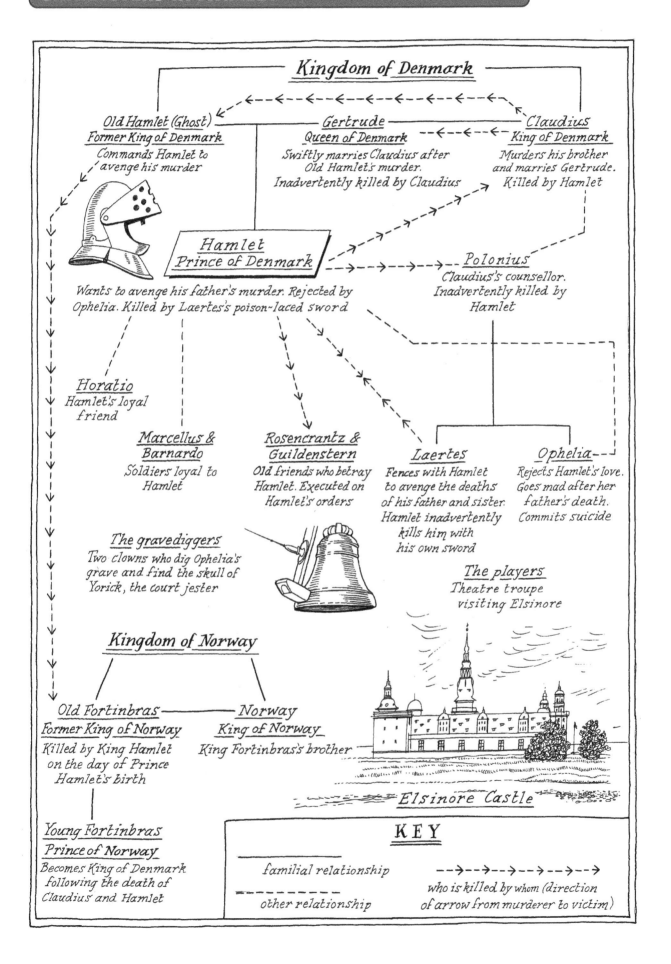

Kingdom of Denmark

Old Hamlet (Ghost)
Former King of Denmark
Commands Hamlet to
avenge his murder

Gertrude
Queen of Denmark
Swiftly marries Claudius after
Old Hamlet's murder.
Inadvertently killed by Claudius

Claudius
King of Denmark
Murders his brother
and marries Gertrude.
Killed by Hamlet

Hamlet
Prince of Denmark
Wants to avenge his father's murder. Rejected by
Ophelia. Killed by Laertes's poison-laced sword

Polonius
Claudius's counsellor.
Inadvertently killed by
Hamlet

Horatio
Hamlet's loyal
friend

**Marcellus &
Barnardo**
Soldiers loyal to
Hamlet

**Rosencrantz &
Guildenstern**
Old friends who betray
Hamlet. Executed on
Hamlet's orders

Laertes
Fences with Hamlet
to avenge the deaths
of his father and sister.
Hamlet inadvertently
kills him with
his own sword

Ophelia
Rejects Hamlet's love.
Goes mad after her
father's death.
Commits suicide

The gravediggers
Two clowns who dig Ophelia's
grave and find the skull of
Yorick, the court jester

The players
Theatre troupe
visiting Elsinore

Kingdom of Norway

Old Fortinbras
Former King of Norway
Killed by King Hamlet
on the day of Prince
Hamlet's birth

Norway
King of Norway
King Fortinbras's brother

Elsinore Castle

Young Fortinbras
Prince of Norway
Becomes King of Denmark
following the death of
Claudius and Hamlet

KEY

——————— familial relationship

----------- other relationship

--->--->--->--> who is killed by whom (direction
of arrow from murderer to victim)

SYNOPSIS

ACT I

THE VILLAIN ON THE THRONE

Valiant King Hamlet has died. His brother has succeeded him as King of Denmark and as husband of Queen Gertrude. The new King is fully in control of the court, despite his hasty and incestuous marriage. Prince Hamlet alone is still in mourning for the late King. In a **soliloquy**, he expresses his revulsion at the state of affairs. A ghost closely resembling the late King appears at the castle. He reveals that his brother seduced the Queen and poisoned him. He commands Hamlet to avenge his murder. Hamlet vows to undertake the task.

Meanwhile, Ophelia, daughter of the King's advisor, Polonius, and with whom Hamlet is in love, is told by her father and by her brother, Laertes, to end the relationship.

ACT II

PLOT AND COUNTER-PLOT

Some weeks have passed and Hamlet continues to behave oddly. Anxious, the King asks the Prince's fellow students, Rosencrantz and Guildenstern, to spy on him. Polonius tells the King about Ophelia's rejection of Hamlet's advances, and suggests that this is the cause of the Prince's 'lunacy' (II.2.49). The men decide to contrive a meeting between Hamlet and Ophelia, so they can eavesdrop on their conversation.

Rosencrantz and Guildenstern admit to Hamlet that they were 'sent for' (II.2.277). When a theatre company arrives, Hamlet requests 'a passionate speech' (II.2.393). The **recitation** deeply moves Hamlet. He asks the actors to perform a play 'something like the murder of [his] father' (II.2.548). He wants it performed in front of his uncle so he can observe the King's reactions.

ACT III

SURVEILLANCE AND CONFESSION

Just before Polonius's plan is put into action, Claudius reveals to the audience that he carries a 'heavy burden' (III.1.54) of guilt. Ophelia pretends to read, whilst Polonius and Claudius hide to listen to her conversation with Hamlet.

Hamlet delivers the 'To be, or not to be' (III.1.56) soliloquy, then encounters Ophelia. He soon realises she is part of a conspiracy, and directs his outrage at both her and the two men he guesses are listening. Whilst Ophelia is saddened by the apparently mad Hamlet, the King is convinced his nephew is sane and dangerous. Polonius proposes to spy on them in the Queen's room, after the play.

Hamlet asks his loyal friend, Horatio, to observe the King during the performance. Hamlet sits beside Ophelia to watch the King. The play is preceded by a mime re-enacting the Ghost's account of the murder, which elicits no reaction from Claudius or Gertrude.

In the first scene of *The Mousetrap*, the Player Queen vows to be forever faithful to her husband. In the interval, Hamlet asks his mother's opinion of the play. She replies, 'The lady doth protest too much methinks' (III.2.211). The second scene represents the murder. When the King rises, displeased, and the performance breaks up in confusion, it is unclear what has upset the King. Hamlet, intoxicated by the experience, gives a soliloquy in which he imagines taking revenge. However, it is not the King he pursues, but his mother.

Hastily, the King makes plans to send Hamlet away. Alone, Claudius struggles to pray, racked with the guilt of his 'foul murder' (III.3, 52). Hamlet passes him on his way to Gertrude's room. He has the perfect opportunity to send the King 'to heaven' (III.3.74), but he pauses: he cannot kill the King at prayer and so proceeds to his mother's chamber.

Polonius hides and listens as the Queen reproaches Hamlet for his behaviour. Hamlet condemns her actions towards his father. Terrified, Gertrude calls for help. Hearing a noise, Hamlet stabs the man in hiding, believing him to be Claudius. Gertrude accuses Hamlet of committing a 'rash and bloody deed' (III. 4.27); Hamlet replies that it is not as bad as killing a king and marrying his brother. The Queen's shocked response establishes her innocence of the murder. Hamlet's criticism of her sins forces her to acknowledge them. Hamlet is visited a second time by the Ghost who comes to 'whet [his] almost blunted purpose' (III.4.110).

ACT IV

MADNESS AND REVENGE

We see Claudius and Gertrude drawing apart. Neither confides in the other. In a **soliloquy**, the King reveals he is sending Hamlet to his death. As Hamlet is about to leave Denmark for England, he encounters the army of Young Fortinbras, en route to fight, simply for glory. Hamlet's initial response is contempt, but upon reflection, he seems to find Young Fortinbras's behaviour glorious and a rebuke of his own lack of action.

With Hamlet off-stage, the focus moves to Ophelia, now mad as a result of her father's death, and then to Laertes. Laertes returns from Paris, seeking revenge for his father's death. The King exploits Laetes's distress and the reappearance of Ophelia refuels Laertes's passion.

Meanwhile, Horatio receives a letter from Hamlet, who has escaped from the ship that was taking him to his execution. A second, similar letter reaches Claudius. He and Laertes unite and plot Hamlet's death. Gertrude enters and reports Ophelia's death by drowning.

ACT V

THE TRAGIC DENOUEMENT

In the graveyard, two sextons (gravediggers) discuss Ophelia's suicide. Hamlet has returned, a different man. He is unaware of his uncle's plot against him.

Handling the skulls in the graveyard, Hamlet reflects on how death is the great leveller. Ophelia's funeral procession interrupts him. Hamlet mocks Laertes's theatrical display of grief and the two fight by her grave.

Hamlet gives Horatio details of his escape. He now feels it would be 'perfect conscience' (V.2.67) to kill the King and damnable to let him live. The Prince is challenged to a fencing match with Laertes. Although he senses underhand tactics, Hamlet is ready to face death.

The play ends with an exciting and cleverly contrived fencing match. It results in the deaths of all the principal **protagonists**, followed by brief, powerful tributes to young Hamlet. Horatio is left to tell the Prince's story. Young Fortinbras assumes power in Denmark.

CRITICAL VIEWPOINT **A03**

'As he endeavours to act aright, we approve and esteem him. But his ... constitution renders him unequal to the contest: he displays ... weaknesses and imperfections ...: he thus becomes an object not of blame, but of genuine and tender regret.' William Richardson, *Some of Shakespeare's Remarkable Characters* (1783).

CHECK THE BOOK **A03**

Having performed *Hamlet* on the stage, Macready recalls: 'End of the play was good. Energy! Energy! Energy!' Macready's Diaries, 1833, in *Responses to Shakespeare*, ed. John Adler (1997).

ACT I SCENE 1

SUMMARY

- It is midnight and bitterly cold. On the battlements of Elsinore Castle, Barnardo, Marcellus and the scholar Horatio take over the watch from Francisco.
- The soldiers tell the sceptical Horatio about the Ghost they have seen on two previous nights.
- The Ghost appears; dressed in full armour, it closely resembles Old Hamlet, the late warrior-king of Denmark. Offended by Horatio's challenge, it stalks away.
- We learn that Young Fortinbras of Norway threatens to invade Denmark. He hopes to recover by force lands lost by his dead father in a ceremonious combat with Old Hamlet thirty years ago. We hear of Denmark's frantic preparations for war.
- The Ghost reappears. Horatio questions it formally but before it can answer, the cock crows, the Ghost 'start[s] like a guilty thing' (line 148) and vanishes.
- The men decide to tell Young Hamlet what they have seen.

ANALYSIS

WHO'S THERE? THE PROBLEM OF THE GHOST

Urgently and economically, using fragments of **colloquial** conversation, Shakespeare establishes the edgy atmosphere of a bitterly cold midnight watch, full of anxiety and dread. The verse does not flow. Broken rhythms generate a mood of unease, apprehension and confusion. The play begins with a question rich in **ironic** implications and in the next twenty lines come six more questions. Francisco feels 'sick at heart' (line 9) and this evocative and puzzling phrase initiates a stream of **imagery** of physical and mental disease which will characterise the whole play. The phrase prepares us for Prince Hamlet's melancholy in the following scene.

Horatio is established as a scholar, an upright Christian and a sceptic: he is a reliable witness, a moral touchstone (someone we can trust) and an educated commentator. He signals to the audience that there can be no doubt of the Ghost's being 'something more than fantasy' (line 54); he confirms its striking resemblance to the last King of Denmark, the heroic warrior, King Hamlet. But the movements of the Ghost, at one moment 'majestical' (line 143) at another 'start[ing] like a guilty thing' (line 148), signal its ambiguous nature. We cannot tell if it is good or bad or something morally more complicated. Throughout the scene, the men refer to the Ghost as 'it', a 'thing'; although awestruck and terrified, they do not defer to the Ghost as if it actually were the old King. Horatio accuses the Ghost of usurping of the 'fair and warlike form' (line 47) of Old Hamlet. Working out the morally correct response to the Ghost and the information it brings will be the central theme of the play.

STUDY FOCUS: REGIME CHANGE – TWO IDEOLOGIES A04

The way this scene develops suggests, misleadingly, that the play will explore a struggle between the sons of the old kings. It also suggests a tension between different systems of value. Old Hamlet and Old Fortinbras (the name means 'strong arm') were warrior kings with medieval ideas of honour and integrity. Old Hamlet is described in **epic** language: 'So frowned he once, when in an angry parle. He smote the sledded Polack on the ice.' (lines 62–3) Young Fortinbras's opportunistic and lawless attack is very different in character from his father's ceremonious challenge to Old Hamlet. We wait to see how Young Hamlet will behave. The scene offers a perspective on events at odds with the one we will be given at court in what follows. Talk of 'post-haste and romage in the land' (line 107) suggests a Denmark in turmoil: it is the perspective of a group of characters who owe their duty and love to Young Hamlet. They maintain this loyalty to him throughout: the King never learns about the Ghost. In a play which will be about treachery and deception, these men alone never betray the Prince.

GLOSSARY

44	**harrows me**	tears me apart, cuts me up
46	**usurp'st**	trespasses, defies the authority of God
107	**post-haste and romage**	frantic, desperate activity and turmoil
154	**extravagant and erring**	wandering beyond permitted bounds, unruly
166	**russet mantle**	cloak made of coarse, reddish brown material, such as a farmer might wear

ACT I SCENE 2

SUMMARY

- Claudius, the new King of Denmark, addresses the court confidently on the occasion of his hasty marriage to Gertrude following the sudden death of his brother, King Hamlet.
- He deals with Young Fortinbras's threatened invasion using diplomacy.
- He grants Laertes's suit to be allowed to return to France. Laertes is the son of Claudius's first minister, Polonius.
- Claudius and Gertrude accuse Hamlet of mourning his father excessively and Hamlet is denied permission to return to Wittenburg.
- Left alone on stage, the grieving Hamlet expresses his melancholy and his contempt for the King and Queen.
- Horatio, Marcellus and Bernardo tell Hamlet about the Ghost.

ANALYSIS

THE SMILING KING

'[O]ne may smile, and smile, and be a villain' (I.5.108)

After the darkness, tension and confusion of the opening scene, there is light, colour and the whole Danish court assembled in a mood of celebration. The dramatic contrast achieved by **juxtaposing** these two scenes could hardly be greater. Contrary to our expectations, we discover that neither Young Fortinbras nor Young Hamlet has succeeded his father as king; in both Norway and Denmark, the old king's brother is on the throne. Exactly how this came about we never learn; Hamlet tells us later that Claudius 'Popped in between th'election and my hopes' (V.2.65). Just as Norway is a feeble ('impotent and bed-rid', line 29) substitute for Old Fortinbras, so Claudius is a very different character from his famous warrior brother: we see them in successive scenes and this allows us to register how different they look.

The scene opens with a long rhetorical flourish in which Claudius seeks to ingratiate himself with the court by creating an impression of confident control, security and propriety. Yet immediately there are false notes. Claudius has not just taken his brother's throne, he has married his widow. Shakespeare's audience would regard such a marriage as incestuous. And it has happened so quickly that funeral and marriage seem inappropriately confused: 'With mirth in funeral and with dirge in marriage' (line 12). The King's confident, carefully balanced **antithetical** statements are intended to convey reasonableness: 'in equal scale weighing delight and dole' (line 13). But although the fluent movement of the verse tries to carry the listener along with it, the oiliness of his speech is similar to the 'glib and oily art' which characterises the insincere gushings of Goneril and Regan in the opening scene of *King Lear* (see **Extended commentary: Act I Scene 2, lines 1–67**). The rest of the court, Claudius tells us, 'have freely gone/With this affair along' (lines 15–16); certainly they seem to have no memory of the old war hero. Only Hamlet is wearing mourning.

STUDY FOCUS: HAMLET THE DISSIDENT `A02`

As far as the audience is concerned, Hamlet has already undermined the new King's authority. The play is called *The Tragedy of Hamlet, Prince of Denmark*, not *Claudius, the King*. The audience has come to see one more famous actor tackle the most celebrated role in drama. When this scene opens, the audience looks not at Claudius but at the man standing apart, dressed in black. His silence is more articulate, more authoritative, than all of Claudius's clever words; his alienation counts for more than the court's compliance ('the censure of the which one must ... o'erweigh a whole theatre of others', III.2.22–4).

THE FALLEN QUEEN

If Hamlet is offended by his uncle's complacency, his anger is provoked much more fully by Gertrude's behaviour, especially when she accuses him of being an actor: 'Seems madam? nay it is, I know not seems'(line 76). Surrounded by people pretending – Claudius claiming the memory of his 'dear brother' is 'green' (lines 1–2) yet expressing not a single word of grief; his mother behaving as if she never had a loving husband; the court silent about the incestuous marriage – Hamlet is furious that Gertrude should accuse *him* of pretending. Surely it was his mother who was acting the bereaved widow just a week or two previously?

When Hamlet describes the 'actions that a man might play' (line 84) he seems to be recalling his mother's funereal bearing when, just weeks before remarrying, and therefore presumably in an adulterous relationship with Claudius, she wept 'like Niobe, all tears' (I.2.149). Gertrude's **platitudinous**: 'all that lives must die,/Passing through nature to eternity' (lines 72–3) sounds as insincere and shallow as a greetings card sentiment by virtue of the cheap **rhyming couplet**. For Hamlet, as later for the gravedigger (V.1), equivocation, the misuse of language, is a barometer of hypocrisy and vice.

STUDY FOCUS: CLAUDIUS THE SPIN DOCTOR `A02`

Hamlet simply refuses to respond to Claudius's **specious reasoning** in lines 87–117. The King tries to make light of Hamlet's hostility, spinning his refusal to speak to him as 'a loving and a fair reply' and 'This gentle and unforced accord of Hamlet' (lines 121–3). In order to end the scene with a confident flourish, Claudius associates himself with rowdy drinking: 'No jocund health that Denmark drinks today/But the great cannon to the clouds shall tell,/And the king's rouse the heaven shall bruit again,/Re-speaking earthly thunder' (lines 125–8). The **imagery** suggests a man playing a part, presenting himself as an earthly Jove the Thunderer, the Roman king of the gods; the effect is to reveal him as a loud and over confident braggart. He will repeat the flourish in the final scene.

HAMLET'S FIRST SOLILOQUY

The major artistic advance Shakespeare made in *Hamlet* was in developing the audience's understanding of the central **protagonist's** inner life. Whereas Brutus in *Julius Caesar* has about fifty lines of **soliloquy**, Hamlet has approximately two hundred. Throughout the play, Hamlet's soliloquies will dramatise the idea of a man wrestling to make sense of complex thoughts and feelings.

Hamlet's first soliloquy contrasts dramatically with Claudius's glib, flowing lines. The listless tempo of the words 'How weary, stale, flat and unprofitable' (line 133) conveys Hamlet's almost suicidal melancholy. The frequent interjections of dismay convey the young man's distress. There is nothing here which sounds rehearsed. The verse starts and stops, punctuated by expressions of pain and confusion: 'heaven and earth,/Must I remember?' (lines 142–3). The disjointed rhythm and dislocated progress of Hamlet's thoughts convey to us his inner turmoil. We seem to eavesdrop on someone in the very process of thinking: 'But two months dead – nay not so much, not two' (line 138).

The terms in which the Prince remembers his father are revealing. He was not just an 'excellent' (line 139) king, but superhuman, at the opposite end of the human spectrum from Claudius: 'Hyperion to a satyr' (line 140). The picture Hamlet paints of his father's love for his mother is on an **epic** scale: he was so loving to her 'That he might not beteem the winds of heaven/Visit her face too roughly' (lines 141–2). This conjures up an **image** of a huge protective figure shielding Gertrude from all dangers. Hamlet's bewilderment and disgust at his mother's hasty and incestuous remarriage is revealed in his comparison of her to an experienced and lusty post-horse. This is present not only in the imagery but in the sounds of Hamlet's words. Hissing **sibilants** convey the young man's repulsion as he imagines his mother and his uncle in bed together: 'Oh most wicked speed, to post/With such dexterity to incestuous sheets' (lines 156–7). Gertrude's shameful conduct has made him lose faith in all women: 'frailty, thy name is woman' (line 146).

Hamlet feels bound to suffer in silence: 'But break, my heart, for I must hold my tongue' (line 159). For the audience, Hamlet's words are **ironic**. They know a ghost, resembling his father and dressed in steel, is haunting the castle. Even knowing nothing of the conventions of **Revenge Tragedy**, the audience would realise that Hamlet will not be permitted simply to suffer. One important detail in this **soliloquy** helps us understand the moral framework within which Hamlet will struggle. Before he mentions his father, Hamlet acknowledges a greater authority: 'the Everlasting' (line 131) whose moral code forbids suicide and outlaws revenge.

CONTEXT

The 'canon 'gainst self-slaughter' (line 132) is the Sixth Commandment, which forbids all murder, including suicide. Unlike Claudius, Hamlet feels bound by such an order.

GRADE BOOSTER

Although the name Claudius appears in the list of characters, it is used nowhere in the play. It is used in these Notes as an alternative to 'the King' or 'Gertrude's husband' or 'Hamlet's uncle/step-father'. It is a good idea to avoid repeating the same term in the same paragraph.

GLOSSARY

13	**delight and dole**	happiness and sadness
72–4	**common … common**	**word play** on two meanings of the word: Gertrude means that people die every day, Hamlet that his mother's behaviour is vulgar, not what you'd expect of a queen
94	**impious stubbornness**	refusing to behave as God would expect you to behave
129	**solid**	most modern editors prefer 'sullied' to 'solid'; critics have argued about whether Hamlet is distressed because his flesh is too tough or because it is too contaminated
150	**that wants discourse of reason**	lacking language and thus the ability to think

EXTENDED COMMENTARY

ACT I SCENE 2, LINES 1–67

The harlot's cheek, beautied with plastering art,
Is not more ugly to the thing that helps it
Than is my deed to my most painted word. (III.1.51–3)

A familiar Shakespearean theme is the discrepancy between appearance and reality. Putting on a face, face painting and being two faced are all aspects of acting, 'seeming', pretending to be what you are not. Claudius's opening speech appears relaxed, level-headed, eloquent and persuasive. But Shakespeare signals to the audience, long before they hear Claudius confess it, that the King's public mask conceals a troubled mind and a corrupt soul. The speech is so polished and so carefully structured that it is evidently rehearsed. Claudius's performance takes in the court but it does not take us in. How does Shakespeare make us suspicious of this charming, smiling speaker?

It would be difficult to imagine a greater contrast with the chopped, nervous rhythms which characterised the opening of the play than the opening of Act I Scene 2. Claudius's first three sentences occupy, respectively, seven, nine and nine lines of flexible and flowing verse. In the first two long sentences, one point leads to the next with seemingly effortless poise, to be rounded off with a condescending flourish: 'Though … Yet … Therefore … nor … for all, our thanks' (lines 1–16). Claudius sugars over the questionable marriage, carrying the court with him. Deliberately, he reminds everyone that until very recently Gertrude was his sister-in-law and is now his wife. It is as if he is testing the court to see if anyone dares breathe the word 'incest'. He pauses and, in many productions, receives at this point the polite applause his performance expects. Claudius deals with affairs in a businesslike way. Unlike his dead brother, the new King is no warrior; he halts Young Fortinbras's incursion with diplomacy. He is confident enough to dismiss Fortinbras, who holds, 'a weak supposal of [his] worth' (line 18) – using this as proof of the young man's folly.

In employing the royal plural ('our', 'us', 'ourselves', 'we') so frequently, the new King sounds like someone trying to convince himself he is not a usurper, 'A cutpurse of the empire and the rule,/That from a shelf the precious diadem stole/And put it in his pocket' (III.4.99–101). Yet Claudius does not sound to the court like a man wracked by his conscience: he presents himself as someone whose judgement controls his passions. He says 'discretion' (line 5) has overcome his natural grief for his 'dear brother' (line 1). Sensibly, he has balanced happiness and distress: 'In equal scale weighing delight and dole' (line 13). The **blank verse** flows and his sentiments sound plausible, until we ask ourselves whether emotions can be measured out like currants. Shakespeare gives Claudius just enough hollow phrases to alert the theatre audience to his hypocrisy. What is 'wisest sorrow' (line 6)? How would 'defeated joy' (line 10) feel? Can a person have 'one auspicious and one dropping eye' (line 11) unless he is two-faced? Surely 'mirth in funeral' and 'dirge in marriage' (line 12) would be grotesque? No one on stage asks these common-sense questions. The rhythm, the music of Claudius's verse carries him through, while the imagery Shakespeare gives him tells us a different story.

In his stage-managed dealing with Laertes, the King parades a caring, indulgent self. He flatters Laertes, using his name four times in just nine lines. Happy to play the King's game, Laertes answers him in appropriate language. Shrewdly, he refers not to the dead King's funeral, but to the new King's coronation as the reason he left France 'willingly' (line 52). In rewarding Laertes for his servile performance, Claudius is signalling to

CONTEXT **A04**

A **Freudian** slip? Shakespeare's audience would notice that Claudius links his brother's death ('he that died today') to 'the first corse' (line 105). The very first murder was committed by the jealous Cain, who killed his virtuous brother Abel (Genesis 4:8).

CONTEXT **A04**

In **Renaissance** literature, kings are often compared to the Sun. Hamlet compares his father to Hyperion, the sun god.

Hamlet that deference is what he demands. The exchange contrasts dramatically with what follows.

That Claudius deals with three items of business before confronting the 'elephant in the room', his black-suited nephew, is another hint from Shakespeare that the King feels far more uneasy than he seems to be. His comfortable control of affairs is abruptly checked by the Prince's cryptic but evident hostility. There is a striking discord between the steady rhythm and melodious tone of the **blank verse** we have been hearing and the Prince's witty and staccato responses; Hamlet's words are harsh and oblique. He speaks in riddles so that he can be rude to the clever Claudius whilst giving little away to the court. 'A little more than kin and less than kind' (line 65) – Hamlet is 'more than kin' now he's both Claudius's nephew and his stepson. He is 'less than kind' in two senses of the word: he is neither 'kindly' disposed towards his uncle, nor does he think he is of the same 'kind', meaning the same species.

They spar a second time, Hamlet continuing to speak in a private language where a word has many different meanings: 'I am too much i'th'sun' (line 67). His incestuous uncle's fawning, calling him his 'son', revolts him. He is having too much of the word 'son' and also of the 'Sun' itself. Shortly after this episode, Hamlet will express his longing for death, to be literally out of the sun. As the proud son of King Hamlet, he is too much his father's son to submit to his uncle. Shakespeare is very fond of **puns**: they invite us to recognise ambiguity; that things may not be as simple as they seem and warn us to use language carefully.

ACT I SCENE 3

SUMMARY

- Laertes warns his sister about Hamlet and her own sexuality.
- Polonius gives his departing son advice on how to conduct himself.
- Polonius orders Ophelia to reject Hamlet unless he offers more. She obeys.

ANALYSIS

DISEASE AND PROSTITUTION

Laertes sounds caring when he warns Ophelia to be wary of Hamlet's love since it may not last – as a prince, Hamlet has only limited scope to choose a partner. However, there is something of his father's mercenary mentality in suggesting that she should conserve her virginity like a valuable property ('chaste treasure' line 31). But it is when Laertes proceeds to talk about her own sexuality that his language becomes more surprising. Desire is 'danger' (line 35), the world slanders even the virtuous, while infection ('canker', line 39) and 'contagious basements' (line 42) threaten the young. The vehemence of this **imagery** reminds us of Hamlet's reaction to his mother's marriage in Act I Scene 2. It becomes part of the pervasive feeling that 'Something is rotten in the state of Denmark' (I.4.90).

Later, when he arraigns (finds fault with) Gertrude in the closet scene, Hamlet will claim that her sexual depravity poisons the climate: 'blurs the grace and blush of modesty,/Calls virtue hypocrite, takes off the rose/From the fair forehead of an innocent love/And sets a blister there' (III.4.41–44). This shocking image, of a prostitute's branded forehead, feeds into the presentation of Ophelia and helps to explain Hamlet's vehement language to her in the nunnery episode. Dismayed by his mother's betrayal of his father, Hamlet had concluded 'frailty, thy name is woman' (I.2.146). In the play scene he will comment that 'woman's love' is of brief duration (III.2.135). In Act III Scene 1, he will accuse Ophelia of 'paintings' (line 137) like a harlot's cheek. This scene, in which her brother and then her father treat Ophelia as property liable to spoil, prepares us for the shocking exchanges between Hamlet and Ophelia later in the play.

STUDY FOCUS: THE SUBPLOT   **A02**

For by the image of my cause, I see
The portraiture of his (V.2.77–8)

The subplot of *Hamlet* revolves around three characters who can be seen as externalising and illuminating simplified aspects of Hamlet himself:

- Ophelia – her passivity, her descent into madness and her suicide following the death of her father
- Laertes – his response as a **Revenge Hero** to Polonius's murder
- Polonius – his habit of losing his thread, of being engrossed by details.

It is useful to bear in mind these comparisons when thinking about how Shakespeare has constructed the play. Are there any other characters who share aspects of Hamlet's personality?

FATHER AND DAUGHTER

It is important to notice that Ophelia never talks about being in love with Hamlet: it is always his love for her which is explored. Despite his swearing his love 'With almost all the holy vows of heaven' (line 114), something Hamlet is unlikely to do lightly, the cynical Polonius accuses him of 'unholy suits' (line 129).

When Polonius questions Ophelia, she has no hesitation in 'unlocking' the secret she pledged to keep exclusive a line earlier (lines 85–6), or in obeying her father's order to deny Hamlet further audiences. In Act II Scene 2, Hamlet calls Polonius a 'fishmonger' (line 172), a cant (slang) term for bawd or pimp. In this scene we hear Polonius talk in crudely commercial terms about his daughter whom he sees as a valuable property to be sold at the highest possible price:

you have tane these tenders for true pay,
Which are not sterling. Tender yourself more
    dearly ....
Set your entreatments at a higher rate ...
Do not believe his vows, for they are brokers,
Not of that dye which their investments show (lines 106–128).

It is no wonder that Hamlet calls him a 'fishmonger'.

> **CRITICAL VIEWPOINT** **A03**
>
> 'Ophelia – poor Ophelia! O far too soft, too good, too fair, to be cast among the briars of the working-day world, and fall and bleed upon the thorns of life!' Anna Brownell Jameson, *Characteristics of Shakespeare's Women* (1832).

> **CHECK THE FILM** **A03**
>
> In his film of *Hamlet*, Kozinstev emphasises Ophelia's lack of freedom using two powerful **images**. We see her being taught a stiff, formal dance, like a puppet. Her cumbersome, wire-framed farthingale (underskirt made of hoops) also suggests someone living in a cage.

STUDY FOCUS: SUBMISSIVE OPHELIA   A04

Feminist critics cite this scene as evidence of the powerlessness of women in a patriarchy (male-dominated world). But Ophelia (whose name means 'serving woman') is dramatically different from many other Shakespearean girls (e.g. Juliet, Desdemona and Cordelia) who resist bullying fathers and even a tyrannical king. She seems to have no will or opinions of her own 'I do not know my lord what I should think' (line 104). Ophelia's rejection of Hamlet's love and her subsequent complicity in the scene in which Claudius and Polonius spy on him add to his emotional turmoil and disillusionment with people.

A. C. Bradley suggests that Ophelia's behaviour is limited by Shakespeare for the benefit of the plot:

Now it was essential to Shakespeare's purpose that too great an interest should not be aroused in the love-story .... If (Ophelia) had been an Imogen, a Cordelia, even a Portia or a Juliet, the story must have taken another shape.
A. C. Bradley, *Shakespearean Tragedy* (1904)

What do you think about Ophelia's behaviour in this scene and her role in the play?

GLOSSARY

31	**your chaste treasure open**	Laertes describes Ophelia's virginity as a valuable property not to be squandered
99	**tenders**	Wordplay. Ophelia means 'expressions' (of love); Polonius means 'offers to buy something'

ACT I SCENES 4–5

SUMMARY

- Hamlet joins Horatio and Marcellus on the watch; he explores how nations and individuals soil their reputations.

- The Ghost appears and 'courteously' beckons Hamlet to follow him.

- The Ghost tells Hamlet that he is his father's spirit. He describes his suffering and orders Hamlet to avenge his murder by Claudius. He tells him to spare the adulterous Gertrude.

- Hamlet dedicates himself to the task and swears his friends to secrecy. He tells them he may adopt 'an antic disposition' (I.5.172).

ANALYSIS

SOMETHING ROTTEN IN THE STATE OF DENMARK

Alliteration, **assonance** and **mimetic rhythms** abound in the passage in which Hamlet describes Claudius's heavy drinking: 'doth wake …/Keeps wassail, and the swaggering up-spring reels,/… drains his draughts of Rhenish down …/This heavy-headed revel' (I.4.8–17). These effects, together with the description of the trumpet's 'braying' create an impression of bestiality and vulgarity. It develops the theme of disease and introduces the related theme of poisoning. We recall Hamlet's description of Denmark's being: 'an unweeded garden/… things rank and gross in nature/Possess it merely' (I.2.135–7). Hamlet's reflection is that nations, like individuals, 'in the general censure take corruption/From [one] particular fault' (I.4.35–6); in other words the Danes' reputation is soiled by their habit of heavy drinking in the same way that a man's fame can be tarnished by one particular weakness. Many critics see this **interlude** as typical of Shakespearean tragedy: Othello, Macbeth, Lear and Coriolanus are all heroes with 'one defect' (I.4.31). Whether the simple formula fits Hamlet is for you to explore.

COSMIC PERSPECTIVES

On its third appearance, the Ghost finally has a voice and holds centre stage. Its impact now is even more terrifying and puzzling than before. Hamlet's immediate response is to call for heavenly protection: 'Angels and ministers of grace defend us!' (line 39). There is no doubt in his mind that the drama is now on a cosmic scale: the Ghost's presence confuses the distinctions between past, present and future; between this world and the next; between the living and the dead; between Earth, Heaven and Hell. Hamlet recognises the potential ambiguity of the apparition:

Be thou a spirit of health, or goblin damned,
Bring with thee airs from heaven or blasts from hell,
Be thy intents wicked or charitable (I.4.40–2).

These balanced, ways of seeing the Ghost spell out precisely Hamlet's ethical dilemma. The technical term for presenting sharply contrasting ideas in this way is **antithesis**. We are invited to weigh up the evidence on either side.

Marcellus and Horatio function briefly as a **chorus**. Marcellus predicts that the Ghost will uncover a filthy secret: 'Something is rotten in the state of

> **CONTEXT** A03
>
> At the beginning of Seneca's **tragedy** *Oedipus*, Thebes is plunged into a catastrophic plague as a result of the king's regicide and incest.

> **CONTEXT** A04
>
> The fascinating 'heavy-headed revel' (I.4.17) passage was cut from the Folio text (see **The texts of *Hamlet*** in **Part Five: Literary background**), possibly because after the James I became king, mention of the Danes' reputation for drunkenness might have been regarded as provocative because his wife was Danish.

Denmark' (I.4.90) whilst Horatio has faith that 'Heaven will direct it' (I.491). We are reminded of Hamlet's **choric rhyming couplet** in I.2: 'Foul deeds will rise/Though all the earth o'erwhelm them to men's eyes' (I.2.256–7). **Choric utterances** like these help us to see that the human drama takes place on a cosmic stage.

STUDY FOCUS: THE PROBLEM OF THE GHOST A03

It can be argued that the problem of the Ghost is the problem of the play. In *Macbeth*,  Shakespeare explores what happens when someone is given 'more than mortal knowledge' (*Macbeth*, I.5.3). Similarly, Hamlet is tempted by 'thoughts beyond the reaches of our souls' (I.4.56).

A simplistic reading of the Ghost would suggest that it is a wicked spirit intent on corrupting Hamlet's soul. Shakespeare presents something more sophisticated: the Ghost is what it seems to be, his admired father's spirit who tells him the shocking truth about the events which happened before the play. Even though it's true, such knowledge has the potential to lead Hamlet to damnation. Hamlet's words: 'I do not set my life at a pin's fee,/And for my soul, what can it do to that …?' (I.4.65–6) are profoundly **ironic**. It is Hamlet's soul, not his body which is at risk. Hamlet thinks of his father as godlike in Act I Scene 2 and Act III Scene 4. Act I Scene 5 suggests he still has human weaknesses and inconsistencies.

CONTRADICTIONS

The Ghost's powerful **narrative** is full of vivid detail but his instructions to Hamlet are a mass of contradictions. He tells his son he is forbidden to describe Purgatory but proceeds to give him information and orders which are surely also prohibited. His demand for vengeance is sinful in Christian terms and the secrets that he died with are 'more than mortal knowledge' (*Macbeth*, I.5.3). Hamlet began by asking the Ghost 'Whither wilt thou lead me?' (I.5.1). This reminds us that Horatio warned Hamlet that what awaited him might be temptation, might be enough to send him mad. Some critics have suggested that we can understand Act I Scene 5 best by thinking of it as a temptation scene.

In psychological terms, the information Hamlet is given is bound to trouble him. On the one hand, the Ghost tells him that sinners are punished cruelly in the afterlife: 'Oh horrible, oh horrible, most horrible!' (I.5.80) but on the other, commands him to undertake a deed which would certainly send him to Hell. He describes Gertrude's adultery, commands Hamlet to cleanse the royal bed of 'luxury and damnèd incest' (I.5.83) but orders him: 'Taint not thy mind, nor let thy soul contrive/Against thy mother aught. Leave her to heaven' (I.5.85–6).

STUDY FOCUS: THE POISONED EAR A02

Some critics argue that the Ghost is poisoning Hamlet's mind; certainly his orders are full of double messages. What authority does the Ghost have to decide who should go to Heaven and who to Hell? Hamlet's impassioned response, his 'wild and whirling words' (I.5.133), is hardly surprising. The Ghost describes his murder so graphically that it cannot be forgotten – but in describing the poisoning in this way, could the Ghost be said to be pouring poison into Hamlet's ears?

HAMLET: AN UNLIKELY REVENGE HERO

It is no wonder Hamlet struggles to find his moral bearings: 'O all you host of heaven! O earth! what else?/And shall I couple hell?' (I.5.92–3). Duty to his father demands that he stick to the Ghost's 'commandment' (I.5.102) but we have already heard Hamlet (I.2.131) referring to the Everlasting's very different set of commandments. How is he to reconcile the two?

At the close of I.4, Horatio expresses his uncomplicated Christian faith: 'Heaven will direct it' (I.4.91). In Act V, Hamlet will come to a similar conclusion. But to reach that point, he will travel an extraordinary, meandering mental journey. That Hamlet is an unlikely **Revenge Hero** is signalled to us in his revealing response to his father's orders: 'Haste me to know it, that I with wings as swift/As meditation or the thoughts of love/May sweep to my revenge' (I.5.29–31). Few Revenge Heroes would use 'meditation or the thoughts of love' to complete this heroic **simile**.

STUDY FOCUS: A VOICE FROM BENEATH A03

Many critics are puzzled by the playful banter between Hamlet on stage and the Ghost moving about beneath it. Rather than attempt to make psychological sense of this episode, it is more fruitful to consider Shakespeare's dramatic purposes here. A playwright's job is to suspend the audience's disbelief. But what could be less convincing than someone shouting commands from under the stage, pretending to be something supernatural and terrifying? We could argue that in this scene Shakespeare deliberately ridicules the limitations of stagecraft in order to reduce the audience's scepticism.

KEY QUOTATION: ACT 1 SCENE 5 A01

The time is out of joint: O cursèd spite
That ever I was born to set it right. (I.5.189–90)

- Hamlet's immediate reaction to his mission is to realise the enormity of the task that he has been given: time itself has been disrupted by his father's murder.

- It is a much larger task than simple vengeance. It is his responsibility to restore 'The sanctity and health of this whole state' (I.3.21). Hamlet wonders if he is equal to the task.

- We will see that he also feels it is his duty not to leave Gertrude 'to Heaven' (I.5.86) as the Ghost instructed but to try and persuade her to acknowledge her sins and to repent. Therefore 'set[ting] it right' is not just a matter of bloody revenge.

CRITICAL VIEWPOINT A03

Peter Stallybrass (in Howard and Shershow, *Marxist Shakespeares* (2001), p. 25) argues that: 'In figuring his father as mole [I.5.161], Hamlet enacts a radical metamorphosis: from human to animal; from omnipotent monarch to blind burrower; from **ideological** figurehead to a worker in the ground.'

CHECK THE BOOK A03

Goethe believed that Act I Scene 5 lines 189–90 hold 'the key to Hamlet's whole procedure … The effect of a great action laid upon a soul unfit for the performance of it' (*Wilhelm Meister's Apprenticeship*, 1796).

ACT II SCENE 1

SUMMARY

- This scene takes place some weeks after the events of Act I.
- Polonius sends his servant, Reynaldo, to spy on his son, Laertes, in Paris.
- Ophelia reports Hamlet's strange appearance and behaviour to her father.

ANALYSIS

SURVEILLANCE

Denmark's a prison (II.2.234)

The episode with Reynaldo is in this scene partly to signal to the audience that some weeks have passed since the end of Act I. Laertes has been in Paris long enough to need more money; the 'notes' (line 1) Polonius gives him may include letters from Ophelia she promised to send in Act I Scene 3 (lines 3–4). The name 'Reynaldo', meaning fox-like, draws attention to the sly and underhand tricks Polonius tells his man to use to spy on his son. The words 'let him ply his music' (line 71) imply that Polonius hopes Reynaldo will catch Laertes doing something he shouldn't. His tactics – 'By indirections [to] find directions out' (line 64) – are similar to those that the King and his spies, Rosencrantz and Guildenstern, will use when they attempt to discover what Hamlet has on his mind. To the idea that something is 'rotten' in Denmark is now added the idea that it is full of spies, deception and persecution. If Hamlet is pretending to be mad in the **dumbshow** with Ophelia, it marks a surprising development in the personality of the man so offended by the idea of 'seeming' in Act I Scene 2.

STUDY FOCUS: LOSING DIRECTION   A03

In this episode, Shakespeare lightens the tone by developing a side of Polonius which makes him not simply unpleasant but delightfully ludicrous too. Full of his own importance and intoxicated by words, he has a tendency to lose the thread of his argument: 'what was I about to say?/By the mass I was about to say something. Where did I leave?' (lines 49–50). Each director of *Hamlet* has to decide how much of a pedantic fool, how much of a tyrant to make Claudius's chief courtier appear.

A PUZZLE

Hamlet's **dumbshow**, described by Ophelia in lines 76–98, is one of the most puzzling episodes in the play. The language in which she describes the Prince 'Pale as his shirt … As if he had been loosèd out of hell/To speak of horrors' (lines 79–82) suggests Hamlet goes to Ophelia's closet immediately after his terrifying interview with the Ghost, perhaps with the hope of sharing his secret. However, the Reynaldo episode and the arrival of the ambassadors and Rosencrantz and Guildenstern in the next scene, establish that this incident occurred several weeks later. This leads some critics to suggest that the whole incident shows Hamlet doing what he anticipated doing in Act I Scene 5, putting on an 'antic disposition' (I.5.172). They interpret Hamlet's disorderly appearance as Hamlet playing with Polonius and the King (to whom he knows Ophelia will report), by wearing the conventional costume of a distracted lover. They argue that Hamlet is buying time and scope for his revenge by appearing to be mad and therefore harmless.

Certainly it is out of character for Hamlet (though not for Ophelia) to be at a loss for words and the fact that the foolish and self-important Polonius is so convinced that the Prince is 'Mad for [her] love' (line 83) suggests **paradoxically** that it *is* an act. Yet some details can fit a different sequence of events. Upon receiving the Ghost's 'commandment' (I.5.102), Hamlet vowed he would pursue revenge single-mindedly: 'I'll wipe away all trivial fond records …' (I.5.99–106). This episode could be read as him saying goodbye to Ophelia. On the other hand, his close study of her: 'such perusal of my face/As a would draw it' (lines 88–9) foreshadows Hamlet's dismay with Ophelia's deceitfulness in Act III Scene 1 'God hath given you one face and you make yourselves another' (III.1.137–8). On this reading, Hamlet's sigh 'so piteous and profound/As it did seem to shatter all his bulk,/And end his being' (lines 92–4) might not be a theatrical gesture but express genuine dismay.

PASSIVE OPHELIA?

The way Polonius deals with his daughter, showing no interest in what she is feeling, reminds us of the Ghost's one-sided conversation with Hamlet in the previous scene.

Here again, **feminist critics** comment that Ophelia is allowed no scope for following her own wishes. Others, contrasting her with Juliet, accuse her of a complete lack of spirit.

CONTEXT **A04**

It is worth remembering that Shakespeare was often careless about chronology: *Othello* is famous for its inconsistencies. He might well have written this episode without being aware that other textual details suggest it took place several weeks after the encounter with the Ghost.

KEY QUOTATION: ACT II SCENE 1   A01

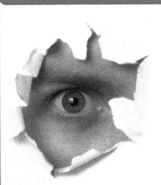

Polonius instructs Reynaldo to 'By indirections find directions out' (line 64).

- The phrase distils the atmosphere of deception which characterises Claudius's Denmark.
- It describes the way Polonius and Claudius use spying and disguise to try and discover what is on Hamlet's mind.
- It could also be used to describe Hamlet's use of feigned madness and the play-within-the-play to probe the consciences of Gertrude and Claudius.

CHECK THE FILM **A03**

Examine the different ways directors Grigori Kozintzev, Laurence Olivier and Kenneth Branagh re-present Ophelia's account of Hamlet's distracted behaviour.

REVISION FOCUS: TASK 1

How far do you agree with the following statements?

- Polonius is a shrewd and caring father to his children.
- Hamlet's mind is perplexed by his circumstances.

Examine the text carefully to help you clarify your ideas and then draft the opening paragraph of a response to each statement.

ACT II SCENE 2

SUMMARY

- Claudius, disturbed by Hamlet's 'transformation' (line 5), welcomes Hamlet's friends, Rosencrantz and Guildenstern, and instructs them to spy on him.
- Polonius reports to the King that he has discovered the cause of Hamlet's 'lunacy' (line 49) and Gertrude offers her own interpretation of her son's 'distemper' (line 55).
- The ambassadors Claudius sent to Norway return successful.
- The King, acting on Polonius's advice, sets up a meeting between Hamlet and Ophelia on which he and Polonius will eavesdrop. Hamlet taunts Polonius, calling him 'a fishmonger' (line 172).
- Hamlet forces Rosencrantz and Guildenstern to confess the King sent for them.
- The players arrive; the First Player delivers the Hecuba speech.
- In his second **soliloquy**, Hamlet reprimands himself for delay and shares with the audience the idea of *The Mousetrap*.

ANALYSIS

FRIENDSHIP BETRAYED

The mock disbelief in Claudius's words (lines 7–10) suggests that the King fears Hamlet may suspect foul play. So, when he speaks of finding a 'remedy' (line 18) for Hamlet's problem, Claudius may be already wondering if he will have to get rid of this potential avenger.

Claudius is decisive, ruthless and pragmatic: he has sent 'hast[ily]' (line 4) for Hamlet's close friends at Wittenberg to 'use' (line 3) them; he makes no apologies for 'sift[ing]' (II.2.58) Polonius. He needs answers and will use any means to secure his position. The Queen, too, is less comfortable than her polished manners to Rosencrantz and Guildenstern suggest. The woman who appeared so at ease with herself in Act I Scene 1 now reveals that she, like her son, sees the marriage as 'o'erhasty' (line 57). There are very few intimate exchanges between King and Queen in this play. This rare insight (lines 54–8) suggests tensions which are not usually displayed. There are also suggestions of maternal concern in Gertrude's description of her 'too much changèd son' (line 36) and in her words 'look where sadly the poor wretch comes reading' (line 166). Rosencrantz and Guildenstern, like Ophelia before and later, have no hesitation in allowing themselves to be used against their supposed friend. Hamlet's isolation and victimisation make the audience more likely to sympathise with him.

CONTEXT A04

Polonius's comment 'This is too long' (line 456) may show Shakespeare anticipating criticism of *Hamlet*. The play takes almost twice as long to read through as *Macbeth*.

DENMARK AT RISK

Many critics refer to the diplomatic solution to the threat posed by Young Fortinbras as evidence of Claudius's clear-headed diplomacy. Yet there is **dramatic irony** in Claudius's granting Fortinbras 'quiet pass' (line 77) through the kingdom. As a direct result of Claudius's crimes, at the end of the play, Young Fortinbras will gain control of Denmark where his father failed to do so. For the country, Claudius's reign, beginning with regicide, will be an even greater disaster than Macbeth's was for Scotland. Denmark will fall into foreign hands.

STUDY FOCUS: POLONIUS AS BAWD A02

Shakespeare now develops the comic potential of Polonius's vain and verbose character. If 'brevity is the soul of wit' (line 90), Polonius is a 'foolish prating knave' (III.4.216). Hamlet's letter which Polonius produces is as ambiguous as the **dumbshow**. It is impossible not to feel the prominent word 'beautified' (line 110) foreshadows Hamlet's attack on Ophelia in Act III Scene 1 in which he accuses her of face-painting and deceit. Yet the remainder of the letter sounds sincere and tender. Polonius confirms that Ophelia has 'All given to mine ear' (line 126) every detail of Hamlet's wooing. When Polonius proposes using his daughter as a decoy, his language: 'loos[ing] [his] daughter' (line 160) like a caged bird, develops the idea of Polonius as a pimp. 'I'll board him presently' (line 168) **puns** on the word 'bawd'. By talking about 'loosing' Ophelia, Polonius **paradoxically** concedes that most of the time he keeps her locked up.

METHODICAL MADNESS: HAMLET AS FOOL

We could argue therefore that Hamlet's apparently mad greeting of Polonius as a 'fishmonger' (brothel keeper, line 172) is entirely appropriate. Hamlet's 'antic disposition' (I.5.172) sounds more like the freedom of the Fool to voice uncomfortable truths than a pretence of insanity. Hamlet's biting observations have the honesty and directness which has been lacking since the accession of Claudius; in her madness (Act IV) Ophelia will also express ugly truths she was unable to voice before. In Claudius's court, as even Polonius agrees, to be honest is 'to be one man picked out of ten thousand' (line 177). Madness can be defined as being in a minority of one.

Yet the language in which Polonius, Claudius and Gertrude describe Hamlet's behaviour: 'transformation' (line 5), 'lunacy' (line 49), 'distemper' (line 55), 'the madness wherein now he raves' (line 148), 'turbulent and dangerous lunacy' (III.1.4) and 'wildness' (III.1.40) suggest that even before the explosive nunnery scene, Hamlet's behaviour is interpreted as something more than clever jesting or depression. These terms may function as stage directions suggesting to the actor how 'wildly' he should present Hamlet at this stage in he play. Or perhaps they reveal a touch of paranoia in those listening to him? Would we, the audience, describe Hamlet's behaviour in such terms? The tone of his exchanges with Polonius, when not being **satiric**, recalls the melancholy of Act I Scene 2. Hamlet would like to be in his grave (line 202), to part with his life (lines 209–10).

FELLOW STUDENTS

In the Prince's witty student banter with Rosencrantz and Guildenstern (lines 215–58) we catch a glimpse of Hamlet's former intellectual energy. Yet even here the disturbing ideas that '[Fortune] is a strumpet' (line 226–7) and 'Denmark's a prison' (line 234) colour their exchanges. Hamlet's famous line 'for there is nothing either good or bad but thinking makes it so' (lines 239–40) has many possible meanings. He probably does not believe, as he implies Rosencrantz and Guildenstern do, that all truth is relative; rather, that people have a duty to think and thus work out the difference between good and bad.

The idea is lost on his companions. Sensing his friends' unease, Hamlet makes them confess that they were sent for by the King. What follows (lines 280–291) has the tone and character of a soliloquy. It develops the idea of the unweeded garden from the soliloquy in Act I Scene 2. But Hamlet presents his negative view of things as mysterious and morbid; he struggles against seeing the world merely as 'a foul and pestilent congregation of vapours' (lines 285–6). His message to Claudius is that he doesn't know why ('wherefore I know not', line 280) he is depressed. Hamlet tells the spies he's giving nothing away to his 'uncle-father and aunt-mother' (lines 344–5) and warns them he is 'but mad north-north-west' (line 347): that he is mad only occasionally. He is taunting Claudius by telling him his madness is partly an act. Hamlet, like the King, is using his fellow students in a game of bluff.

CHECK THE BOOK A03

One of the difficulties facing each director of the play is to decide exactly when Hamlet comes on stage in this scene and how much, if any, of the plotting between Claudius and Polonius he overhears. John Dover Wilson, in *What Happens in Hamlet*, suggests that Hamlet is listening to this conversation.

CHECK THE PLAY A03

In the first half of *King Lear*, the 'all-licensed Fool' (I.4.198) voices uncomfortable truths everyone else is too wicked, too frightened or too blind to admit; Hamlet never talks gibberish in the way that Edgar, pretending to be Mad Tom, does in Act III of *King Lear*.

DECADENT DENMARK

The arrival of the actors brings a breath of fresh air into the prison of Denmark. Hamlet is immediately energised as the plan to stage *The Mousetrap* comes to him: *'He that plays the King shall be welcome'* (line 298). Yet the reason why this company whose 'endeavour keeps in the wonted pace' (line 324) is forced to tour is symptomatic of a country in decline. Hamlet cites more evidence in lines 335–6. In Act V we will hear that there are many 'pocky corses' (V.1.140) nowadays; Osric is presented as a typically decadent courtier, 'the drossy age dotes on' (V.2.166).

THE POWER OF PLAYING

At the Prince's request, the Principal Player recites a powerful **narrative** poem presenting Hamlet's favourite episode from the Trojan War. The focus is not upon the slaughter of the King but upon the grief of his loyal Queen, Hecuba. One moment in the speech is a curious foretaste of Hamlet's next **soliloquy** in which he berates himself for delay: 'seemed i'th'air to stick … Did nothing.' (lines 437–40). The **image** foreshadows the episode in the Chapel where Hamlet's impulse to kill Claudius fights with his need to think things through.

STUDY FOCUS: HAMLET'S SECOND SOLILOQUY | A02

The player's intense but acted passion shames Hamlet into exploring why he 'can say nothing' (line 521). When the Ghost set him the task, he suggested that Hamlet would be 'duller … than the fat weed/That rots itself in ease on Lethe wharf' (I.5.32–3) if he failed to act. Hamlet now responds to that taunt, worrying that he is indeed 'dull and muddy-mettled' (line 519). In the course of the speech, he scathingly describes himself as 'a rogue and peasant slave' (line 502), 'A dull … rascal' (line 519), 'a coward' (line 523), 'villain' (line 524), 'pigeon-livered' (line 529), 'an ass' (line 535), 'like a whore … a very drab,/A scullion' (lines 538–40). He feels bitterly ashamed he is not behaving as his kingly father's son should. Hamlet resolves to test the truth of the Ghost's story by having the actors perform a play which closely re-presents the Ghost's account of his murder. Guilty people watching plays have been shocked into confessing their crimes: 'The play's the thing/Wherein I'll catch the conscience of the king' (lines 557–8). The soliloquy ends with a ringing **rhyming couplet** in which Hamlet appears to have regained his momentum.

KEY QUOTATION: ACT II SCENE 2 | A01

'For if the sun breed maggots in a dead dog, being a god kissing carrion' (lines 179–80)

- This disturbing image develops the theme of disease. How can something as pure as sunlight generate maggots? By 'kissing', coming into contact with, contaminated flesh.

- The image recalls Hamlet's father, whom he compared to Hyperion, and his mother from whose depravity Hamlet believes he has contaminated, 'sullied flesh' (I.2.129, see **Act I Scene 2 Glossary**).

- The idea of purity being corrupted will be developed in the nunnery episode and the closet scene.

- Hamlet warns Polonius (lines 182–3) and Ophelia in the next scene (III.1.119–20) that she can expect to be only 'a breeder of sinners'.

CONTEXT | A04

The **melodramatic** speeches that Hamlet shares with the First Player are written in a quaint, old-fashioned **blank verse** style **parodying** that of Shakespeare's popular predecessor, Christopher Marlowe. Significantly, Hamlet chooses an episode describing Pyrrhus avenging the slaughter of his father which focuses upon the behaviour of his victim's loyal wife.

CRITICAL VIEWPOINT | A03

Some critics see Hamlet's first expression of doubts about the Ghost's honesty and intentions: 'The spirit that I have seen/May be a devil' sent 'to damn me' (lines 551–6) merely as an excuse for a lack of action. Others see it as evidence of the scruples which subconsciously have held Hamlet back from taking revenge.

CHECK THE FILM | A03

Notice the way in which Kozinstev's magnificent film of *Hamlet*, with its imagery of massive stone walls, bars, the heavy portcullis and Ophelia's severely controlled behaviour, continually reinforces the idea of Elsinore as a prison.

ACT III SCENE 1

SUMMARY

- This scene takes place the next day. Hamlet's 'crafty madness' (line 8) is discussed; as Ophelia is prepared to act as a decoy, Claudius reveals his guilty feelings for the first time.
- Hamlet delivers his fourth soliloquy: 'To be, or not to be ...' (line 56).
- Claudius and Polonius eavesdrop on Ophelia and Hamlet's bitter conversation. At some point Hamlet realises it is a set-up.
- Ophelia expresses her dismay at Hamlet's 'ecstasy' (line 154).
- Convinced that Hamlet is not mad but possibly meditating revenge, Claudius decides with 'quick determination' (line 162) to ship him off to England.
- Polonius proposes spying on Hamlet again, this time in the Queen's room. Claudius agrees, pretending again that he thinks Hamlet is mad and therefore needs watching.

ANALYSIS

THE KING UNSETTLED

Claudius's concern that his spies should come up with something beyond Polonius's diagnosis reveals his troubled state of mind before *The Mousetrap* and prepares us for his agonised soliloquy (III.3). Here, he talks of Hamlet's 'turbulent and dangerous lunacy' (line 4) although we have seen nothing that deserves that description. Guildenstern deepens the King's suspicion that Hamlet's behaviour is '[put] on' (line 3) by accusing him of 'crafty madness' (line 8). The King's unexpected, powerful and shocking aside (lines 50–4) shows him to be a much more psychologically developed and interesting character than the complacent smiling villain he appeared to be in Act I Scene 2. It increases our expectation that the play will reveal that the Ghost has been telling the truth. The imagery Claudius uses makes a connection between the willing part Ophelia is playing as a decoy and his own deceptions; imagining himself as a prostitute being publically whipped foreshadows the curious way both Hamlet and Ophelia address him as a woman in Act IV.

STUDY FOCUS: 'TO BE OR NOT TO BE' – THE THINKING MAN'S SOLILOQUY A03

The dramatic purpose of this episode is to establish Hamlet as characteristically detached, reflective and moral – as somebody completely unlike the active, simple-minded heroic figures of Old Hamlet and Old Fortinbras, his 'unimprovèd' (I.1.96) son Young Fortinbras, and the rash Laertes. Just a few hours before *The Mousetrap*, the play designed to 'catch the conscience of the king' (II.2.558), we see Hamlet absorbed in abstract reflection. It is a bleak but surprisingly calm, philosophical consideration of the popular **Renaissance** theme of whether our troublesome life is worth living. It is strikingly different from Hamlet's previous soliloquies; where they are full of nervous energy and abrupt changes of direction, here there is a dejected tone and tempo. This might be Hamlet reading aloud from a philosophical essay. He might indeed be, as Q1 (see **The texts of *Hamlet*** in **Part Five: Literary background**) has it, 'poring upon a book' as Polonius instructs Ophelia in imitation to pretend to do. This famous speech contains probably the best-known lines in the whole of literature and is notoriously challenging for any actor to make sound fresh and engaging. Because we all 'know' it, it is also difficult for us to read it carefully.

CRITICAL VIEWPOINT A03

'No one but Shakespeare could have interrupted an exciting dramatic intrigue with a passage like this.' (John Dover Wilson, *What Happens in Hamlet* (1935), p. 128). 'Unlike the other soliloquies, this one shows no sign of belonging to the particular scene in which it appears.' (L. L. Schücking, 'The Meaning of Hamlet', 1939, in Alex Newell, *The Soliloquies in Hamlet: the Structural Design* (1991), p. 77.)

CHECK THE BOOK A03

Q1, which is probably based upon an acting text, moves this famous soliloquy and the nunnery episode to Hamlet's earlier appearance 'poring upon a book' (Q1 Scene 7 line 109) before the 'fishmonger' episode (II.2.172) and thus before the second soliloquy. Some modern productions adopt this change, arguing that it not only makes better dramatic but better psychological sense too.

KEY SOLILOQUY OR DISTRACTION?

Is this **soliloquy** simply irrelevant to the action of the play or central in exploring Hamlet's character? We have seen Hamlet repeatedly longing for death. Some critics suggest this is world-weariness; others identify it as alienation from a world that causes him extraordinary and specific pain. Hamlet has suffered very real, traumatising shocks in the course of the play. Mourning the sudden death of the father he idolised, he has been visited by a terrifying Ghost who has revealed that his father was murdered by his uncle; his mother who appeared grief-stricken at the funeral he now believes to have been in an adulterous relationship with her brother-in-law. Now, against all propriety, she is married to him. Instead of Hamlet succeeding his father, as he expected to do all his life, his Uncle is on the throne. Apart from Marcellus, Barnado and Horatio, nobody seems to remember Old Hamlet just a few weeks after his death. Only the Ghost has expressed any reservations about Claudius's behaviour whilst two of Hamlet's closest friends have taken sides with the King. Ophelia, whom Hamlet seems to have loved, has unaccountably rejected him and refuses to talk to him. To add to all these problems, Hamlet does not know whether the Ghost is a benign or a wicked informant.

A WORLD OF PAIN

Why is none of this material examined directly in this central soliloquy? The phrase 'The pangs of disprized love' (line 72) which might **allude** to Ophelia's rejection of him is simply one item in a list of generalised disappointments true of any human society. It would be stretching points impossibly to see Hamlet as someone bearing 'fardels' or 'grunt[ing] and sweat[ing] under a weary life' (lines 76–7); the Prince appears to be reflecting on the human condition, not analysing his immediate situation. He never uses the words 'I' or 'me'; the ideas he explores are expressed as general truths: 'Thus conscience does make cowards of us all' (line 83). No detail demonstrates just how detached Hamlet's mind appears to be from everything that has happened to him than his statement that 'no traveller returns' (line 80) from beyond the grave. If the audience can still hear the Ghost's words 'Remember me' (I.5.91), Hamlet, it seems, cannot.

THE MORALITY OF SUICIDE

However, it is the problem of the Ghost which shapes the direction of this soliloquy. What Hamlet addresses initially is whether, in the face of suffering, he is morally right to contemplate suicide, something he longed for in his first soliloquy and expresses a desire for on three subsequent occasions. Although it is a passage many people know by heart, its expression is not straightforward.

The assumption is that we all wish to behave nobly and must work out whether taking our own life or putting up with our suffering is more praiseworthy. However, the **metaphor**, 'take arms against a sea of troubles,/And by opposing end them' (lines 59–60) is perhaps deliberately confused. Some argue it captures Hamlet's feelings of being unequal to the task that has been assigned to him. He feels that trying to set the world to rights would be like committing suicide; the **imagery** recalls King Canute's hopeless trial of strength, as he tried to hold back the sea. But in the remainder of the speech, the argument against suicide is explored not so much as an ethical as a psychological issue. If death were like a deep sleep, suicide would be a very attractive alternative to the 'thousand natural shocks' (line 62) we all suffer. But when we sleep, we dream; which suggests that death isn't simply oblivion; what we suffer in life may be less awful than what we may suffer in the afterlife: the Ghost has shown that to be true. 'And thus the native hue of resolution/Is sicklied o'er with the pale cast of thought' (lines 84–5).

Suddenly we see how this reflection is linked with Hamlet's thinking about the Ghost's 'commandment' (I.5.102) and his reluctance to commit murder: 'enterprises of great pitch and moment/With this regard their currents, turn awry/And lose the name of action' (lines 86–8). It is, after all 'conscience' which has kept Hamlet from taking revenge. However we read the speech, it serves as a powerful dramatic contrast to the passionate exchanges which follow. For further discussion see **The problem of the Ghost** in **Part Three: Themes**.

STUDY FOCUS: THE NUNNERY EPISODE [A02]

Although Gertrude is on stage during the planning of the spying, she takes no part in it. This helps the audience to focus upon Claudius as Hamlet's enemy and prepares us for Gertrude's change of loyalty in the second half of the play. Meanwhile Ophelia, from appearing to be Hamlet's girlfriend, has distanced herself from him further by allowing herself to be used by Claudius.

There are striking similarities between Hamlet's passionate exchanges with Ophelia here and those he has with Gertrude in Act III Scene 4. If Hamlet's enthusiasm for revenge is at best half-hearted, his eagerness to confront the women in his life who he feels have betrayed him and morally compromised themselves is explosive. They represent the 'cue for passion' which unleashes 'horrid speech' (II.2.513–15). The progress of the two episodes differs, however, because of the presence of Claudius and Polonius throughout this one. In Act III Scene 4 the eavesdropper is removed at the beginning of the meeting; in this episode it is the listeners who effectively send Hamlet away at the end.

CONTEXT [A04]

When Hamlet advises Ophelia to enter a 'nunnery' (lines 119–26), whether he is suggesting she enter a convent to escape the corrupt world of Elsinore or, believing she has sold herself already, is suggesting she work in a brothel is a matter for debate: in Elizabethan times, the word 'nunnery' could mean either.

FAIR OPHELIA

Hamlet's immediate response to coming so unexpectedly upon Ophelia is affectionate. The very sounds of his words 'Soft … fair Ophelia … Nymph … orisons' (lines 88–9) convey a tender, not an aggressive, instinctive reaction. Here, as at her funeral (V.1.209), he describes Ophelia as 'fair' (line 89). 'Fair' is a complex word of particular weight in Shakespeare's *Sonnets*: 'Fair, kind and true' (Sonnet 105, lines 9–10) comprise the qualities we most admire in those we love: beauty, honesty, gentleness, truthfulness and loyalty. Certainly Ophelia looks 'fair'; Hamlet has until now regarded her as lovely in appearance *and* character. Now Hamlet is puzzled, frustrated and wounded that having at last allowed him into her company, her impersonal language blocks any proper communication between them, hence his observation: 'I never gave you aught' (line 96). In treating him as if he were someone else, Ophelia has ceased to be herself. She is acting, posing as his wronged sweetheart in the process of betraying him.

HAMLET'S FURY

When Ophelia tells him a direct lie, Hamlet explodes with fury, directed partly at her, partly as those he guesses are listening; his bizarre self-accusation: 'I am very proud, revengeful, ambitious' (line 122) is surely intended for Claudius's ears. If we believe Hamlet when he says in Act V that he 'loved Ophelia' (V.1.236) then we can understand why he is so shaken by her betrayal. He sees Ophelia as frailty and deceptiveness personified: 'I have heard of your paintings … You jig, you amble … and make your wantonness your ignorance' (lines 137–40). Yet Hamlet's interpretation of Ophelia's behaviour is no more extreme than Polonius's as he refers to her reading her prayer book: 'colour/Your loneliness … with devotion's visage,/And pious action, we do sugar o'er/The devil himself' (lines 45–9). It is Hamlet's fury which is terrifying.

TAUNTING THE KING

It is not clear from the text at what point Hamlet realises he is being tricked and listened to. Certainly by the time Ophelia lies to him by telling him that her father is 'At home' (line 127), Hamlet knows he is being set up. Each director of the play must decide which of Hamlet's words should be directed at Ophelia and which at those listening from behind the arras. However, there can be no doubt that what he says at the end of this episode, 'Those that are married already, all but one shall live' (lines 141–2), is a direct threat to the King.

STUDY FOCUS: A LOST OPPORTUNITY A02

Alone with the audience for the only time in the play, Ophelia reveals little of her inner self. Her expression of grief for Hamlet's 'ecstasy' (line 154) is expressed in generalised language; her tribute to him does not describe the man we have been watching on stage and by interpreting his behaviour as madness (a diagnosis the shrewd Claudius rejects) Ophelia avoids any examination of the part she may have played in causing Hamlet's distress or deserving his criticism. Whether we should blame Ophelia for this lack of honesty or Shakespeare for failing to develop the character is a point you could debate.

CHECK THE FILM A03

The staging of this scene poses interesting problems for every director. At what point does Hamlet realise that a trap has been laid, that Ophelia is lying and that the King and Polonius are listening? Watch as many different versions of the scene as you can, noting exactly how the director conveys to us the moment at which Hamlet's suspicions are aroused and how he reacts.

THE RUTHLESS RESPONSE

As far as Claudius is concerned, the honey trap has worked: Polonius's theory of Hamlet's odd behaviour being love-sickness is proved incorrect: Hamlet is neither mad nor energised by thoughts of love. Convinced that Hamlet is meditating revenge, Claudius acts with characteristically 'quick determination' (line 162) to send this dangerous young man to England. He packages the trip to Polonius as a health cure holiday; we will discover that his intentions are anything but charitable. Polonius himself will discover 'to be too busy is some danger' (III.4.33). His plan to eavesdrop upon Hamlet a second time costs him his life and swings the play into a wholly new direction.

KEY QUOTATION: ACT III SCENE 1 A01

How smart a lash that speech doth give my conscience!
The harlot's cheek, beautied with plastering art,
Is not more ugly *to the thing that helps it* [compared with the pretty face it puts on]
Than is my deed to my most painted word. (lines 50–3, author's italics)

- Claudius identifies with the harlot, linking the sharpness of the lash with which she is whipped to the sharp prick of his conscience. He feels that his deceptions, putting on a false face, are like hers ('beautified with plastering art'). Both disguise their sinful selves with an attractive cover.

- This is an example of an extended and complex **metaphor**.

- In Shakespeare's day, harlots (prostitutes) were often whipped in public.

- Face-painting, lying and disguise are all aspects of dishonesty which the play explores. The relationship between appearance and reality is one of the major themes in Shakespeare's works.

- This shocking **image** links Claudius's 'seeming' with the game Ophelia is about to play.

- It is the first time the King has revealed an inner, troubled self.

ACT III SCENE 2

SUMMARY

- It is some hours later. Preparing for the play-within-the-play, Hamlet coaches the actors.

- He declares his love and admiration for Horatio; he talks crudely and bitterly to Ophelia.

- Hamlet and Horatio monitor Claudius's reaction to the performance. The **dumbshow** represents the events described by the Ghost but also shows the Queen's seduction after the murder.

- The first scene of the play focuses upon the Queen's vows of monogamy. Gertrude's verdict is that 'The lady doth protest too much' (line 211).

- The second scene presents the poisoning of the King. The murderer is his nephew. Hamlet **narrates** what will happen next and Claudius leaves 'marvellous distempered' (line 273).

- Hamlet is elated, convinced that the Ghost has been proved right; Horatio reserves judgement.

- Hamlet mocks Rosencrantz, Guildenstern and Polonius, and then, preparing to visit his mother, he delivers a brief, **melodramatic soliloquy**.

ANALYSIS

ADVICE TO THE PLAYERS

It is unlikely that Shakespeare would devote such attention to the advice to the players if the thoughts were not his own; the play-within-the-play episode displays a professional man of the theatre's insight and expertise. *The Murder of Gonzago* is deliberately made to sound quaint by being written in **rhyming couplets**. In his advice to the actors and his declaration of his love for Horatio, Hamlet praises restraint and discretion: very different sentiments from those in his soliloquy in Act II Scene 2 where he was impressed by the actor's passion.

UNCONDITIONAL LOVE

Following his distressing exchanges with Ophelia, Hamlet expresses heartfelt love and admiration for his one true friend, Horatio. Volatile and often passionate himself, Hamlet admires the composure of the poor scholar who 'in suffering all ... suffers nothing' (line 56), who is not 'passion's slave' (line 62). Characteristically, Horatio says nothing; that he loves Hamlet unconditionally emerges in his unwavering loyalty and his impulsive attempt at suicide when Hamlet dies in Act V. Hamlet asks Horatio to help him judge Claudius's reaction to the play: in a conversation we have not seen, he has shared the Ghost's story with his friend.

RIDDLES

Once more 'idle' (line 80), resuming his 'antic disposition' (I.5.172), Hamlet speaks in riddles to Claudius and even more coarsely than before to Ophelia; he sits next to her rather than his mother to observe Claudius more easily. His exchange (lines 86–94) with Polonius is a moment of dark comedy. It is probable that the two actors playing Hamlet and Polonius were the same people who had played Brutus and Caesar in Shakespeare's previous **tragedy**. Hamlet's comment 'It was a brute part of him to kill so capital a calf there' (line 93) is a moment of **dramatic irony**; in a few moments the audience will see Richard Burbage kill John Heminges (or possibly Robert Armin) once again.

STUDY FOCUS: THE CONSCIENCE OF THE QUEEN   A02

Hamlet told us in Act II Scene 2, 'The play's the thing/Wherein I'll catch the conscience of the king' (II.2.557–8), but his production is designed to work first on the conscience of his mother. He calls the play 'The Mousetrap' (line 216); later Hamlet will imagine Claudius in bed calling Gertrude 'his mouse' (III.4.184). When he kills Polonius believing him to be the King, he calls him not a mouse but 'a rat' (III.4.24).

In a barbed exchange, Hamlet makes the connection between Ophelia's rejection of him and his mother's infidelity to her husband: 'look you how cheerfully my mother looks, and my father died within's two hours' (lines 112–13). The Player Queen gives dramatic expression to the idea 'frailty, thy name is woman' (I.2.146). The first part of the play revolves around her three declarations of uncompromising marital fidelity. Pointedly, the couple have been married thirty years: we learn Hamlet is thirty in the graveyard scene. That detail alerts Gertrude to the play's ulterior purpose. When he asks her opinion of the play, Hamlet foreshadows the moral grilling he will give his mother in the next scene. She understands the taunt and criticises the playwright for preaching too much.

GOADING CLAUDIUS

Hamlet announces that the murderer, Lucianus, is the king's nephew, not his brother. Fearing that the play will not sting Claudius into 'proclaim[ing] [his] malefactions' (II.2.545) Hamlet seems to be rewriting it as a brazen threat. As the performance proceeds, with no obvious reaction from Claudius, Hamlet becomes increasingly agitated, interrupting more and more excitedly until his final outburst (lines 237–41). It is a desperate attempt to provoke a response from a man who has his conscience, in public, completely under control. The play is another version of Hamlet's threat in the nunnery episode, 'all but one shall live' (III.1.142); a clumsy warning to Claudius that his life is in danger. This is the second occasion on which Hamlet has had the word 'revenge' bellowed into Claudius's ear. It is as if he wants to provoke Claudius to act so he will not have to. This is exactly what happens.

SUCCESS OR FAILURE?

When the performance breaks up, Hamlet is euphoric: 'I'll take the ghost's word for a thousand pound' (line 260). But Horatio's judgement of Hamlet's success is that he's earned only 'Half a share' (line 253) in a company; he neither confirms nor denies that the King

has reacted like a guilty man. Hamlet turns away from Horatio to taunt Rosencrantz and Guildenstern and then Polonius. Guildenstern reports that the King is mad with anger, and that the Queen is 'in most great affliction of spirit' (lines 282–3) and wishes to see him. To the spies, Hamlet explains his 'distemper' (line 305) as frustrated ambition: another message for Claudius's ears.

SPEAKING DAGGERS

Alone on stage Hamlet prepares to face his mother. Elation gives way to **melodramatic** language mimicking that of Lucianus (lines 231–6), the nephew about to murder his uncle: ''Tis now the very witching time of night … Now could I drink hot blood' (lines 349–51). Yet his next move is not to hunt out Claudius but his mother: 'I will speak daggers to her but use none' (line 357) – the cruel **irony** of which is that in her room he will kill Polonius and set in train a sequence of events over which he has no control.

GLOSSARY

22	**make the judicious grieve**	dismay people who appreciate good acting
50	**lick absurd pomp**	Shakespeare often compares flatterers to dogs who slobber over their masters to get what they want
99–107	**shall I lie in your lap? … country matters … to lie between maid's legs … Nothing**	Hamlet's crude abuse makes an impression on Ophelia; it surfaces in the bawdy language of her second song in Act IV Scene 5
122	**miching mallecho**	dastardly deeds, sneaky villainy
169	**Purpose is but the slave to memory**	an ironic comment upon Hamlet's delayed revenge
226	**it would cost you … mine edge**	Hamlet continues to punish Ophelia with gross sexual **images**
273–5	**marvellous distempered … with choler**	Guildenstern interprets Claudius's mood as angry, not guilty
301	**were she ten times our mother**	Gertrude is Hamlet's mother twice over, having married his stepfather

CHECK THE FILM **A03**

In Laurence Olivier's 1948 film, courtiers look at one another in horror as they realise their King has committed regicide.

ACT III SCENE 3

SUMMARY

- Claudius accelerates his plan to ship Hamlet to England.
- Sounding like press officers, Rosencrantz and Guildenstern justify the King's decisive action.
- In **soliloquy**, we hear Claudius struggling with his guilty conscience.
- With Claudius at his mercy, Hamlet explores in his sixth soliloquy why he is unable to kill the King.

ANALYSIS

THE FALL OF KINGS

If Denmark is a prison, it is suffering a major disturbance; for the first time Claudius's easy control of affairs has been seriously undermined. Feeling vulnerable, Claudius acts decisively to 'fetters put about this fear/Which now goes too free-footed' (lines 25–6). His henchmen's justification for whatever the King decides to do (lines 7–23) could sound merely like flattery. But Rosencrantz's speech (lines 11–23) is stylistically unlike anything else in the play. For a moment he sounds like a **chorus** commenting on what is essentially a domestic drama in **epic** language. As the play moves towards its fatal **denouement**, we see the larger significance of this family upheaval. Rosencrantz may believe he is talking about the threat to Claudius but the catastrophic ruin following the fall of a King applies equally to the murder of Old Hamlet. Rosencrantz and Guildenstern will be amongst those caught up in 'the boisterous ruin' (line 22).

STUDY FOCUS: CLAUDIUS – A TRAGIC HERO? **A02**

Claudius's unexpected soliloquy is one of Shakespeare finest achievements; exploring a character utterly different from Hamlet's, we have here the germ from which Macbeth will develop. In a play already longer than anything he had produced before, Shakespeare does not have the scope to develop Claudius's inner self in Acts IV and V. But this dramatisation of a guilty consciousness gives us a satisfying insight into the man who had appeared to be a one-dimensional smiling villain. There is nothing comparable in any other **Revenge Tragedy**. You may like to try comparing the characters of Claudius and Macbeth. What traits and motivations do they share?

CHECK THE BOOK **A02**

Compare Claudius's soliloquy with the steady-eyed despair in Macbeth's final soliloquies (*Macbeth*, V.3.19–29; V.5.17–27).

CLAUDIUS'S DILEMMA

Claudius is clear and frank about his situation. His confession is comprehensive and unflinching: he confirms the essence of the Ghost's account, identifies his own tragic weakness: 'mine own ambition' (line 55), yet is unable to repent. He testifies to the nature of the moral universe in which we must read the play: 'In the corrupted currents of this world/Offence's gilded hand may shove by justice,/... But 'tis not so above' (lines 57–60). The man who appeared to be a **Machiavellian** pragmatist is revealed as a Christian trembling at the prospect of divine judgement. He conveys vividly the anguish of his position in the **imagery** of a bird trapped on a sticky branch: 'Oh limèd soul that struggling to be free/Art more engaged' (lines 68–9). In these closing lines (64–72) his self-control unwinds, his fluent sentences give way to anguished exclamation: 'Oh wretched state! Oh bosom black as death!' (line 67). It is at this point of despairing vulnerability that Hamlet comes across the praying Claudius.

STUDY FOCUS: HAMLET'S SIXTH SOLILOQUY A02

With unparalleled dramatic confidence, Shakespeare **juxtaposes** Claudius's anguished soliloquy with another of Hamlet's. Nothing could demonstrate more powerfully the range and scope of Shakespeare's ability to create vividly realised but utterly different characters. Each soliloquy has its characteristic thought-pattern, tone and rhythms. Although both men are thinking about crime and punishment, Heaven and damnation, Old Hamlet and Gertrude, Shakespeare makes Hamlet and Claudius sound completely different.

Hamlet's sixth soliloquy is brisk and superficially straightforward. It begins with tripping **monosyllables**: 'Now might I do it pat' (line 73) and presents Hamlet, who was focused on his coming interview with his mother, momentarily distracted by this unexpected opportunity to carry out the Ghost's 'commandment' (I.5.102). The highly unusual situation of Claudius's passivity leaves Hamlet scope to reflect before he acts: 'That would be scanned' (line 75). Had he encountered Claudius at this moment in any other context, his energetic response to *The Mousetrap* might perhaps have propelled him to take revenge. A few minutes later, when he thinks Claudius is hiding behind the arras, he has no hesitation in killing him. Hamlet's refusal to complete his revenge at this point will have catastrophic consequences.

CRITICAL VIEWPOINT A03

Dr Johnson was dismayed by Hamlet's callousness in this speech. For a critic much closer in time to Shakespeare's than our own, Hamlet's desire to send Claudius to hell was 'too horrible to be read', Dr Johnson, *Notes on the Plays* (1765).

DIVINE JUDGEMENT

As we saw in Claudius's soliloquy, talk of Heaven, Hell and judgement is much more than a verbal convention in this play: the drama unfolds with a cosmic perspective, the life to come is perceived as intensely as the present one. When Hamlet weighs up whether to send Claudius either to Heaven or Hell, he is intensely serious; he has no doubt that such places exist. And yet many critics argue that what we hear is Hamlet rationalising: satisfying his obligation to his father in the very act of refusing to do the Ghost's bidding, he argues that killing Claudius now would be 'hire and salary, not revenge.' (line 79). But as a sincere Christian, he cannot possibly kill a man at prayer.

GRADE BOOSTER A03

Hamlet is by nature a thinking man utterly dissimilar from the rash Laertes who will play the part of Revenge Hero in the second half of the play. Laertes would have no hesitation in 'cut[ting] his throat i'th'church' (IV.7.125); Hamlet in precisely that situation delays. It is a matter of critical debate whether Hamlet's own explanation for his sparing Claudius is convincing. Try writing out different arguments for Hamlet's lack of action here. Which do you find most persuasive?

There is a wonderful **irony** in the delayed **rhyming couplet** which closes Claudius's soliloquy. Whilst Claudius sees his prayer as ineffectual, we know it has saved his life. Hamlet will finally kill Claudius when he is 'about some act/That has no relish of salvation in't' (lines 91–2). We can only assume that whilst 'flights of angels sing [Hamlet] to [his] rest' (V.2.339), Claudius's feet 'kick at heaven' (line 93).

KEY QUOTATION: ACT III SCENE 3 A01

And like a man to double business bound
I stand in pause where I shall first begin
And both neglect. (lines 41–3)

- The King describes a will paralysed, torn between conflicting inclinations. He knows he should repent his crimes but cannot renounce what they have won him: the crown and the Queen. He knows that God will judge and punish him but cannot make the sacrifice which would earn him his 'mercy' (line 46).
- The way Claudius describes his dilemma fits Hamlet's situation too. How can he reconcile his duty to avenge his father and his 'holy ... fear' (III.2.8) of damnation? It is like a commentary on the behaviour we are about to see (lines 73–96): a moment which recalls that when Pyrrhus's sword 'seemed i'th'air to stick' (II.2.437).
- The **caesura** after 'neglect' produces a pause which mimics the act of hesitation.

ACT III SCENE 4

SUMMARY

- Polonius urges Gertrude to 'lay home' (line 1) to Hamlet and eavesdrops on their conversation.
- Gertrude attempts to reprimand Hamlet but he angrily admonishes her. Her fearful cry is taken up by Polonius; Hamlet kills him, believing he has killed the King.
- Discovering his error, he expresses contempt for Polonius and his interfering.
- Hamlet accuses his mother of involvement in Old Hamlet's murder and of incest. Gertrude's response suggests she knew nothing of the assassination; Hamlet chastises what he sees as her sexual depravity.
- The Ghost reappears to whet Hamlet's 'almost blunted purpose' (line110) and to entreat him to support the Queen. Unable to see the Ghost, Gertrude thinks Hamlet is mad.
- Hamlet convinces her of his sanity and urges her to keep away from Claudius's bed. He then plays devil's advocate, telling her to reveal his plans to Claudius.
- Gertrude promises not to reveal Hamlet's secrets.

ANALYSIS

A DRAMATIC TURNING-POINT

The closet scene is one of the dramatic climaxes of the play and the turning-point of the whole drama. It is the only time we see mother and son alone together; apart from a brief exchange during *The Mousetrap* this is the first conversation they have had since Act I Scene 2. Although Hamlet seems curiously unaffected by his murder of Polonius, the deed proves disastrous: it initiates the secondary **Revenge Tragedy** in which Laertes is the chief **protagonist** and brings about the deaths of Ophelia, Laertes, Rosencrantz and Guildenstern, Gertrude, Claudius and Hamlet himself.

Whatever motivation Gertrude has in agreeing to rebuke her son, control of the interview is immediately seized by Hamlet. He mocks the rhythm and the words of her reprimands, turning the finger of accusation from his own behaviour to hers:

Gertrude: Hamlet, thou hast thy father much offended.
Hamlet: Mother, you have my father much offended.
Gertrude: Come, come you answer with an idle tongue.
Hamlet: Go, go, you question with a wicked tongue.
(lines 9–12)

The technical term for such to and fro **dialogue**, two characters swapping lines of verse, is **stichomythia**.

Where Hamlet has little appetite for revenge, this interview, like the one with Ophelia, serves a purpose that he cares about passionately. He is much more eager to try and save a soul than to carry out an execution. He can be 'cruel only to be kind' (line 179).

THE DEATH OF POLONIUS

The interruption of their conference by Polonius's murder is curious. Hamlet's spontaneous, bloody reaction, 'Dead for a ducat … is it the king?' (lines 24–6), is a dramatic contrast to his declining to take Claudius's life just a few minutes earlier. Accused by Gertrude of a 'rash and bloody deed' (line 27), he in turn blames the old counsellor for being a 'rash, intruding fool' (line 31). Although he says later he 'will answer well/The death I gave him' (lines 177–8) he shows the body little respect: 'I'll lug the guts into the neighbour room' (line 213).

This is perhaps an echo of the story as found in Saxo Grammaticus's tale where the eavesdropper's body is fed to the pigs. (Saxo Grammaticus was the twelfth-century author of a history of Denmark in which the story of Amleth, a son who revenges his murdered father, first appears.)

Accused by Gertrude of a 'bloody deed' (line 27), Hamlet throws back the phrase at his mother and retorts in a jeering **couplet**: 'A bloody deed? Almost as bad, good mother,/As kill a king and marry with his brother' (lines 28–9). Gertrude's shocked echo, 'As kill a king?' (line 30) and the 'wringing of [her] hands' (line 34) signal not only her innocence of the deed, but her shock in discovering that her new husband murdered her first. It prepares the ground for her switching loyalties from her husband to her son at the end of the scene.

Her son's strength of feeling succeeds in breaking down the front with which Gertrude has suppressed her guilty feelings hitherto. She confesses that when she looks into her soul she sees 'such black and grainèd spots/As will not leave their tinct' (lines 90–1). We are reminded of Claudius's confessing that he had a 'bosom black as death' in the previous scene (III.3.67).

STUDY FOCUS: TWO BROTHERS, TWO HUSBANDS **A02**

There follow two episodes of passionate intimacy unlike any other in the play. Whereas in Hamlet's furious encounter with Ophelia, monitored by Polonius and Claudius, Ophelia's conduct was constrained, this one brings a response: Gertrude has scope to react.

The **juxtaposition** of the two brother's pictures is presented in vivid language: we seem to see the pictures as they are described. It is an elaboration of Hamlet's comparing them to 'Hyperion' and 'a satyr' in his first **soliloquy** (I.2.140). Old Hamlet is in his son's eyes the embodiment of a superhero, a mixture of the qualities of several Roman gods with Hyperion's curls, Jove's forehead, Mars's eye, Mercury's bearing, 'new-lighted on a heaven-kissing hill' (line 59); he is himself 'a fair mountain' (line 66). Meanwhile Claudius is seen as a 'moor' (line 67), 'a paddock … a bat, a gib' (line 191). He is also an infectious 'mildewed ear/Blasting his wholesome brother' (lines 64–5). This disease **metaphor** reminds us of the gruesome poisoning. Hamlet sees Gertrude's adultery and incest as 'apoplex[y]' (paralysis or stroke, line 73): the source of infection and corruption in Denmark (see lines 40–51).

AN INTERRUPTED CADENCE

At line 180, as in the nunnery scene (III.1.129) we have a false **cadence**; Hamlet seems to finish chastising Gertrude before embarking upon a fresh assault. In both cases this may signal untidy revision or Shakespeare's being unable to control his invention. Hamlet renews his attack by playing devil's advocate, urging his mother to inform Claudius about his true state of mind and reveal his suspicions of his 'schoolfellows' (line 203) whom he promises to 'blow … at the moon' (line 210). But Gertrude is a changed woman. She promises to keep Hamlet's secrets.

STUDY FOCUS: FATHER, MOTHER AND SON **A02**

Many twentieth-century productions presented this encounter between Hamlet and his mother with **Freudian** overtones but it can be argued that Hamlet's passion is more that of the zealous preacher than a would-be Oedipus: the scene is another take on Claudius's desperate failure to repent (III.3). Hamlet sees himself as heaven's 'scourge and minister' (line 176) and his speeches are peppered with the terms a confessor might use: 'for love of grace … trespass … Confess yourself to heaven … Repent … virtue … vice … devil … angel … Refrain … abstinence … And when you are desirous to be blessed,/I'll blessing beg of you' (lines 145–73). Hamlet is desperate to save his mother's soul by forcing her to acknowledge her sins, repent and refrain from further wickedness. The passage contains the most disturbing of all the play's disease **images**: pretending Hamlet's criticism of her conduct is mere 'madness' (line 142) will 'skin and film the ulcerous place,/Whiles rank corruption, mining all within,/Infects unseen' (lines 148–50). Failure to repent will 'spread the compost on the weeds/To make them ranker' (lines 152–3). This **metaphor** recalls Hamlet's description of Denmark as 'an unweeded garden' in his first **soliloquy** (I.2.135).

When the Ghost intervenes, not this time 'in complete steel' (I.4.52) but 'in his habit as he lived' (line 136), Hamlet accuses himself before the Ghost confirms that he has let time slip (lines 106–10). Gertrude's graphic description of her son's terror (lines 118–23) is full of maternal concern and tenderness. Presenting Hamlet's family together on stage at this critical point in time makes for a memorable dramatic moment.

STUDY FOCUS: GERTRUDE'S MISSING SOLILOQUY **A02**

Shakespeare might have given Gertrude a soliloquy here. It would help us gauge exactly the effect the traumatic experiences in the closet scene have had on her. We have little sense of Gertrude as an individual or a very fully developed personality beforehand. Lacking a substantial soliloquy following it, we can judge her only by her behaviour. Using Claudius's soliloquy as a model, think about what Gertrude might say at this critical turning-point about her relationships with her son and her husband. Perhaps she might also explore her feelings for Old Hamlet? Remember that Gertrude's ideas and expression should be consistent with the way Shakespeare has presented her.

KEY QUOTATION: ACT III SCENE 4 **A01**

'reason panders will' (line 88)

- Hamlet argues that Gertrude's behaviour is more shocking than sexual misconduct in the young because at her age 'judgement' (line 70) not appetite should control her behaviour.
- To see 'reason' turning a blind eye to immorality is like watching a trusted and virtuous person behaving like a 'pander', a pimp.
- The phrase develops the theme of prostitution as a symptom of the moral pollution emanating from Gertrude's marriage to Claudius.

REVISION FOCUS: TASK 2

How far do you agree with the following statements?

- Claudius's self-awareness makes him more like a tragic hero than a villain.
- Gertrude is not developed as a dynamic character.

Draft the opening paragraphs for essays on each of these statements. Using close textual analysis, explore the arguments for and against each proposition.

CHECK THE FILM **A03**

Examine how in his 1948 film, Laurence Olivier suggests Hamlet's Oedipal fixation with his mother in this scene. For an analysis of Olivier's film of *Hamlet*, see Peter S. Donaldson's essay 'Olivier, Hamlet and Freud' in Robert Shaughnessy (ed.), *New Casebooks: Shakespeare on Film* (1998).

CONTEXT **A04**

The obscure image 'Unpeg the basket …' (lines 194–7) seems to be an **allusion** to a story about an ape that stole a basket full of birds which it opened on the roof of a house. When the birds flew away, the ape climbed into the basket and tried to copy the birds. Instead of flying free, it fell and broke its neck. Hamlet is warning Gertrude not to let his secret out of the bag lest she suffer the ape's fate.

ACT IV SCENE 1

SUMMARY

- This scene follows immediately on from the last; act and scene divisions in modern editions are not Shakespeare's own.
- Distraught, Gertrude tells Claudius that Hamlet 'in ... brainish apprehension' (line 11) has murdered Polonius.
- Claudius declares that Hamlet is dangerous to everyone and must be sent away to England immediately. He hopes this will prevent people blaming him for the murder.
- He dispatches Rosencrantz and Guildenstern to recover Polonius's body and take it to the chapel.

ANALYSIS

A STUDY IN ALIENATION

This scene follows two powerful episodes in which we have seen the King and then the Queen acknowledge their sins and reveal the tormented consciences which struggle beneath their bland exteriors. Gertrude's distress is a complex response to her discovery that her husband had murdered his brother and to her son's forceful reprimand of her sexual conduct. She is also disturbed by the puzzling episode in which he claimed to be talking to her dead husband. That scene (III.4) concluded with a new intimacy established between Gertrude and Hamlet and in this scene we see her distancing herself from Claudius, using grief for Polonius's death as a means of concealing the true nature of her distress. She describes Hamlet's ruthlessness as madness even though he has just shown her he is 'essentially ... not in madness,/But mad in craft' (III.4.188–9) and bent on revenge.

CRITICAL VIEWPOINT A03

'Though Gertrude is still nominally the wife of Claudius, she is no longer, psychically or sexually, in ... union with him. She has ... consented to rejoin Hamlet in the paternal triangle, thus re-establishing the family configuration in its original form', John Russell, *Hamlet and Narcissus* (1995), p. 138.

CHECK THE PLAY A03

It is interesting to compare this scene where a married couple drift apart to *Macbeth* Act III Scene 2 where we see the tragic **protagonists** suffering similar anxieties but no longer confiding in one another.

GLOSSARY

2	**translate**	explain
11	**brainish apprehension**	mad delusion
17	**providence**	foresight, taking care of this dangerous person
18	**out of haunt**	under guard
22	**divulging**	becoming public knowledge
23	**pith of life**	life itself
29	**The sun no sooner shall the mountains touch**	a poetic description of sunrise. It is after one a.m. (the Ghost's usual time for appearing) when this scene takes place
38	**our wisest friends**	we have no idea who these people are; Polonius had been Claudius's only counsellor

EXTENDED COMMENTARY

ACT IV SCENE 1, LINES 1–45

A powerful sound effect, Gertrude's sobbing, links Acts III and IV. As Claudius realises, 'There's matter in these sighs' (line 1). Yet the drama of this scene arises from Gertrude's refusing to 'translate' (line 2) 'these profound heaves' (line 1). Without a **soliloquy** revealing what Gertrude is thinking, we must judge her by her behaviour.

This is the one intimate conversation between Claudius and Gertrude in the whole play. At all other moments, apart from their brief exchange in Act II Scene 2, conversations between Gertrude and Claudius are public: what they say is conditioned by the other people present. What is remarkable about this moment of intimacy is that the couple share virtually nothing of what has just happened to each of them. Like his wife, Claudius is fresh from a painful moral crisis, explored in his soliloquy following *The Mousetrap*. He can share nothing of this with Gertrude. As far as he knows, she does not suspect that he murdered his brother. He signals a new separateness from her by referring to Hamlet as her son, no longer pretending that Hamlet is his. When at the end of the play he refers to Hamlet once more as 'Our son' (V.2.264) it is hypocritically, after he has prepared the poisoned wine for him. Shakespeare presents husband and wife as suffering in mutual isolation beneath a pretence of intimacy. They exchange words but not confidences. In fact, they tell each other lies.

Despite Hamlet's demonstration to her of his sanity a few minutes earlier, Gertrude develops the fiction that her son is: 'Mad as the sea and wind, when both contend/Which is the mightier' (lines 7–8). She tells Claudius nothing about Hamlet's belief that his father was murdered or about his intentions to 'blow' his captors (and perhaps him too) 'at the moon' (III.4.210). To justify sending him to England for everyone's safety, Claudius also pretends he still believes his nephew is a 'mad young man' (line 19) whose 'liberty is full of threats to all,/To you yourself, to us, to everyone' (lines 14–15). It suits the King's purpose to pretend that there could be neither rhyme nor reason in Hamlet's murder of Polonius. He acknowledges that 'It had been so with us had we been there' (line 13) without exploring any possible reason Hamlet might have for wanting to kill him. Claudius cannot share his fears of Hamlet as a potential **Revenge Hero** with Gertrude. If we believe what he says to Laertes later, 'The queen his mother/Lives almost by his looks' (IV.7.11–12), her affection for her son would make any plot to have him killed out of the question. Her son's behaviour must therefore be presented as irrational and indiscriminately dangerous. Gertrude dare not reveal to Claudius that Hamlet reacted with such coolness to Polonius's corpse, so we have the invention: 'a weeps for what is done' (line 27). She goes along with the idea that Hamlet is out of his mind and therefore not guilty of murder.

Claudius is uneasy for other reasons too. He cannot afford a scandal and does all he can to 'bear all smooth and even' (IV.3.7). With a shrewd eye on managing public opinion, he rehearses with all his 'majesty and skill' (line 31) what sounds like a modern-day press release: 'so much was our love … Even on the pith of life' (lines 19–23). The statement is as fluently hypocritical as his opening speech in Act I Scene 2. He is planning, after all, to send Hamlet to his death. In fact, Claudius's 'smooth and even' (IV.3.7) manner is commented upon by Hamlet himself in Act V Scene 2 when Claudius's order to kill his nephew has been uncovered by him. Hamlet describes Claudius's command as 'Larded with many several sorts of reasons' (V.2.20). Claudius projects himself as a 'reasonable' man and we have seen how persuasive he can sound even when his conduct is underhand. Here he applies his customary 'double varnish' (IV.7.131) to the order. Hamlet describes his request as 'larded' with persuasive arguments; the **image** suggests the greasy **rhetoric** with which the smiling villain disguises his sinister intentions. It develops the theme of appearances not reflecting reality which runs through the play.

At line 32, Claudius summons his spin doctors, Rosencrantz and Guildenstern, and presents them with the official version of events: 'Hamlet in madness hath Polonius slain' (line 34). He instructs them to 'speak fair' to the failed assassin as if he were a madman rather than a son bent on revenge (line 36). The King apparently has other counsellors besides Polonius but who these 'wisest friends' (line 38) are we never learn. Clearly the priority is to prevent rumours from unsettling the population.

At this point in the text, there are some words missing from Q2 (lines 41–4 are missing entirely from F). (See **The texts of *Hamlet*** in **Part Five: Literary background**.) Editors conjecture that the lost words are something like: 'So haply Rumour …' The image of Rumour personified whispering and broadcasting (Claudius will later talk of 'buzzing') the news The King wishes to suppress is probably inspired by the way Virgil describes Rumour in Book IV of *The Aeneid*:

Rumour raced at once through Libya's great cities,
Rumour, compared with whom no other is as swift.
She flourishes by speed, and gains strength as she goes:
first limited by fear, she soon reaches into the sky,
walks on the ground, and hides her head in the clouds.
Earth, incited to anger against the gods, so they say,
bore her last, a monster, vast and terrible, fleet-winged
and swift-footed, sister to Coeus and Enceladus,
who for every feather on her body has as many
watchful eyes below (marvellous to tell), as many
tongues speaking, as many listening ears.
She flies, screeching, by night through the shadows
between earth and sky, never closing her eyelids
in sweet sleep: by day she sits on guard on tall roof-tops
or high towers, and scares great cities, as tenacious
of lies and evil, as she is messenger of truth. (lines 173–88)

In *Hamlet*, Rumour (or slander) is even swifter than this terrifying bird. Shakespeare refashions Virgil in contemporary, hi-tech imagery:

Whose whisper, o'er the world's diameter,
As level as the cannon to his blank,
Transports his poisoned shot, may miss our name
And hit the woundless air. (lines 41–4)

Shakespeare gives the impression of our living in a global village, with the vivid image of information reaching everywhere at once. It is a strikingly modern notion of how quickly news travels.

GRADE BOOSTER **A01**

When analysing passages from the play you should be cautious about using technical terminology for its own sake: students often lose marks for identifying a bit of **alliteration** or **dramatic irony** without explaining how that contributes to the dramatic *effect*. Perhaps the most important thing to identify is **tone**: is the passage meant to sound serious or comic? Straightforward or ironic? Does the speaker sound angry, agitated, serene, confused, aggressive or tender?

ACT IV SCENES 2–3

SUMMARY

- Hamlet has hidden Polonius's body; he toys with Rosencrantz and Guildenstern.
- Claudius reflects on his situation; Hamlet's popularity means he must proceed cautiously.
- Hamlet's flippant, abusive manner continues in his exchanges with Claudius.
- In a second brief **soliloquy**, Claudius reveals his plans to kill the Prince.

ANALYSIS

PLOT AND COUNTERPLOT

After the intensity of the closet scene and the strained conversation between King and Queen, Shakespeare lightens the mood now and quickens the pace, presenting Hamlet in a scurrilous, **satiric** mode, a development of his flippant attitude to Polonius's death in Act III Scene 4. He leads Rosencrantz and Guildenstern on a wild goose chase 'Hide fox, and all after!' (IV.2.27) as they search for the body and riddles with them in hostile contempt for one-time friends who have sold themselves to his enemy. Rosencrantz is no more than 'a sponge' (line 14), the fragment of an apple in the corner of the King's mouth; opportunists, Rosencrantz and Guildenstern will regret their bargain (lines 10–19).

Hamlet's mood recalls other moments of heightened emotion: after the visit of the Ghost (I.5.114–63) and at the conclusion of *The Mousetrap* (III.2.246–348). His eccentric behaviour is a **parody** of his solitary mourning in Act I Scene 2, his satire a continuation of his games with Polonius in Act II Scene 2 and Act III Scene 2. All this lends these scenes a darkly comic tone: Claudius's attempts at gravity being scuppered by Hamlet's refusal to act appropriately. It is a comic version of their unrelenting and deadly hostility to one another. Claudius is acting too: his unlawful plan to have Hamlet beheaded by the English king is not something he can share with either the court or Gertrude. But Hamlet, as he revealed in the closet scene, is one step ahead: he has no doubts about what Claudius intends: 'I see a cherub that sees [your purposes]' (IV.3.45).

STUDY FOCUS: THE SHAPE OF THINGS TO COME A02

Our expectations are being shaped for a new stage in the drama; Shakespeare begins to separate the virtuous and vicious characters as he moves the play towards its dramatic climax. He simplifies Claudius as the villain of the piece, Hamlet as the popular hero (IV.3.4), so that in Act V we will be in no doubt where our sympathies should lie. Public opinion is becoming agitated; Claudius cannot put Hamlet on trial. '[T]he distracted multitude' (IV.3.4) will shortly rise against Claudius when Laertes returns. Although we are given no more than these hints, the King's position is now shown to be less secure than it had appeared previously. In two brief soliloquies, we hear Claudius becoming nervous and ruthless; he acts characteristically 'with fiery quickness' (IV.3.40). He makes use of the central **imagery** of the play, describing Hamlet as a 'disease' (IV.3.9): 'For like the hectic in my blood he rages,/And (England) must cure me' (IV.3.62–3). Hamlet's ludicrous leave-taking of the King as his 'dear mother' (IV.3.46) is a curious foretaste of the farewell the crazy Ophelia will bid him (IV.5.71). Talk of worms and beggars anticipates the **memento mori** reflections in the graveyard scene (V.1).

ACT IV SCENE 4

SUMMARY

- We meet Young Fortinbras leading his army across Denmark on its way to fight for 'a little patch of ground' (line 18) in Poland.
- Hamlet is perturbed by the situation.
- He then delivers his final soliloquy in which he appears to revise his judgement.

ANALYSIS

THE OTHER PRINCE

In the opening scene, Horatio described Young Fortinbras: 'Of unimprovèd mettle, hot and full' (I.1.96). His appearance here develops this **characterisation** and his presence serves as a preparation for his arrival at the end of the play when he will claim the kingdom.

Young Fortinbras is evidently a chip off the old block. Just as his father, 'pricked on by a most emulate pride' (I.1.83), challenged Old Hamlet to a combat, risking and losing not only his life but all his lands, so now his son risks the lives of 'two thousand souls and twenty thousand ducats' (line 25) to fight for a patch of worthless ground in Poland. Like his father, he is fighting simply for fame, the soldier's religion. Hamlet's immediate response is an expression of contempt. He diagnoses such reckless waste as yet another example of disease and corruption in the world: 'This is th'imposthume of much wealth and peace,/That inward breaks, and shows no cause without/Why the man dies' (lines 27–8).

STUDY FOCUS: A NECESSARY SOLILOQUY? 〔A02〕

There is some evidence that Shakespeare decided to cut most of this scene as a result of his experiences of presenting *Hamlet* on the stage: it is one of the major cuts in F (see **The texts of *Hamlet*** in **Part Five: Literary background**). *Hamlet* is already Shakespeare's longest play and, coming at such a late stage, the richest and most interesting soliloquy puts a considerable strain not only upon the actor playing *Hamlet* but also upon the audience. Cutting these lines does not necessarily mean Shakespeare thought them redundant or inferior to what he left; simply that, as drama, they were expendable. When we study *Hamlet* as a text, with plenty of time to examine the soliloquy closely, we may feel that what happens in Act IV Scene 4 is central to our reading of the whole work.

GLOSSARY

22	**A ranker rate, should it be sold in fee**	a better price if it were sold outright
27	**imposthume**	an abscess inside the body
32	**inform against me**	give evidence against me
36–7	**he that made us with such large discourse,/Looking before and after**	God gave us the capacity to reflect on what we have done and to weigh what we should do
40	**Bestial oblivion**	being like an animal, unaware of anything
40	**craven scruple**	cowardly nit-picking

CRITICAL VIEWPOINT 〔A03〕

'Shakespeare has been remarkably skilful in his management of tone in the soliloquy as a means on the one hand of stressing again that Hamlet is a man of considerable intellect … and on the other of revealing … the turbulent desire for revenge in him', Alex Newell, *The Soliloquies in Hamlet* (1991) p. 77.

CHECK THE FILM 〔A03〕

When making his film of the play in 1948, Laurence Olivier cut this soliloquy, finding it impossible to deliver with any animation. Kenneth Branagh presents it with great gusto as the rousing conclusion to the first half of his 1996 film.

EXTENDED COMMENTARY

ACT IV SCENE 4, LINES 32–66

Hamlet's final **soliloquy** and the one in Act II Scene 2 have a similar emotional logic but here Shakespeare gives us a much more detailed insight into the processes of Hamlet's tortured thinking. Again, he moves from procrastination to resolving to act, and his concluding **rhyming couplet** rings with determination: 'Oh from this time forth,/My thoughts be bloody or be nothing worth' (lines 65–6). But this is **ironic**. As so often, Hamlet's actions contradict his words. His thoughts appear to move convincingly to that bloodthirsty conclusion but the speech is a mass of contradictions. It is the supreme example of Shakespeare showing that what someone *says* is not always what he *believes*.

The speech begins with striking imagery: 'How all occasions do inform against me' (line 32). Hamlet feels he is on trial; one event after another comes in to give evidence against him. Who does he feel is his judge? The answer comes indirectly in the next image: 'And spur my dull revenge!' (line 33). He compares his revenge to a dull (spiritless) horse. No matter how much it is spurred, it will not get going. This interesting word 'dull' recalls the Ghost's: 'And duller should'st thou be' (I.5.32). Mention of the 'Polack' (line 23) reminds us of one of his father's **epic** victories (see I.1.63). Throughout the play, Hamlet has felt answerable to two incompatible authorities, his father and God 'the Everlasting' (see I.2.131).

Hamlet goes on to try to define what separates man from animals. God gave humans reason and the duty to use it. Thinking, making moral choices is what distinguishes mankind from beasts, makes men 'god-like' (line 38). We have seen Hamlet is what Shakespeare suggests a person should be, a thinker, but now he asks whether his thinking is healthy. He cannot be charged with 'Bestial oblivion' (line 40). Does he have the opposite tendency:

> some craven scruple
> Of thinking too precisely on th'event –
> A thought which quartered hath but one
>   part wisdom
> And ever three parts coward
> (lines 40–3)?

To be a coward is surely to be less than a man? This leads Hamlet to question himself further – a man should fear nothing, shouldn't he?

But Shakespeare has gone to elaborate lengths in this play to show us there is not only life after death but divine punishment for those who sin. God-fearing men are good men, not bad. What can Hamlet make of this? That it is a son's duty to obey his earthly father because that is how things are in a pagan universe, or that he must remember that there is divine justice? Hamlet cannot articulate this problem; to do so would be to accuse his father of being a devil who asks his son, in the name of loving duty, to do what would cost him his soul. So, when Hamlet continues:

> I do not know
> Why yet I live to say this thing's to do,
> Sith I have cause, and will, and strength, and means
> To do't' (lines 43–6)

clearly this is not the case. He may have 'cause', the physical 'strength' and at times the 'means' to take revenge. What he does not have is the 'will'.

CRITICAL VIEWPOINT A03

'Hamlet talks far more than any other character in Shakespeare.' Sir Sidney Lee, *A Life of William Shakespeare* (1898) in Victor Kiernan, 'Hamlet', in *Eight Tragedies of Shakespeare, A Marxist Study* (1996), p. 64.

Hamlet proceeds to contradict himself explicitly: 'Examples gross as earth exhort me' (line 46). This is illogical. The word 'gross' means 'foul, disgusting, savage, bad'. 'Exhort' means 'encourage, persuade, shove on'. A gross example cannot exhort you to do anything except the opposite. Hamlet was instinctively appalled by what the Captain told him Fortinbras's army was about to do. Now, a few lines later, he seems to feel their behaviour exhorting him to do something similarly honourable, not in the Christian but in the Roman sense of the word (see **Revenge: A question of honour** in **Part Three: Themes**).

Hamlet completes his speech by rewriting what he has just seen. The passage raises many questions. Who is this 'delicate and tender prince' (line 48)? Surely not the Fortinbras described by Horatio or the man we see? Hamlet is projecting himself into Fortinbras's situation, imagining himself playing the kind of role his father might have wished him to play. What can the phrase 'divine ambition' (line 49) possibly mean? Is it not a contradiction in terms? The principal Christian virtue is humility, not ambition. It can be seen as 'divine' only through Roman or secular, courtly eyes where fame is the only kind of afterlife. What is most revealing is the repetition of the word 'straw' (line 55) which Hamlet had used so contemptuously a few moments earlier. Here, he uses it in an attempt to justify the unjustifiable, equating greatness not with Christian virtue but with the pursuit of fame. Somehow Hamlet has 'reasoned' himself into seeing the world upside down. He starts to sound very much like the hot-blooded Laertes. Yet even as he does so, we detect a false note. '[F]ame' is, after all, 'a fantasy and a trick' (line 61), a deceit. And who would fight for an 'egg-shell' (line 53)?

ACT IV SCENE 5

SUMMARY

- We hear of a pitifully distracted girl whose ramblings are unsettling Claudius's subjects; Horatio advises the reluctant Gertrude to speak to her.
- In a brief **soliloquy**, the Queen reveals that her sinful state makes her apprehensive of 'some great amiss' (line 18).
- Mad Ophelia appears 'playing on a lute, her hair down, singing' (Q1 – see **The texts of *Hamlet*** in **Part Five: Literary background**).
- Laertes returns, leading a revolt, to avenge the murder of his father.
- Claudius promises to satisfy Laertes that he, Claudius, is not to blame.

ANALYSIS

A DOUBLE REVENGE TRAGEDY

In *Hamlet*, Shakespeare presents two **Revenge Tragedies**. In the first, which begins in the play's opening scene, we watch Hamlet wrestle with the Ghost's 'commandment' (I.5.102) to avenge is murder. In the second, which begins in Act IV Scene 5, we see the way Laertes responds to his father's murder. In Act V, Shakespeare brings the two dramas together, counterpointing the language, behaviour and values of two very different **Revenge Heroes**. (See **Part Four: Structure**.)

A SECOND EXPOSITION

Act I serves as the exposition of Hamlet's drama: establishing the circumstances of Old Hamlet's death and introducing the themes which later will be developed. Act IV Scene 5 is a **parody exposition**: another father has been murdered and we look forward to seeing how his children will respond. In Hamlet's absence, Shakespeare develops Polonius's children as stylised **foils** to two aspects of the Prince's personality. Ophelia's is largely a pitiably passive, Laertes's a rashly active response to the death of a father. Where Hamlet was alternately melancholy and elated, and contemplated suicide, Ophelia goes mad and kills herself. Where Hamlet was instructed by the Ghost to undertake revenge and would not, Laertes plays the conventional Revenge Hero, free of all the ethical scruples which complicate Hamlet's performance in that role. The naivety and simplicity of Polonius's two children's behaviour bring out the complex nature of Hamlet's.

Hamlet's drama begins with the premeditated murder of his heroic father, King Hamlet. Laertes's father, the foolish, self-important meddler, Polonius, is killed by accident when eavesdropping on Claudius's behest. Old Hamlet is buried with great ceremony (I.4.47–50); Polonius is buried 'hugger-mugger' (line 83). Hamlet is visited by a terrifying Ghost who reveals the circumstances of his death and commands his son to avenge him. Laertes hears of his father's death by 'buzzers' (rumours and gossip, line 89); he is 'persuade[d to] revenge' (line 168) by the distracted behaviour and plaintive songs of his mad sister and by the scheming of the wicked King. Both Revenge Heroes believe it is their duty to pursue revenge but whereas Hamlet is paralysed by a tangle of contradictory moral commands, Laertes is impulsive, single-minded and simple-minded. The two heroes' collision in Act V represents Shakespeare's **critique** of the Revenge Tragedy formula he inherited. He transforms a crude and confused set of conventions into challenging adult drama.

STUDY FOCUS: GERTRUDE'S REALIGNMENT A02

Hamlet begins with edgy fragments of conversation and talk of an ominous supernatural visitor. This second part of the play also begins obliquely: it is not clear who the distracted, pitiable girl is whose behaviour is disturbing onlookers. Gertrude refuses to speak to her until Horatio advises her that it may prevent political instability. Seeing Gertrude with Horatio as her improbable respected advisor, signals to us the Queen's strategic and moral realignment in Part II. Although she supports Claudius when Laertes bursts in, she plays no part in the subsequent plotting against her son and at the climax of the play fatally defies the King to toast Hamlet with the poisoned cup. In her only brief soliloquy, consisting of two **rhyming couplets** (lines 17–20), Gertrude is shown to be very different from the contented adulteress of Act I Scene 2; burdened by guilt, she foresees 'some great amiss' (line 18). It seems that the closet scene has transformed her.

MAD OPHELIA

Also transformed since we saw her last is Ophelia who is a much more powerful figure mad than she was when she was sane. Most of her lines in Act IV are sung and the plangent (melancholy) beauty of her songs is an important part of the theatrical effect. The responses of those on stage: 'Her mood will needs be pitied' (line 3), 'pretty lady' (line 41) indicate that she is meant to arouse pathos, an emotion which has not been part of the dramatic effect hitherto. Playing her naturalistically as a madwoman with a harsh voice and unable to sing, as some modern productions do, is clearly not what Shakespeare had in mind. Ophelia sings of death and betrayal in stylised, decorative terms: 'a grass-green turf', 'White ... mountain snow' (lines 31–6) and the many references to flowers and herbs culminating in Gertrude's description of Ophelia's drowning, lend these scenes a **pastoral**, out-of-doors flavour quite different from the claustrophobic prison atmosphere of Part I.

But just as Hamlet's 'madness' licensed him, like a Fool, to speak distasteful truths, now Ophelia who before 'did not know ... what [she] should think' (I.3.104) and whose every move was controlled by her father, sings and talks frankly, and often obscenely, about the 'tricks i'th'world' (line 5); if there is not Hamlet's method in her madness, then it is certainly not babble. The Gentleman describes the previously passive Ophelia as 'importunate' (line 2) and we soon understand why initially Gertrude is reluctant to admit her. Her first bizarre enquiry, 'Where is the beauteous majesty of Denmark?' (line 21) has been recognised by many critics as raising one of the most searching questions in the play but its immediate focus is upon Gertrude. When Ophelia sings pointedly of the funeral where a woman's 'true love' (line 23) 'bewept to the grave did *not* go/With true-love showers' (author's italics, lines 39–40) it is impossible to miss the biting **allusion** to Gertrude's hypocrisy at Old Hamlet's interment where she appeared 'Like Niobe, all tears' (I.2.149).

STUDY FOCUS: REASON IN MADNESS A02

Ophelia tells Gertrude twice to 'mark' her words (line 28 and 35). Ophelia's ominous warning: 'we know what we are, but know not what we may be' (line 43) echoes Hamlet's urging Gertrude to 'avoid what is to come' (III.4.151) by repenting and turning away from the 'bloat King' (III.4.183). After all, the wicked baker's daughter was turned into an owl (line 42). Hamlet's crude language to Ophelia in the play scene is now reflected in the bawdy 'By Cock, they are to blame' (line 61) of her second song, about sexual betrayal. Perhaps, just like Hamlet, there is reason in Ophelia's madness?

CHECK THE PLAY A04

The part of Ophelia may have been played by the same boy actor who would play Desdemona. The willow song in Act IV Scene 3 of *Othello* serves a similar function to Ophelia's songs here: the generation of **pathos** before the tragic climax. In both plays the weeping willow is a decorative pathetic detail.

CONTEXT A04

The plants Ophelia mentions are symbolic: fennel = flattery; columbine = adultery; rue = repentance; daisy = broken hearts; violets = fidelity.

CONTEXT A04

The extra syllable 'not' in Ophelia's **cadential couplet** (lines 39–40) looks like a mistake but since it is one detail found in all three printed texts (Q1, Q2 and F – see **The texts of *Hamlet*** in **Part Five: Literary background**) many critics feel it is meant to be a prominent irregularity.

INSURRECTION

Claudius shares with Gertrude disturbing news. In just thirty lines of **narrative** (lines 74–95 and 99–108) Shakespeare telescopes the action so that when Laertes appears, we have a sense of the kingdom falling apart, recalling the 'post-haste and romage in the land' of Act I Scene 1 line 107. There was a suggestion in Act I Scene 5 that in describing his own poisoning, the Ghost was also infecting Hamlet's ear. Claudius tells us now that Laertes's ear has been infected (line 89) by rumours and 'pestilent speeches' (line 90) arising from the murder and his ill-advised secret burial of Polonius. It is striking that Shakespeare should present both **Revenge Heroes** as poisoned in this way. Claudius is at his most desperate and lowest ebb: 'this/Like to a murdering piece, in many places/Gives me superfluous death' (lines 93–5). The messenger's concentrated, powerful narrative presents Laertes in an **epic simile** moving like an unstoppable force: 'The ocean, overpeering of his list,/Eats not the flats with more impitious haste/Than young Laertes in a riotous head/O'erbears your officers.' (lines 99–102). Where Part 1 of the play moved very slowly, Part II, with extreme dramatic economy, moves at a cracking pace.

> **CONTEXT** **A04**
>
> Claudius's hypocrisy in voicing the **ideology** of the divinity of kings when he himself has slaughtered the Lord's anointed marks him as the most **Machiavellian** of all Shakespearean monarchs. And for the moment, the bluster works.

STUDY FOCUS: A VERY DIFFERENT REVENGE HERO — A02

The parallels and differences between the two Revenge Heroes are boldly presented: Laertes is Hamlet simplified. With not the remotest claim to the throne, he has no sooner returned than the populace wish to make him king. He confronts Claudius boldly and clearly, without concealing his fury in riddles: 'O thou vile king,/Give me my father … That drop of blood that's calm proclaims me bastard' (lines 116–18). We never hear a word about Polonius's wife, Laertes's mother, but Shakespeare makes a parallel: restraint, delay, pausing to reflect all cry 'cuckold to my father, brands the harlot …/between the chaste unsmirchèd brow/Of my true mother' (lines 118–21). We can  only wonder how the adulterous King and Queen feel at Laertes's unconscious **allusion** to their situation. Note that the branding **image** Laertes uses is exactly the one Hamlet used to his mother in the closet scene (III.4.42–4).

REVISION FOCUS: TASK 3

Consider these two statements:

- Claudius is at his best in an emergency.
- Laertes is no match for the sophisticated and cunning King.

Draft the opening paragraphs of essays based on the discussion points above. Refer closely to the language of this scene.

ACT IV SCENE 6

SUMMARY

- Hamlet has escaped from the ship that was taking him to his execution in England.
- He warns Horatio to join him as quickly as he would 'fly death' (line 20).

ANALYSIS

DRAMATIC EXPEDIENCY

Shakespeare now advances the plot quickly at the cost of some credibility. Hamlet's letter, which Horatio reads aloud for the audience's benefit, describes a sequence of events which would otherwise occupy far too much stage time. The picture of Hamlet bravely boarding a pirate vessel and the subsequent fates of Rosencrantz and Guildenstern show Shakespeare sacrificing plausibility for the sake of the drama. It is a tidy but clumsy trick to prepare the ground for the dramatic climax.

Hamlet is the only major character we see with the common touch. He talks easily to the actors, the pirates, the sailors and the gravedigger. It is plausible that, as Claudius says in the next scene, 'the general gender' love him (IV.7.18).

STUDY FOCUS: FORTUNE A02

The fabulous, romantic event of Hamlet's escape is so out of character with the rest of the play that it startles us. That is the dramatic point: the episode illustrates the operation of Fortune (chance, accident, luck) in the shaping of human destinies, the lesson of which will influence Hamlet's outlook in the coming scenes. Like his friends the actors, the pirates readily help Hamlet; his description of them as 'thieves of mercy' (line 17) makes them seem to be part of the workings of a benevolent God. We never discover what 'good turn' (line 18) Hamlet is to do his rescuers and we could argue that Shakespeare's attempt to make their charity seem credible is clumsy.

The style of Hamlet's letter has a clarity and energy about it which reflects a new outlook in the writer. Whether it be the sea, the working of providence or simply Hamlet's escaping the stench of the prison of Denmark, the Hamlet we meet in the last act will be in many ways a different person from the tortured young man we have been watching up to now.

KEY QUOTATION: ACT IV SCENE 6 A01

Hamlet urges Horatio to join him as he 'wouldest fly death' (line 20).

- It is indicative of the change which has come over Hamlet that he now feels life is preferable to death.
- It is also moving since we shall hear Claudius plotting to cut that life short in the next scene.

CONTEXT A04

Hamlet managed to jump ship 'in the grapple' (line 15). To make hand-to-hand fighting possible between ships, grappling irons were thrown to haul the boats alongside one another.

CONTEXT A03

In Shakespeare's romance *The Tempest*, written at the end of his career, he uses a sea storm symbolically as a kind of baptism. Characters' old selves die and emerge sea-changed – the better for their immersion, their symbolic drowning.

ACT IV SCENE 7

SUMMARY

- Claudius has been describing to Laertes the circumstances of Polonius's death.
- He explains that he could not hold the Prince to account in public because of the Queen's love for her son and Hamlet's popularity with the Danish people.
- Claudius is about to reveal what action he did take, when a letter arrives from Hamlet informing Claudius of his return 'naked' (line 43) and 'alone' (line 51).
- Claudius and Laertes plot Hamlet's death, Claudius testing Laertes's resolve to avenge his father.
- Gertrude enters and in a poetic **set piece** describes Ophelia's death by drowning.
- Claudius tells Gertrude he has been placating Laertes whereas in fact he has been stirring him up.

ANALYSIS

CONTEXT

Claudius uses astrological **imagery** to describe his relationship with Gertrude: 'as the star moves not but in his sphere,/I could not but by her' (lines 15–16). The medieval astronomers believed that each planet was moved by its own spherical force-field.

CLAUDIUS IN CONTROL

Shakespeare writes some of his most vigorous conversation in the first part of this scene which functions as a parallel 'temptation scene' to the one in which Hamlet received his orders from the Ghost. With the Prince off stage, Shakespeare has scope to develop, briefly but fully, the personalities of his **antagonists**. The scene begins **in media res** and pushes the action along swiftly whilst foregrounding the psychological and symbolic contrasts between the two **Revenge Heroes**. Claudius has regained his poise and controls the progress of the scene until he is interrupted by Gertrude with her account of Ophelia's drowning.

PLOTTING AND POISON

Whilst we have been listening to Horatio reading Hamlet's letter, Claudius appears to have put his case to Laertes very effectively: he now has him eating from his hand. The King's declaration of love for Gertrude (lines 12–16), though it adds poignancy to the final scene, is clearly less than the truth: he has plotted already and is about to plot again the death of the son by whose looks he claims the Queen lives (lines 11–12).

Although not physically present, Hamlet shadows the proceedings and when his letter arrives, its language: 'naked' and 'alone' (lines 43 and 51): sounds like a provocation to Claudius to move against him. The resourceful Claudius no sooner registers this setback to his plans than another is 'ripe in [his] device' (line 63); the King is decisive, unscrupulous and practical. Although he admits it will be a device to trick the Queen into believing Hamlet's death is an accident, he plans to exploit Laertes's desire for revenge to secure his own position. In Act V Scene 2 Hamlet backs up what at first sight seems an unlikely story: that the sinisterly named Lamord ('death') had praised Laertes's fencing skills so much that Hamlet longed to fight him, 'envenom[ed]' with the kind of 'emulate pride' (I.1.83) which animated his father. Laertes will use an envenomed sword to kill him.

OPHELIA'S SUICIDE

The **lyrical**, eighteen-line **narrative** poem in which Gertrude represents Ophelia's death is another instant **anthology** piece and may well have been composed earlier than the play. Its lyrical beauty is consistent with the way Ophelia has been presented, mainly in song, in Act IV.

Many critics have commented upon the speech's 'unreality'; it does not sound like Gertrude talking, and what she says she observed raises problem after problem. Her account is too sweet, too rich, too utterly improbable to fit either the situation or the **narrator**. But we have noted already Shakespeare's stylisation of Ophelia's response to her father's death and, given Gertrude's stated loyalty to her son, it could be argued that she sanitises Ophelia's suicide deliberately to spare Laertes' feelings and thus not add to Hamlet's danger. Gertrude deliberately blames everything in Ophelia's surroundings for her death, rather than the girl herself. In the next scene, we will hear the straight-talking common folk speak less charitably about the event.

This moment of **pathos** is followed immediately by the King's crude lie to his wife: 'How much I had to do to calm his rage' (line 192). It completes the audience's alienation from the scheming Claudius and prepares for the pathos of Hamlet's death by treachery.

CONTEXT A04

There are many paintings of this scene, the most famous of Ophelia's death scene which are by the Victorian painter Millais and the French nineteenth-century artist Alexandre Cabanel. The English composer Frank Bridge re-presented it as a tone poem (a one-movement symphonic work on a literary theme).

STUDY FOCUS: REVENGE WITHOUT BOUNDS A02

Before he proceeds with his plot, Claudius questions Laertes to see if his desire for vengeance is robust or whether in his grief is 'like the painting of a sorrow,/A face without a heart' (lines 107–8): the phrase recalls Gertrude's accusing Hamlet of pretend grief in Act 1 Scene 2. When he asks Laertes what he would do to prove himself a loyal son, Laertes responds without hesitation: 'To cut his throat i'th'church' (line 125) as if he too had been watching the play and seen Hamlet unable to kill Claudius at prayer (III.3). None of the scruples which inhibited Hamlet's revenge affect Laertes; he is the only character in the play who does not seem to live in a Christian universe. Clearly shocked by the young man's atheism, Claudius proceeds to engineer a plot with him. Like similar schemes in many **Revenge Tragedies**, this one involves deception and poison; it is of a piece with the King's murder of his brother. Despite his anguish in the Chapel (III.3) Claudius has no hesitation in planning to kill another member of his family. And Laertes, who makes such an issue of his 'honour', has no hesitation in behaving disreputably. By contrast, Claudius confirms that Hamlet is: 'Most generous, and free from all contriving' (line 134). The polarisation of good and bad characters is complete.

KEY QUOTATION: ACT IV SCENE 7 A01

That we would do,
We should do when we would for this 'would' changes,
And hath abatement and delays (lines 117–19)

- Claudius's observation sounds like a commentary on Hamlet's procrastination.
- The halting rhythm and confusing repetitions capture the way thoughts often get into a tangle.

ACT V SCENE 1

SUMMARY

- Two gravediggers discuss Ophelia's suicide and the way it has been hushed up.
- Hamlet and Horatio contemplate the inconstancy of all things. Contemplating a skull thrown up by the gravedigger, Hamlet learns that it is Yorrick's, Old Hamlet's Fool. Reflecting on the fate of the man who was dear to him in his childhood lends poignancy to Hamlet's meditations.
- Ophelia's funeral procession arrives; Laertes's ranting display of grief for Ophelia enrages Hamlet who proclaims he genuinely loved her and the two men fight by her graveside.

ANALYSIS

THE MESSAGE OF THE SKULL

The Globe's simple stage used the minimum of props yet the power of this scene is achieved largely by spectacle. Hamlet holding the skull of Yorrick is the most widely recognised **tableau** in the whole of drama and this is also the best-known **memento mori** scene in literature. 'Memento mori' is Latin for 'remember you are mortal', 'don't forget that you, too, will die'. Remembering that we will die helps us to see what is and is not important. What we see at the beginning of this scene is as important as what we hear. Amidst skulls and gravestones, we encounter two comic gravediggers: they are at the same time characters in this play and universal gravediggers who are symbols of death. In this scene, as before, the context is Christian. Throughout the play we have been made aware that all the major players save Laertes believe in an afterlife where they will be judged on their conduct on Earth and sent either to Heaven or Hell. This scene crystallises the debate which Hamlet has been having with himself since his first appearance about how a man should behave in a world answerable to God.

THE UNIVERSAL GRAVEDIGGER

The first half of this scene, written in **colloquial prose**, is the longest comic sequence in *Hamlet* and serves as a dramatic contrast to what follows. It provides a welcome change of tone and pace three hours or more into a very long play. The humour is profoundly serious as well as funny: it represents a different way of exploring the themes of suicide, appearance and reality, disease and corruption, fame and thinking, which have until now been the subject of more sophisticated debate. Shakespeare gives half the lines to the first gravedigger, half to Hamlet; this time the Prince does not adopt 'an antic disposition' (I.5.172), he adopts the stance of the Clown, the impartial observer, the outsider who sees the unvarnished essence of things, what T. S. Eliot calls 'the skull beneath the skin' ('Whispers of Immortality') and speaks his mind fearlessly.

Illiterate, 'rude' and working-class, the first gravedigger is an 'ancient gentlem[a]n' (lines 24–5) tracing his profession back to Adam. The singing sexton is a figure who is timeless and unchanging; like the Porter in *Macbeth*, the gravedigger in *Hamlet* is the great leveller: 'knock[ing] ... about the sconce with a dirty shovel' (lines 85–6) all classes of men and women. This is the man who has dug the grave in which Yorrick lay, and in which Ophelia is to be buried. Soon he will deal with Hamlet, Laertes, the King and the Queen. His song is about the stages of human life that lead everyone to his rough, indiscriminate care. He refers familiarly to Adam and to the Day of Judgement. He has been there from the beginning of human history, long before Alexander and Caesar, Claudius and Hamlet came into the world, and will be busy until the final trumpet.

CONTEXT — A04

The comic gravedigger in Hamlet was probably played by Robert Armin. He almost certainly played a similar role in *Macbeth*: the Porter of Macbeth's castle who also represents the Porter of the gates of Hell. You may like to compare the words, behaviour and impact of the two roles (*Macbeth*, II.3.1–42). Both figures deal with all classes of people and are especially hard on 'equivocators' (liars).

In their conversation, the gravedigger reminds Hamlet of his father and the temporary heroic glory which the name Hamlet stood for. He began the job 'that day that our last King Hamlet o'ercame Fortinbras' (lines 120–1). The gravedigger has outlived both of them. His career in Denmark began the very day Hamlet was born and he will take care of him when he dies.

EARTH TO EARTH

Gertrude's pretty **narrative** (IV.7) of Ophelia's drowning is bluntly discredited by the first gravedigger who is in no doubt that 'she drowned herself wittingly' (lines 10–11). The opening **dialogue** (lines 1–50) is peppered by terms such as 'Christian burial', 'salvation', 'scripture', 'church' and 'doomsday' which assert the play's religious context. Hamlet's first extended speech refers to Abel's murder and the politician 'that would circumvent God' (line 67) reminding us of Claudius's crime and his agonised attempt to pray (III.3).

STUDY FOCUS: A SEA CHANGE A02

The Hamlet who returns from his sea voyage is strikingly different from the man we saw leaving Elsinore. What has brought about this second 'transformation' will be revealed in the next scene. Hamlet has no **soliloquies** in Act V, he is no longer crippled by indecision; he can share his most intimate thoughts with Horatio. He sees things with a clarity and definition which make his death by treachery feel like a tragic waste. Although Horatio suggests there is still an echo of the man who was guilty of 'thinking too precisely on th'event' (IV.4.41) in his meditation on the fate of Alexander: ''Twere to consider too curiously to consider so' (line 174) Hamlet argues his case convincingly. The skull of Yorrick, the jester he loved as a boy, and upon whom he perhaps models his Fooling, prompts him to consider the fates of heroic figures even greater than his famous father. If even Alexander and Caesar, the most renowned of emperors, end up no more than a 'quintessence of dust' (II.2.290) perhaps his father is also diminished in terms of Eternity.

It is noticeable that the Ghost's 'commandment' (I.5.102) does not figure in Hamlet's thinking in Act V. In contemplating the fact that Alexander and Julius Caesar, warriors far greater than his father, are now no more than dust, Hamlet is exorcising the Ghost's hold over him. His irreverent song marks a release from his obligation to that awesome warrior whose 'commandment' (I.5.102) he has felt obliged to carry out but could not. If Caesar is insignificant, his father becomes invisible. Later in the scene the Prince celebrates this freedom by announcing: 'This is I,/Hamlet the Dane' (lines 224–5). He appreciates the ultimate insignificance of the man who at the beginning of the play he compared to a god.

RANTING LAERTES

A major theme in *Hamlet* is the immorality of pretence, 'seeming', hypocrisy and deception. In Act IV Scene 7 Laertes promised 'a speech of fire that fain would blaze' (line 190). Now we hear that language. It is full of **hyperbole**: we sense that Laertes is trying to create an effect of wild grief with a 'phrase of sorrow' (line 222) rather than feeling it. We recall his father's self-important blustering. Laertes is especially fond of inflated statistics: 'Oh treble woe/Fall ten times treble on that cursèd head' (lines 213–14). Theatrically he leaps into Ophelia's grave and asks to be buried in a pile of dust which reaches the heavens (lines 218–21). Infuriated by 'the bravery [showiness] of his grief' (V.2.79), Hamlet bursts forward, challenges the Laertes whose 'grief/Bears such an emphasis' (lines 221–2) and mocks his inflated **rhetoric**: 'forty thousand brothers … with all their *quantity* of love' (author's italics, lines 236–7); his 'millions of acres' (line 248) cannot match Hamlet's genuine affection. He accuses Laertes of whining, mouthing, acting, trying to 'outface' (line 245) him, indulging in extravagant gestures: 'Woo't drink up eisel, eat a crocodile?' (line 243). We are reminded of his scathing attack on Ophelia for face-painting (III.1). He seems to have forgotten entirely that he has killed Laertes's father: 'What is the reason that you use me thus?' (line 256). Both Claudius and Gertrude, who know better, excuse

Hamlet's fury as 'madness' (lines 239 and 251). Gertrude through increased tenderness for her son, and Claudius, anxious not to disrupt the plan to kill his nephew, pretend that Hamlet's criticism is meaningless. Hamlet storms off, full of contempt for this conspiracy of deceit: 'The cat will mew, and dog will have his day' (line 259)

CONTEXT **A04**

With the words 'an act hath three branches' (lines 9–10) Shakespeare's clowns are making **satiric** fun of a famous contemporary case of suicide. This is examined in the Arden edition of *Hamlet* edited by Harold Jenkins (1982).

STUDY FOCUS: A DEATHLY CARNIVAL **A02**

Political criticism points to the **subversive** nature of the comedy which opens the final act of the play. The gravedigger plays Hamlet at his own word games and outlives all the high-born characters he serves. Michael D. Bristol points out that:

> Against the perspective of death and burial, all claims to hierarchical superiority are nullified, … economic, political or moral systems become the objects of laughter … In the grave-diggers' world-view, Doomsday is a horizon that corresponds to the overthrow of social inequality. '"Funeral Bak'd meats": Carnival and the Carnivalesque in *Hamlet*', reprinted in Susan Zimmerman (ed.), *New Casebooks, Shakespeare's Tragedies* (1998)

In other words, Shakespeare's gravedigger encapsulates two connected ideas: that of death being the great leveller – it makes no distinction between rich and poor, nobles and commoners – and that of carnival and clowning, where irreverence and humour can break down social barriers and the order of the world is turned upside down.

GLOSSARY

2	**her own salvation**	a joke. The gravedigger means 'damnation': a suicide would go to Hell
16	**Argal**	The gravedigger means 'ergo' (Latin for therefore)
67	**one that would circumvent God**	somebody who thought he could cheat, deceive God
74	**chopless**	missing the bottom jaw
75	**mazard**	skull
77	**loggets**	skittles
93	**this box**	coffin
140	**pocky**	rotten with sexual disease, falling to bits
174	**to consider too curiously**	to reason too fastidiously
176	**Alexander**	Alexander the Great, perhaps the greatest soldier of all time, famous for his beauty
180	**Imperious Caesar**	Julius Caesar, who conquered Britain
199	**crants**	wreathes
228	**splenitive**	hot-tempered. Not the way we usually think of Hamlet
254	**when that her golden couplets are disclosed**	when her chicks are hatched

ACT V SCENE 2

SUMMARY

- Hamlet reveals that whilst at sea he discovered the plot against him and sentenced Rosencrantz and Guildenstern to death and damnation.
- Hamlet concludes that justice and conscience dictate that Claudius must die.
- Claudius's courtier, Osric, invites Hamlet to a fencing match with Laertes; Hamlet **parodies** Osric's verbal affectations.
- Despite grim intimations, Hamlet accepts the challenge. Before the match, he apologises to Laertes.
- Laertes strikes Hamlet with the poisoned foil and is in turn fatally wounded with it; Gertrude defies Claudius and drinks from the poisoned cup Claudius prepared for her son.
- Dying, the Queen and Laertes accuse Claudius; Hamlet kills the King.
- In grief for Hamlet, Horatio tries to commit suicide.
- Hamlet begs Horatio to tell his story 'aright' (line 318); he nominates Young Fortinbras successor to the Danish throne.
- Young Fortinbras arrives; Horatio summarises the action of the play.
- Fortinbras takes control and orders a soldier's funeral for Hamlet.

ANALYSIS

A KIND OF WILD JUSTICE

Coming at the end of Shakespeare's longest work, this scene is full of invention and variety; it is by far the longest in the play. If the audience is feeling tired, Shakespeare evidently is not; he presents us with a satisfying and dramatically exciting working-out of the major issues. We saw how in Act IV Shakespeare began to separate the virtuous and wicked characters. In Act V this process continues so that by the end of it, Claudius is isolated as the source of all corruption and wickedness in Denmark. It was his seduction of the Queen and murder of the King which set in motion the tragic juggernaut which destroys all the major players. Laertes feels a twinge of conscience for the first time just before the fencing match (line 274) and by the time he dies he has pardoned Hamlet for killing his father and himself, and he and Hamlet have 'Exchange[d] forgiveness' (line 308). Gertrude shows Hamlet maternal affection and fatally defies her husband. In killing Claudius, Hamlet avenges not only his father but also his mother, Laertes and himself. It is Laertes who spells out the rightfulness of his own death: 'I am justly killed with mine own treachery' (line 287) and reveals the King's moral corruption to the assembled court. It is significant that when Hamlet kills Claudius he denounces him for incest first and his murders second. Bacon condemned revenge as 'a kind of wild justice' ('Of Revenge', 1625). At the end of *Hamlet*, most people would agree that justice has been seen to be done.

Hamlet claims that all that matters is being prepared for the judgement that awaits us after death: 'If it be now, 'tis not to come; if it be not to come, it will be now; if it be not now, yet it will come – the readiness is all' (lines 193–5). The simplicity of what Hamlet says here (almost entirely in **monosyllables**) is a mark of its humility and sincerity. He is discussing all this calmly with Horatio, no longer passionately turning it over in his own mind. Now when he considers the morality of taking Claudius's life, there is a similar clarity:

GRADE BOOSTER **A03**

How should this exciting **denouement**, where action largely replaces talking, be staged? Is Osric involved in Claudius's scheming or an impartial referee? Does Gertrude realise she is drinking poison when she defies her husband? When does Hamlet realise he is again 'benetted round with villainies' (line 29)? How does the court react when the King is assassinated? Is Fortinbras's entry presented as something sinister or as a fresh start for an unfortunate country?

CONTEXT **A04**

At sea, mutineers were punished by being put into iron shackles, hence 'mutines in the bilboes' (line 6).

CONTEXT A04

Sons did not automatically succeed their fathers in Denmark but Hamlet suggests that Claudius got himself chosen as King by devious means: 'Popped in between th'election and my hopes' (line 65).

He that hath killed my king, and whor'd my mother,
Popped in between th'election and my hopes,
Thrown out his angle for my proper life,
And with such cozenage – is't not perfect conscience
To quit him with this arm? And is't not to be damnèd
To let this canker of our nature come
In further evil? (lines 64–70)

Hamlet uses the possessive pronoun 'my' four times and 'our' once: the cause is Hamlet's own, no longer a duty to a remote ghost. By presenting young Hamlet here as a man of simple faith and as so witty and alive in the exchange with Osric, Shakespeare accentuates the grief we will feel when we lose our engaging hero.

STUDY FOCUS: HAMLET'S SECOND TRANSFORMATION A02

Hamlet's vivid **narrative** to Horatio could not be more coherent or succinct: stylistically nothing could be less like the tormented and confused **soliloquies** in Act II Scene 2 and Act IV Scene 4. His experiences at sea have given Hamlet a new perspective on things. Something prevented him sleeping, prompted him 'rashly' to open the King's commission (line 6). Without hesitation, he amended the document and thanks to heaven's 'ordinan[ce]' (line 48) was able to seal it with Old Hamlet's signet ring, the first benefit he has enjoyed from being his father's son. Hamlet now recognises that sometimes 'indiscretion' (line 8) serves us better than over scrupulous thinking. He and Horatio are in no doubt that the directing intelligence in such cases is God's: 'There's a divinity that shapes our ends,/Rough-hew them how we will –/That is most certain' (lines 10–12). It is an endorsement of the simple faith Horatio expressed at the beginning of the play: 'Heaven will direct it' (I.4.91). The Hamlet who has returned to Denmark has a new philosophical strength. He has a grasp not only of his own situation but also of the universe in which he operates. As the plans for the fencing match are made and Hamlet senses deception taking place, he expresses forcefully his faith and trust in God: 'Not a whit. We defy augury. There is special providence in the fall of a sparrow' (lines 192–3).

CONTEXT A04

Hamlet's words are an **allusion** to Christ's words in St Matthew's Gospel: 'Are not two sparrows sold for a farthing? And none of them doth light on the ground, without your father .... Feare ye not therefore: ye are of more value than many sparrows.' (Matthew 10 vv29–31) Tyndale's Translation of the New Testament, 1534

THE DENOUEMENT: KILLING THE KING

There's such divinity doth hedge a king
That treason can but peep to what it would,
Acts little of his will (IV.5.124–6)

Where previously we have seen Hamlet wrestling with his conscience, now he believes 'quit[ting]' (line 68) the King who is clearly the author of so many crimes would be 'perfect conscience' (line 67); indeed, to let the man who infects the country, 'this canker of our nature' (line 69), do more evil would be 'damn(able)' (line 68). There is no need for an agonised soliloquy; Hamlet has achieved a moral certainty which few in the audience would take issue with; as long as Claudius lives, he will be involved in 'cozenage' (line 67). Hamlet's way forward is clear. It is now just a matter of opportunity: 'The interim's mine' (line 73). This is the second moment in the play when Hamlet talks about Claudius having seized the throne from him 'Popped in between th'election and my hopes' (line 65). Having asserted himself as the rightful King, 'Hamlet the Dane', in the previous scene (V.1.224), he now sees his responsibilities to the state as being as important as any obligation to the Ghost. Killing Claudius would not be private vengeance but the dispensing of justice and restoring the health of Denmark. Hamlet executes Claudius only when everyone has seen that he deserves it. The immediate response of the court to the deed is the cry: 'Treason, treason!' (line 302). But Laertes's testimony 'He is justly served' (line 306) and Horatio's explanations will fully justify Hamlet's apparently wild and lawless act. No other villain in Shakespeare is guilty of so many crimes as Claudius: adultery, regicide, usurpation, incest, attempted murder and manslaughter. As the conscientious Horatio observes: 'Why, what a king is this!' (line 62).

A PROBLEMATIC APOLOGY

Many commentators have been unhappy about Hamlet's apology to Laertes (lines 198–216). Given Hamlet's evident sanity here and his scrupulous concern at all times for the truth, his laying of the blame for his offences on 'madness' (line 204), which he characterises as an alter ego, a false self, rings hollow. We know that his killing of Polonius was not 'a purposed evil' (line 213) but his claiming innocence on the grounds of madness is surely dishonest? We have seen throughout the play that Hamlet's madness has in all likelihood been a convenient fiction, subscribed to for various reasons by Claudius, Gertrude and the Prince himself. Yet here, Shakespeare surely intends Hamlet to sound sincere. The tone of the final lines is moving but the reasoning seems unsatisfactory. The apology is one of the Prince's most perplexing utterances.

But perhaps the fiction of the 'antic disposition' (I.5.172) is maintained here because Hamlet is still unsure how he will deal with the cunning and unscrupulous King. We must remember he does not know how the match will end; despite his faith in God, he believes he still has to find some way of restoring the country.

STUDY FOCUS: WHAT SORT OF TRAGEDY IS *HAMLET*? A02

Throughout the play, Hamlet has found it impossible to translate the Ghost's 'commandment' (I.5.102) into action. No matter how vehemently he believed that he should take revenge, something held him back. Now he finds himself in an action initiated by others: 'Or I could make a prologue to my brains/They had begun the play.' (lines 30–1). There has been no chance to analyse or question things: the initiative has been seized by Claudius. The mechanism which will lead to Hamlet's death will '[Fall] on th'inventors' heads' (line 364), those of Claudius and Laertes. What will look to Young Fortinbras's eyes like 'havoc' (line 343) has method in it: the working out of what we call poetic or divine justice. Hamlet's death will be the price paid for unchecked villainy. Had the court scrutinised Claudius's marriage rather than 'freely gone ... along' (I.2.15–16) with it, Denmark would not have fallen into Norwegian hands. Rather than resembling the shape of Shakespeare's later **tragedies** where the **protagonist** suffers for his egotistical blindness, *Hamlet*, in this respect, is more like *Romeo and Juliet* where the wickedness of others brings about the death of protagonists we admire. Where Othello, Lear and Macbeth pass judgement on themselves, Hamlet leaves it to Horatio to 'report [him and his] cause aright' (line 318), and for us to judge. Fortinbras sounds the note of tragic waste: 'For he was likely, had he been put on,/To have proved most royal' (lines 376–7).

DRAMATIC VARIETY

The dramatic qualities of the fencing match are not apparent on the page. What takes a few seconds to read accounts for many minutes of stage time. After a play in which most of the activity has been in intellectual wordplay, this exciting sword-play comes as the latest of so many varied ingredients. Some productions show Hamlet realising he has been wounded and deliberately exchanging the foils and striking Laertes. This is not supported by the text, which generates far greater **pathos** by leaving Hamlet totally innocent of what is going on until Laertes tells him.

Yet for all the seriousness of the final chapter of this tragedy, it is enlivened by the play's funniest episode. Hamlet's exchanges with Osric present a comically concentrated version of the many similar exchanges Hamlet has had with others who abuse language. Hamlet's sensitivity in this matter was already apparent in Act I Scene 2, where he showed such hostility to Claudius calling him his 'son' (I.2.67), and to Gertrude's unfortunate use of the words 'common' and 'seems' (I.2.74 and 76). For much of the play, it was Polonius whose inflated sense of his own importance and cynical abuse of his daughter led him to **rhetorical** excess (see I.3 and II.2). Earlier in Act VI (V.1.116–18) Hamlet had commented that the gravedigger's fondness for wordplay was a symptom of the decadence of the times

CONTEXT A04

Boethius's *Consolation of Philosophy* was a hugely influential book in the Middle Ages and the **Renaissance**. Boethius shows how the goddess Fortune who appears to distribute good and bad luck indiscriminately is in fact the handmaiden of God: testing the virtuous and giving the wicked scope to ruin themselves.

CRITICAL VIEWPOINT A03

'Hamlet senses that he too has become part of a larger process: the plot of Providence as scripted by the divine Playwright.' James L. Calderwood, *To Be And Not To Be, Negation and Metadrama in Hamlet* (1983).

and in his exchanges with Laertes (lines 222–59) it was his **hyperbolic** ranting which provoked Hamlet.

Now, as a dramatic **foil** to the climactic fencing match, the mood is closer to **farce**. Osric is an upstart courtier, 'spacious in the possession of dirt' (line 87), who has little to say but attempts to make a showy impression in his speech by dressing it up in as many words as possible. By the word 'impawned' (line 135) Osric means 'wagered' but this is obviously an affected way of saying it since Hamlet mocks him for using it; likewise Osric makes himself ridiculous by using the word 'carriages' (line 137). In his description of Laertes in particular (lines 101–5), Osric praises Laertes extravagantly and in the process misuses English ludicrously. Hamlet employs similar ornate terms, such as 'definement' (definition, line 106) and 'verity of extolment' (justifiable praise, lines 108–9), and thus **parodies** and completely baffles Osric in response. When Hamlet out-Osrics Osric, the courtier is completely floored by **tautology**: 'Why do we wrap the gentleman in our more rawer breath? … What imports the nomination of this gentleman?' (lines 114–19).

STUDY FOCUS: THE TRAGIC EPITAPH A02

Horatio's poignant farewell to his friend, 'Now cracks a noble heart. Good night, sweet Prince,/And flights of angels sing thee to thy rest' (lines 338–9), usually expresses the feelings of the audience. But when he describes events in lines 359–65 we need to ask whether his account leaves out anything central to our understanding of what has happened. The audience has been privy to many things that Horatio has not. How would you sum up the tragic epitaph?

REVISION FOCUS: TASK 4

Consider the following statements:

- The Hamlet Shakespeare presents in Act V is in many ways a different man from the Hamlet we saw earlier in the play.
- *Hamlet* is a play in which Shakespeare **satirises** the misuse of language.

Draft the opening paragraphs of essays based on the discussion points above.

CHECK THE FILMS A04

Watch as many different productions of the final scene as possible, carefully noting what is cut, what is emphasised, what the directors and actors add in terms of stage business, music and lighting to generate the particular mood of their reading of the play's finale. Think about how you would present the scene.

CONTEXT A04

In Classical Roman and Greek literature, suicide is presented not as a sin but as an heroic way for someone to end his/her life. Thus in Shakespeare's Roman works, Lucretia, Brutus and Cleopatra are praised for taking their own lives. By identifying with the 'ancient Roman' (line 320) Horatio momentarily follows a different ethical code from his usual Christian one. Yet a few lines later he calls on 'flights of angels' (line 339) to sing Hamlet to his rest.

CHARACTERS

HAMLET

WHO IS HAMLET?

- Prince Hamlet is the son of his namesake, Old Hamlet, the previous King of Denmark.
- Hamlet was born on the day of his father's famous victory over King Fortinbras of Norway, thirty years before the play begins.
- He is a scholar at the Protestant University of Wittenberg.
- His mother, Gertrude, has hastily remarried after Old Hamlet's sudden death.
- His uncle, Claudius, has married Gertrude and seized the throne.
- Hamlet loves Ophelia, daughter of Claudius's right-hand man, Polonius.

A COMPLEX REVENGE HERO

Shakespeare was attempting something new and daring in this play. No character in literature had ever been explored so fully in his actions and reflections; Hamlet's **soliloquies** are a searching examination of how we think about difficult issues in critical situations. Each of his seven soliloquies has its own colour and rhythms: you will find analyses of each of them in **Part Two** of these Notes. What Shakespeare shows us are the different ways the mind works under pressure: not logically, like a computer, but torn this way and that by reason, feeling and by the tricks of language itself. There is no play of *Hamlet* without the Prince; the amount of stage time Shakespeare allots him means that other characters are presented much more sketchily. In his later (and shorter) **tragedies**, Shakespeare gives the tragic **protagonist** much less stage time so he can develop other characters more fully. *Hamlet* remains Shakespeare's most extended study of personality.

| CONTEXT | A04 |

Shakespeare chooses Wittenburg as Hamlet's university (the place where Martin Luther launched the Protestant Reformation) with its emphasis upon biblical authority and individual responsibility.

THE STARTING POINT

Hamlet's situation as the play opens could hardly be more testing. His father, the widely revered and heroic King whom Hamlet idolised, dies suddenly and, with scandalous haste, his mother gets remarried to his uncle. Whether modern audiences feel such a marriage is incestuous and sinful as the Elizabethans did, is irrelevant. The haste of the marriage is a fact: not only Horatio but also Gertrude confirm that. What dismays Hamlet is that Gertrude always seemed to love her husband and wept copiously at his funeral. That she has remarried so quickly suggests she had been deceiving her husband and everyone else. There is nothing morbid or difficult to understand about Hamlet's melancholy in Act I Scene 2: he has received a complicated moral shock. It is the behaviour of everyone else which is puzzling. Hamlet alone is in mourning; custom dictated at least a year's mourning for the death of a king. Isolated and ridiculed by the hypocritical Queen and the villainous King for play acting and being 'impious', (I.2.94) 'unmanly' (I.2.94) and 'absurd' (I.2.103), Hamlet feels suicidal but is bound by his belief in judgement in the afterlife to suffer in silence.

MELANCHOLY DRAMATISED

But what Shakespeare gives us is something much more life-like than any cool **prose** appraisal of Hamlet's condition can be. The regular verse rhythms of **blank verse** are torn apart by the feeling of helplessness. His recollections do not sound like a list of bullet points but are jumbled up and full of disturbing **imagery**. Shakespeare is trying to pull off a very difficult trick: to present a picture of a troubled mind which is both intelligible to the audience but faithful to the way the mind plays tricks, works illogically, and catches at confusing ideas sometimes directly, at other times at a tangent. Where Laertes thinks in single ideas uncomplicated by conflicting notions of right and wrong, Hamlet is presented as someone almost paralysed by his sense of the complexity and subtleties of things.

STUDY FOCUS: A VOICE FROM BEYOND THE GRAVE A02

Hamlet is presented with the demands of the Ghost when he is already in a dejected state of mind. It must be remembered that Hamlet identifies the Ghost with his father and his immediate response to a voice which he has always respected is simple and straightforward:

> Remember thee? …
> … thy commandment all alone shall live
> Within the book and volume of my brain,
> Unmixed with baser matter (I.5.97–104)

But what Shakespeare explores in the rest of the play is how all that other 'matter' in Hamlet's brain shapes his response to that dubious 'commandment'. Whether his reservations really are 'baser': cowardly, 'unmanly' (I.2.94), 'dull' (IV.4.33) or rather the promptings of that 'god-like reason' (IV.4.38) which distinguishes a man from a beast is what the play asks us to judge.

BETRAYAL

Hamlet's situation is complicated by a further emotional shock. He is presented in the play as someone who sets a high value upon telling the truth: his **soliloquies** could be described as the search for a difficult sincerity. So, when we are told he declared his love for Ophelia 'With almost all the holy vows of heaven' (I.3.114) and he says at her graveside that he loved her sincerely, it rings true. Without explanation, she suddenly rejects him and later allows herself to be used so the King can spy on him. Meanwhile two other former friends (Gertrude claims that 'two men there are not living/To whom he more adheres', II.2.20–1) enlist themselves as spies in the King's service. If Hamlet felt alienated in Act I Scene 2, his situation is a whole lot worse in Act II Scene 2.

By this point there has been a long delay between Hamlet's soliloquies, time enough for the ambassadors to travel to Norway and return. In the interim we are told Hamlet has undergone a 'transformation' (II.2.5); whatever he has done, he has not carried out the Ghost's commandment. He reprimands himself violently for this delay in his 'rogue and peasant slave' soliloquy (II.2.502–58). Some critics argue that the doubts about the Ghost's honesty which Hamlet includes at the end of the speech are a rationalisation of delay: merely an excuse for failing to do his duty. But other critics argue this is to make the mistake of expecting thoughts to move rationally, step by logical step. They suggest that a stubborn, subconscious unease about the validity of the Ghost's request is the key to Hamlet's lack of action. He cannot accuse his father of willing him to damnation but he can, quite properly, suspect devilish temptation. When we remember Laertes's declaration 'I dare damnation' (IV.5.133), we can see how little intelligence has been involved in his arriving at such a rash challenge.

THE MISSION MODIFIED

The Ghost's instructions are complex: see **The problem of the Ghost** in **Part Three: Themes** for a full analysis. Hamlet finds it impossible to carry out the commandment, even when he finds Claudius alone and defenceless at prayer (see **Analysis** in **Part Two: Act III Scene 3**). Nor can he agree to leave his mother to be judged by Heaven as the Ghost instructed. When Hamlet was given his orders, he saw the extent of his task as overwhelming: 'The time is out of joint: Oh cursèd spite,/That ever I was born to set it right.' (I.5.189–90) But 'putting things right' is what he attempts to do instead of simply exacting vengeance. Rather than the 'ambassador of death' as Wilson Knight described him ('The Embassy of Death', in *The Wheel of Fire*, 1930), some critics argue that Hamlet is much more animated by the idea of rescuing his mother, and perhaps Ophelia, from corruption and, finally, of cleansing the kingdom than concentrating on vengeance. See the analysis of the nunnery episode (**Part Two: Act III Scene 1**) and the closet scene (**Part Two: Act III Scene 4**). Hamlet kills the King after deciding that in fact his mission is to carry out a cure rather than simply carry out punishment: it is curative rather than retributive. Hamlet's 'conscience' (III.1.83), which has been the subject of unprecedented study, is what makes him a worthy tragic hero.

CHECK THE BOOK **A04**

'Even though the King were trebly a fratricide, in a Christian sense, it would still be a sin to put him to death with one's own hand, without a trial and without justice.' Herman Ulrici, *Shakespeare's Dramatic Art* (1839).

CHECK THE FILM **A03**

Aristotle stated that tragedy was brought about by a weakness of character in the hero. The words 'some vicious mole of nature' (I.4.24) have led some critics to apply Aristotle's model to Hamlet. Laurence Olivier's 1948 film over-simplifies the play in this way, beginning with the voice-over: 'This is the tragedy of a man who could not make up his mind'.

KEY QUOTATION: HAMLET **A01**

        is't not perfect conscience
To quit him with this arm? And is't not to be damned
To let this canker of our nature come
In further evil? (V.2.67–70)

- Hamlet's conscience has been the focus of dramatic scrutiny throughout the play; finally his sense of duty and his sense of what is morally right are in harmony with one another.

- Retribution for his father's, his mother's, Laertes's and his own death is achieved together with the restoration of Denmark's health.

- The expression is clear and uncluttered; Hamlet's mind is no longer troubled by contradictory motivations and commands.

CLAUDIUS

WHO IS CLAUDIUS?

- Claudius is the younger brother of Old Hamlet, the previous King of Denmark.
- He is now King of Denmark and husband to Gertrude, his brother's widow. Young Hamlet is his nephew and step-son.

A DISCONTENTED YOUNGER BROTHER

Growing up in the shadow of a national hero, 'valiant Hamlet –/For so this side of our known world esteemed him' (I.1.84–5), Claudius was publically mocked whilst his brother was alive (II.2.335–6). Ambitious and in love with his brother's wife, he seduced the Queen and poisoned the King. By marrying Gertrude quickly, he secured the throne as well. Ruthless, pragmatic and decisive, he has many of the characteristics of a **Machiavellian** prince but his major **soliloquy** reveals that his Christian faith and his sense of sin are as strong in him as his villainy.

FIRST IMPRESSIONS

Our first impression of Claudius comes indirectly (I.1). Old Hamlet's death has encouraged Young Fortinbras, 'holding a weak supposal' (I.2.18) of Claudius as a soldier, to try his luck. The impression Hamlet's friends give us is of panic and 'sweaty haste' (I.1.77); shipwrights are forced to work on the Sabbath in an atmosphere of 'post-haste and romage in the land' (I.1.107).

PAINTED WORDS

Yet when we meet the new King, whose position is morally dubious, he exudes confidence and easy control, dealing with affairs systematically until he is stopped by Hamlet's riddles. The **image** projected by this heavy drinker who 'drains his draughts of Rehnish down' (I.4.10) is of a clear-thinking and sensible man: 'You cannot speak of reason to the Dane/And lose your voice' (I.2.44–5). For further discussion of Claudius at the beginning of the play see **Part Two: Act I Scene 2**. Unlike his heroic brother, Claudius behaves like a modern statesman, using diplomacy rather than force to deal with Young Fortinbras. Acutely aware that opinion, at court and more generally, is something which has to be managed, he is quick to gloss Hamlet's rudeness as 'a loving and a fair reply' (I.2.120), his refusal to compromise as 'gentle and unforced accord' (I.2.123). Claudius is a master of spin. The Ghost sees Claudius as a clever and persuasive talker, whose 'witchcraft of his wits' (I.5.43) seduced Gertrude; we will see him meeting every challenge with quick-thinking eloquence.

A TROUBLED CONSCIENCE

Refusing Hamlet permission to return to Wittenberg is an early sign that Claudius wants to keep a potential revenger under observation. As Hamlet's behaviour becomes increasingly problematic, the King has no hesitation in bribing the Prince's fellow students to spy on him or in eavesdropping on his intimate conversation with Ophelia. Claudius sees more to disturb him in Hamlet's 'transformation' (II.2.5) than is explained, describing as 'turbulent and dangerous lunacy' (III.1.4) behaviour which is at worst odd and aggressive. It is another indication that the smiling villain has an uneasy conscience. When Ophelia is used as a decoy, Claudius suddenly reveals his anguish and deceitfulness in a shocking **simile** (see **Analysis** in **Part Two: Act III Scene 1**); beneath the 'smooth and even' (IV.3.7) surface suffers a tormented soul. *The Mousetrap* stings the King into a clear eyed and desperate self-examination (see **Analysis** in **Part Two: Act III Scene 3**). In his agonised

---

CONTEXT **A04**

Brothers in Shakespeare are often enemies. Jealous that in Elizabethan society the eldest son inherited everything, younger brothers are often portrayed by Shakespeare as devious and vicious. Duke Frederick (*As You Like It*), Edmund (*King Lear*) and Antonio (*The Tempest*) are three such villains.

CONTEXT **A04**

The Fourth Commandment forbids work on the sabbath.

---

soliloquy, we have a glimpse of how Shakespeare might have developed the King as a tragic **protagonist**. The God-fearing man who is simultaneously ashamed of his sins and fatally in love with the fruits of wickedness is a prototype of Macbeth.

STUDY FOCUS: SPINNING OUT OF CONTROL — A02

When Gertrude reveals that Hamlet has killed Polonius, we see the King managing public opinion: 'how shall this bloody deed be answered?' (IV.1.16). Claudius realises he is vulnerable to Rumour: 'Whose whisper o'er the world's diameter ... Transports his poisoned shot' (IV, 1. 41–3).

He dresses up his murderous plan as responsible governance: 'How dangerous is it that this man goes loose', aware that public opinion favours Hamlet (IV.3.4) and of the need to be seen 'To bear all smooth and even' (IV.3.7). He rehearses the spin he will put on the affair: 'so much was our love' (IV.1.19) he must 'with all our majesty and skill/Both countenance and excuse' it (IV.1.31–2). But after Act III Scene 4, we see Gertrude gradually distancing herself from the King (**see Extended commentary: Scene 1** in **Part Two: Act IV**). For the first time, Claudius's panic botches the smooth operation and rumour abounds: we hear of suspicious 'ill-breeding minds' (IV.5.15), Claudius talks of 'the people muddied,/Thick and unwholesome in their thoughts and whispers' (IV.5.80–1). Claudius realises that burying Polonius 'hugger-mugger' (IV.5.83) was the sort of mistake a novice villain makes; the air is full of 'buzzers' (IV.5.89) and 'pestilent speeches' (IV.5.90) which threaten his grip on power. When his Switzers (Swiss guards) desert him, Claudius stands alone against the might of Laertes's rebellion.

CONTEXT — A04

Politicians in Shakespeare's time were well aware of the power of rumour, gossip and misinformation to unsettle a state. Shakespeare's *Henry IV Part Two*, is introduced by Rumour himself, 'painted full of tongues'. His job is 'stuffing the ears of men with false reports' (Induction, line 8).

FATAL CRISIS MANAGEMENT

In this crisis, Claudius is at his unprincipled best. Sizing up his man, he confidently puts him down: 'What is thy cause ... That thy rebellion looks so giant-like?' (IV.5.122). Bravely, brazenly, this regicide cites the 'divinity [that] doth hedge a king' (IV.5.124) to defy him and uses his charm and wits to seduce Laertes just as he seduced his queen; we see Laertes eating out of his hand, manipulated into murdering Hamlet (see **Analysis** in **Part Two: Act IV Scene 7**). As we approach the tragic **denouement**, however, Claudius's devious villainy unravels, falling justly 'on th'inventors' heads' (V.2.364). It is appropriate that poison with which he won the queen 'so conjunctive to [his] life and soul' (IV.7.14) should cause her death and help send this wine-loving villain to Hell.

KEY QUOTATION: CLAUDIUS — A01

A cutpurse of the empire and the rule,
That from a shelf the precious diadem stole
And put it in his pocket (III.4.99–101)

- In the closet scene, Hamlet adds the wrongful seizing of the throne to the catalogue of Claudius's sins. He amplifies on this accusation in Act V when he tells us Claudius 'Popped in between th'election and my hopes' (V.2.63).

- These lines undercut the impression of having behaved correctly that Claudius created in Act I Scene 2. There he stated that the Council 'had freely gone with this affair along' (I.2.15–16), that he acted with political integrity in becoming the partner of the 'imperial jointress' (I.2.9), Gertrude.

- Hamlet's imagery presents Claudius as a shifty pickpocket.

GERTRUDE

WHO IS GERTRUDE?

- Gertrude is the widow of Old Hamlet; she is now remarried, to the new King, Claudius, who is Old Hamlet's brother.
- She is Hamlet's mother.

A SHADOWY PRESENCE

Gertrude is largely undeveloped in the action of the play but after the climactic closet scene (III.4), we see her loyalty shift progressively from her husband to her son. This movement culminates in her open defiance of Claudius in Act V Scene 2 when she drinks from the poisoned cup Claudius had prepared for Hamlet. This separation from her husband focuses our sense of wickedness exclusively upon him. In Act V Scene 2, Hamlet places the blame for the 'Wretched queen's' (line 312) fall squarely upon the King who 'whored my mother' (line 64).

THE FALLEN WOMAN

Both Hamlet and the Ghost are shocked by Gertrude's 'falling off' (I.5.47). The Ghost describes Gertrude as his 'seeming virtuous Queen' (I.5.46) and Hamlet recalls how when the King died, the woman who always appeared to be devoted to her husband (I.2.143–5), followed his body 'like Niobe, all tears' (I.2.149). In Act IV Scene 5 mad Ophelia asks disconcertingly, 'Where is the beauteous majesty of Denmark?' (IV.5.21) and one reason why Gertrude initially refuses to see her is because after the closet scene in which Gertrude admits her guilt: 'Thou turn'st my eyes into my very soul' (III.4.89) she is a broken and apprehensive woman. As she becomes progressively alienated from the King (see **Extended commentary: Scene 1 in Part Two: Act IV**), her one, very brief **soliloquy**, consisting of two **rhyming couplets**, distils her sense of sin:

To my sick soul, as sin's true nature is,
Each toy seems prologue to some great amiss.
So full of artless jealousy is guilt,
It spills itself in fearing to be spilt. (IV.5.17–20)

These lines are very different from the dramatically powerful exploration of Claudius's troubled conscience which Shakespeare gave us in Act III Scene 3. Gertrude is given nothing in the way of self-analysis or self-justification and nowhere in the play is there any exploration of her feelings for either of her husbands or for her son. In Act IV, she is presented simply as a 'sick soul' (IV.5.17). When Ophelia sings pointedly of the funeral where a woman's true love 'bewept to the grave did not go/With true-love showers' (author's italics, IV.5.39–40) it is impossible to miss the cutting **allusion** to Gertrude's hypocritical, showy grief at Old Hamlet's funeral.

Ophelia tells Gertrude twice to 'mark' (IV.5.29 and 3) her words and Claudius's insistence that all Ophelia's distress is 'conceit upon her father' (IV.5.45) suggests **paradoxically** that he sees the point of the song. Ophelia's ominous warning: 'we know what we are, but know not what we may be' (IV.5.43) echoes Hamlet's urging Gertrude to 'avoid what is to come' by repenting and turning away from the 'bloat King' (III.4.183).

GRADE BOOSTER A02

The role of Gertrude and Ophelia as the only major female characters in *Hamlet* is an important one. See also **The women in *Hamlet*** in **Part Three: Themes**.

TURNING THE TABLES

Hamlet is incensed when the hypocritical Gertrude accuses him of 'seeming' in Act I Scene 2. She imitates Claudius's 'reasonable' appeals to Hamlet, suggesting that his grief is disproportionate: 'Do not forever ... Seek for thy noble father in the dust' (I.2.70). But in Act II Scene 2, she recognises that her marriage was 'o'erhasty' (II.2.57) and after *The Mousetrap* in which her infidelity is highlighted and the King's guilt suggested we are told she is struck into 'amazement and admiration' (III.2.296).

STUDY FOCUS: THE CLOSET SCENE — A02

In the closet scene, Hamlet again turns the tables on Gertrude when she accuses him of offending his father. Significantly, she is shown to be innocent of her husband's murder, and learning that Claudius killed Old Hamlet perhaps shocks her into separating from her new partner. Once Polonius is disposed of, she is engaged with Hamlet in what could be seen as a **psychodrama**: the battle for Gertrude's soul. But actresses can do little but weep: Shakespeare has given Gertrude so few words with which to respond to Hamlet's grilling. The Ghost, who, touchingly, remains fond of his errant wife, suggested in Act I Scene 5 that Gertrude's lack of concern about her moral position was itself an act, that she was already tormented by 'those thorns that in her bosom lodge/To prick and sting her' (I.5.87–8). Now he urges Hamlet to 'step between her and her fighting soul.' (III.4. 113) (See **Part Two: Act III Scene 4** for analysis of the closet scene.) The fact that Shakespeare has not provided a soliloquy for Gertrude after the closet scene means that we are left to judge her mainly on these hints and her actions rather than on anything she tells us.

A QUALIFIED LOVE

For his part, Claudius tells Laertes that Gertrude is 'so conjunctive to my life and soul,/That as the star moves not but in his sphere,/I could not but by her' (IV.7.14–16); this is supported by his admission in his soliloquy that desire for Gertrude prompted his murder of his brother. Nevertheless, in Act IV Scene 7, recognising that the Queen 'lives almost by [Hamlet's] looks' (IV.7.12), he feels no guilt as a result of cunningly contriving her son's death so that 'even his mother shall ... call it accident' (IV.7.66–7) and his dismay when she drinks from the poisoned chalice is less powerful than his determination to escape detection. His final bit of window dressing: 'She sounds to see them bleed' (V.2.288) gives Gertrude her most heroic moment in defiance: 'No, no, the drink, the drink – O my dear Hamlet –/The drink, the drink – I am poisoned' (V.2.289–90). Some critics argue that this appeal to Hamlet proves decisive. He avenges his mother with a speed than he could not summon up four acts previously to avenge his poisoned father.

> **CHECK THE FILM — A04**
>
> In Laurence Olivier's film of *Hamlet* (1948), we see the Queen sizing up the poisoned cup before she decides to defy the King and drink the poison she guesses has been prepared for her son.

KEY QUOTATION: GERTRUDE — A01

I hoped thou shouldst have been my Hamlet's wife.
I thought thy bride-bed to have deck'd, sweet maid,
And not t'have strewed thy grave (V.1.211–13)

- Together with the Queen's **lyrical** account of Ophelia's suicide, these lines generate a mood of **pathos** in the final stages of the play. This moment recalls the doomed lovers of Shakespeare's earlier **tragedy** *Romeo and Juliet*.

- Gertrude's maternal feelings for her son are developed when she asks Hamlet to apologise to Laertes (V.2.180–1) and in the tender moment when she mops his brow during the fencing match (V.2.265).

POLONIUS

WHO IS POLONIUS?

- Polonius is Claudius's right-hand man, a counsellor.
- He is the father of Laertes and Ophelia, an old man and, presumably, a widower.
- When Hamlet kills Polonius by accident, Claudius tries to hush things up by having Polonius buried in secret, without ceremony.
- Their father's death sends Ophelia mad and prompts Laertes to play the **Revenge Hero**.
- In Act V, Polonius's place in court is taken by Osric.

CLAUDIUS'S RIGHT-HAND MAN

No other courtiers figure significantly in the play until Polonius dies; in Act V some of his **dramatic functions** are assumed by Osric. Claudius is essentially a one-man government. Polonius serves Claudius uncritically; he never mentions the previous King and voices no misgivings about Claudius's accession to the throne. Shakespeare presents him as a man whose desire to serve the King is rooted as much in vanity and a sense of his own importance as in duty.

Laertes tells us he was 'an old man' (IV.5.160) and Ophelia's song (IV.5) suggests he had a white beard. Polonius is largely a stock character: he has no interior life. He is a jealously authoritarian parent who demands absolute obedience from his children, of whom he is groundlessly suspicious. Having given Laertes 'leave to go' (I.2.61), a paternal blessing and a list of moral instructions to follow (I.3), we see him sending a spy to Paris (II.1) to try and catch him misbehaving. This seems to arise from viewing his children as possessions to be kept unsullied rather than from paternal care for their wellbeing. He has no qualms about using lying and deception to investigate things, indeed his preferred method is 'By indirections [to] find directions out' (II.1.64). He proposes using his daughter as a decoy so he and Claudius can eavesdrop on her conversation with Hamlet and when that fails to prove his theory, proposes he snoop on a similar conversation between Hamlet and his mother. He discovers that to be 'too busy is some danger' (III.4.33): the plan costs him his life. Hamlet expresses little regret for killing him. His **epitaph** on Polonius is that he is a 'rash intruding fool' (III.4.31).

'DOTAGE ENCROACHING UPON WISDOM'

Polonius's parting advice to Laertes has appeared in many **anthologies** and represents clear thinking and elegance of expression. It is from this high point that he declines into pompous ramblings. But this does not excuse the grubby aspects of his character. Polonius shows no interest in his daughter's feelings when he prohibits her from seeing Hamlet or after the harrowing nunnery episode. He sees Ophelia as a piece of valuable property to invest (see **Analysis** in **Part Two: Act I Scene 3**). The idea that Polonius prostitutes his daughter is developed in the **imagery** of Act II Scene 2 where he talks of 'loos[ing]' (II.2.160) his daughter and 'board[ing]' (bawding, II.2.168) Hamlet. Hamlet develops this idea by calling him a 'fishmonger' (fleshmonger/bawd, II.2.172); Polonius has no idea of how he is perceived. Hamlet calls him Jephtha after the foolish judge of Israel who sacrificed his daughter.

Despite this, in her madness Ophelia has tender feelings for him: 'I cannot choose but weep to think they would lay him i'th'cold ground' (IV.5.68–9); Gertrude calls him a 'good old man' (IV.1.12) and Claudius calls him 'good Polonius' (IV.5.82) despite burying him without ceremony ('hugger-mugger', IV.5.83). Claudius also tells Laertes he loved his father as he loves himself (IV.7.34) as he manipulates the young man intent on revenging his 'noble father' (I.2.70). But there is nothing corresponding to Hamlet's warm memories of Old Hamlet. Laertes feels personally dishonoured by what's happened to Polonius; he does not appear to be grieving for him.

STUDY FOCUS: POLONIUS AS A COMIC FIGURE A02

Perhaps as a reaction to memorably funny performances in the role by Miles Malleson and Felix Aylmer in the mid twentieth century, many modern actors stress Polonius's stern and sinister aspects and refuse to enjoy the ludicrous aspects of the character. Shakespeare uses the character of Polonius to **parody** Hamlet's habits: his love of **word play** and his tendency to 'think too precisely', 'to consider too curiously' (IV.4.41; V.1.174). Shakespeare generates rich comedy when Polonius regularly gets lost in tedious qualifications, elaborations and circumlocutions (the use of many words when fewer would do). We see this inclination in his first speech: 'wrung from me my slow leave/By laboursome petition' (I.2.58–9). The words lumber along, suggesting someone wordy and full of self-importance. Later, Shakespeare develops this affectation into a comic **set piece**: 'to expostulate … I will be brief' (II.2.86–92). Polonius's elaborate verbal decoration: 'tediousness the limbs and outward flourishes' (II.2.91) illustrate the very fault he is criticising. In his lines that follow, we see that Polonius is incorrigible.

Listening to Polonius lose his thread in deviation and wordiness is funny in itself and contributes to the play's dramatic variety. But it also mirrors Hamlet's own mental muddles and his liability to get lost in quibbles on the meanings of words, in self-expanding **rhetorical** patterns, unnecessary qualifications and speculations leading nowhere.

GARRULOUS SHAKESPEARE?

There is an element of Shakespearean self-criticism here too. In *Hamlet*, the playwright finds so many issues diverting that the progress of the play is continually compromised. When Gertrude demands from Polonius 'More matter with less art' (II.2.95) she could be criticising Shakespeare himself.

Later in the same scene, Shakespeare presents Polonius as a pedant (paying undue attention to learning and rules): 'The best actors in the world, either for tragedy, comedy, history, pastoral, pastoral-comical, historical-pastoral, tragical-historical, tragical-comical-historical-pastoral' (II.2.363–5). We can hear Shakespeare anticipating all those essays which will try to pigeon-hole this play, to reduce its rich dramatic variety to a formula.

KEY QUOTATION: POLONIUS A01

If circumstances lead me, I will find
Where truth is hid, though it were hid indeed
Within the centre (II.2.155–7)

- These words are richly **ironic**. Polonius prides himself on his skills in uncovering the truth but there is no indication that he realises Claudius is a regicide or is troubled by the incestuous marriage. He is incapable of seeing the larger picture.
- He has no inkling of what really troubles Hamlet.

CRITICAL VIEWPOINT A03

For a Jungian reading of Polonius's role as scapegoat, see Elizabeth Oakes, 'Polonius, The Man Behind the Arras', in Mark Thornton Burnett and John Manning (eds.), *New Essays on Hamlet* (1994).

CHECK THE BOOK A03

An anonymous eighteenth-century critic (quoted in David Farley-Hills, *Critical Responses to Hamlet 1600–1900* v.4, 2004) said that 'To mix comedy with Tragedy is breaking through the sacred Laws of Nature nor can it be defended'. Do you agree?

LAERTES

WHO IS LAERTES?

- Laertes is the son of Polonius, the brother of Ophelia.
- After the coronation, he returns to Paris where he is learning the skills of a courtier.
- When Polonius is killed, Laertes returns to Denmark, determined to play the role of a **Revenge Hero**.
- He is manipulated into an underhand plot on Hamlet's life.
- The plot unravels; Laertes kills Hamlet but is fatally wounded with his own sword.
- Laertes and Hamlet are reconciled; Laertes identifies the King as the source of treachery.

STUDY FOCUS: HAMLET'S FOIL · A02

Hamlet says to Laertes, 'I'll be your foil' (V.2.227). In fact, the reverse is true; Shakespeare presents Laertes as a dramatic **foil** to his much more sophisticated central **protagonist**. A striking contrast between Prince Hamlet and Laertes is established on their first appearance in the play; it is elaborated and developed in Acts IV and V when the revengeful Laertes first challenges the King and then becomes his accomplice in the plot that kills the Prince. Laertes is more a set of attitudes than a psychologically developed character like the Prince but Hamlet recognises the superficial parallel in their situations: 'For by the image of my cause, I see/The portraiture of his.' (V.2.77–8) The play systematically contrasts the behaviour of a passionate Revenge Hero who has a limited, secular (not religious) notion of honour with the much more fully developed consciousness of Hamlet. Shakespeare asks us to consider what an educated, modern man would do if he found himself in a **Revenge Tragedy**.

BOUNDLESS REVENGE

Laertes's religion is the Roman and courtly pursuit of fame (see **A question of honour** in **Part Three: Revenge**); his concept of honour concerns his reputation, his standing in the world rather than his standing before God. In Paris, he has been a student not of philosophy but of how to become 'the card or calendar of gentry' (V.2.103–4), the accomplished courtier, something more like 'The glass of fashion and the mould of form,/Th'observed of all observers' (III.1.147–8) that Ophelia oddly describes Hamlet as. He is proud to have been 'talked of' (IV.7.70), given 'a masterly report' by the highly esteemed Lamord for 'art and exercise in [self] defence' (IV.7.95–6). When he learns of Polonius's death, it is not from a ghost but **ironically** by 'buzzers [who] infect his ear' (IV.5.89).

Laertes storms back to Elsinore, intent on revenge. Although he describes Polonius as his 'noble father' (I.2.70), Laertes does not remember him fondly or in terms of reverence like those in which Hamlet recalled his father. What upsets him about his Polonius's death is the fact that his funeral was 'hugger-mugger' (IV.5.83), without the appropriate 'noble rite' (IV.5.83) and 'formal ostentation' (IV.5 210); later, he is equally upset that his sister's funeral should lack sufficient 'ceremony' (V.1.190). He feels the family's honour has been compromised.

Concern for Ophelia's reputation: 'weigh what loss your honour may sustain' (I.3.29) prompts him to warn her not to respond to Hamlet's love; his sister's madness intensifies Laertes's thirst for vengeance: 'Hadst thou thy wits, and didst persuade revenge,/It could not move thus' (IV.5.168–9) and is fed by Claudius who examines Laertes on his fitness to be a Revenge Hero (see **Analysis** in **Part Two: Act IV Scene 5** and **Act IV Scene 7**). 'Splenitive and rash' as Hamlet calls him (V.1.228), Laertes has none of the ethical concerns which make revenge so problematic for Hamlet. He lacks not only the Prince's Wittenberg education but also the critical intelligence which Hamlet argued in his Act IV Scene 4 **soliloquy** distinguishes a man from a beast.

CRITICAL VIEWPOINT · A03

'Laertes is not a whiff of fresh air. He is a hurricane. He rushes into the palace in an uncontrolled rage, roaring for blood, having no idea whom he seeks but ready "swoopstake", to smash all in his way. He defies his sovereign King, his conscience and his God.' Eleanor Prosser, *Hamlet and Revenge* (1967).

CONTEXT · A02

The **image** of Laertes's ear being infected by rumours is a **parody** of Act I Scene 5, the scene in which the Ghost, telling Hamlet about the way he was murdered, can be seen as infecting his son's ear with forbidden knowledge.

THE REVENGER'S CREED

Laertes's beliefs are spelled out in a startling rejection of everything we have seen holding Hamlet back from responding to the Ghost's 'commandment' (I.5.102):

To hell allegiance, vows, to the blackest devil,
Conscience and grace to the profoundest pit!
I dare damnation. To this point I stand,
That both the worlds I give to negligence,
Let come what comes, only I'll be revenged
Most thoroughly for my father. (IV.5.131–6)

Laertes refers to 'hell', the devil, 'conscience', 'grace', 'damnation' and whatever awaits him in the next world only to reject anything that prevents him taking revenge. For Laertes, no thinking is required to arrive at this position. If he is aware of the afterlife and divine judgement, he is so consumed with anger that he will risk anything. There could be no more powerful illustration of the foolishness of acting without thinking. Before Claudius tries to win him over, he suggests that there is an element of childish, **melodramatic** acting about Laertes: 'What is the cause … That thy rebellion looks so giant-like?' (IV.5.121–2)

STUDY FOCUS: A WOUNDED NAME — A02

The King is shocked by Laertes's ruthless determination and happy to exploit it, spurring him on. When he observes 'Revenge should have no bounds' (IV.7.127), the King underlines the idea that moral questioning is incompatible with the pursuit of revenge. Where Hamlet reflects and delays, Laertes is hot-headed and blinded by passion. Claudius flatters Laertes, making much of his reputation, in order to make him more willing to accept his wicked plan. For all his proud talk of standing 'aloof' in his 'terms of honour', and wishing to keep his 'name ungored' (V.2.218–22), Laertes is putty in the hands of the ruthless King, and is easily tempted into deception. There is an ironic **pun** on the word 'ungored'. Laertes means that he is determined to keep his name spotless and pure but he is about to wound Hamlet with a poisoned, 'unbated' (IV.7.137) sword. It will be 'gored' with evidence of Laertes's deceit. (See **Analysis** in **Part Two: Act V Scene 2** for a study of Laertes's role in the tragic **denouement**.)

KEY QUOTATION: LAERTES — A01

Oh treble woe
Fall ten times treble on that cursèd head …
Now pile your dust upon the quick and dead
Till of this flat a mountain you have made
T'o'ertop old Pelion or the skyish head
Of blue Olympus. (V.1.213–21)

- Shakespeare contrasts the sincerity of Hamlet's simply expressed 'I loved Ophelia' (V.1.236) with her ranting brother's **hyperbole**.

- Laertes's distress sounds simulated; his language is artificial, overdone and **melodramatic**: he is more upset by the lack of an impressive funeral than by bereavement.

- His distress is affected. Straining for the effect of grandeur, the imagery attempts to be **epic** but sounds hollow. Leaping into Ophelia's grave is a theatrical gesture.

CONTEXT — A04

The Earl of Essex was a favourite of Queen Elizabeth's and one of her most charismatic, ambitious and reckless courtiers. Sent to subdue the rebels in Ireland in 1599, he returned a failure and, suspecting enemies at court, led a rebellion in 1601 which was immediately suppressed. He was executed for treason. Both Laertes and Young Fortinbras have something of Essex's rashness.

OPHELIA

WHO IS OPHELIA?

- Ophelia is the daughter of Polonius, the sister of Laertes.
- She is the girl Hamlet loved.

PASSIVE OPHELIA

In the first half of the play, 'The fair Ophelia' (III.1.89) is passive, almost non-existent as an independent identity; she is a more extreme version of Gertrude. She addresses the King and Queen only when she is mad. Actresses have to struggle if they wish to inject a note of **irony**, impertinence or defiance into the few words she exchanges with her brother, father or Hamlet. Shakespeare uses this passivity to provoke responses from other characters in the play and from the audience. When Hamlet delivers the judgement 'frailty, thy name is woman' (I.2.146), he is unconsciously commenting upon both his mother and his girlfriend; their behaviour is linked, this time deliberately, just before *The Mousetrap* when he comments on the short-lived nature of 'woman's love' (III.2.135).

The first time we see her, Ophelia is involved in two successive, parallel conversations. Both take broadly similar shape: the men lecture her for forty lines each to which she responds with just seven lines (including two half lines) in each case. Where Juliet and Desdemona defy strict fathers who attempt to stifle their love affairs, in Ophelia's case, there is not even a gesture of a struggle. Ophelia is presented as someone with no point of view; she tells her father: 'I do not know my lord what I should think' (I.3.104) and in Acts I to III, apart from her teasing Laertes about his own constancy, we never see her challenging her subordinate role or acting or thinking independently. Her second appearance is to describe Hamlet's strange visit. This time she has rather more of the speaking lines than her father (twenty-seven to twenty-one) but of these, twenty-two are impersonal **narrative**, their function being to tell us about Hamlet's puzzling behaviour. They do not give us any insight into Ophelia's response to what she has been witnessing; all we learn is that she found the experience frightening. She expresses no feelings or ideas about Hamlet or about having been denied access to him for so many weeks.

DUPLICITOUS OPHELIA

Ophelia promises twice to write to Laertes and perhaps her letters bring him home but she makes no attempt defy her father and communicate with Hamlet. On the two occasions when she could confide to him in an aside, Shakespeare keeps her silent. Ophelia is never presented as actually being in love with Hamlet; the play's focus is entirely on whether he loves her. In her only **soliloquy** she tells us she 'sucked the honey of [Hamlet's] music vows' (III.1.150), revealing she enjoyed his attentions at some stage, but the **metaphor** does not suggest that she returned his love. Instead, she responds to his fury with the fact that she is allowing herself to be used against him by agreeing, rather unconvincingly, to the fiction that he is mad: 'Oh help him you sweet heavens! … Oh heavenly powers, restore him! … Oh what a noble mind is here o'erthrown!' (III.1.130–44).

It is as this point that Claudius, who has been closely monitoring their conversation declares that what Hamlet spoke, 'though it lacked form a little,/Was not like madness' (III.1.157–8). By lack of form, Claudius means its rudeness, its severity to a woman who Hamlet knew was deceiving him. But this idea is not developed; Ophelia displays no sense of shame for having shown her father Hamlet's letters, for having played the decoy or for lying directly to her supposed lover. Instead she talks of him in generalised terms which do not seem to fit the man we have seen in the play, describing him as 'The glass of fashion and the mould of form' (III.1.147). It is difficult to believe that the scholarly, sceptical

Hamlet, so critical of public opinion was at any time a fashion icon. Again, this is not so much a psychological problem but as T. S. Eliot argues, an artistic one. The shortcoming is not Ophelia's so much as the dramatist's.

STUDY FOCUS: A NEW OPHELIA A02

At the end of Act IV and through into Act V, Ophelia is given a limited kind of power, first in her madness, then in the brook and finally in her coffin. Her inability to do anything, which has been a theme since Act I Scene 3, changes into 'madness' (IV.5.156) presented as plaintive songs and apparently pretty nonsense designed to generate **pathos**. This, we could argue, together with Gertrude's stylised presentation of her death, offers decoration in place of a real attempt at psychological explanation. She is portrayed as an innocent victim of the wickedness which pollutes Elsinore. Gertrude describes Ophelia's suicide as unintentional. However, public opinion, as represented by the gravediggers, is sceptical.

A DOCUMENT IN MADNESS

Claudius and Laertes insist upon the 'prettiness' (IV.5.184) of Ophelia's madness but the word the First Gentleman uses to describe her is 'importunate' (IV.5.2); the girl who was so passive in Acts I to III, is now troublesome, assertive, demanding. And although those Ophelia confronts try to discount her 'winks and nods and gestures' (IV.5.11), her songs are a curious mixture of wistful sadness and biting **satire**. They are mostly **metrically** regular and logical, unlike the gibberish Shakespeare gives Mad Tom in *King Lear*, more like Hamlet's use of 'antic disposition' (I.5.172) to play the licensed Fool. (At court, a Fool was allowed to speak satirically, even rudely, in a way other couriers could not. Lear's Fool is a prime example of such a character.) Ophelia threatens to expose the 'tricks i'th'world' (IV.5.5). Claudius's analysis: 'Oh this is the poison of deep grief, it springs/All from her father's death' (IV.5.74–5) is an attempt to camouflage the uncomfortable truths Mad Ophelia voices. If her third song, addressed to Laertes, laments her father's death, the first two are directed elsewhere. The St Valentine's song is a bawdy, satiric jibe at faithless seducers; it seems to echo Hamlet's harsh treatment of Ophelia for betraying him. The song she sings to Gertrude accuses the Queen of that very hypocrisy Hamlet **alluded** to when he described her false tears at his father's funeral (I.2.149).

In asking where 'the beauteous majesty of Denmark' (IV.5.21) is, Ophelia sounds almost like a **chorus** voicing a more general criticism of the Queen. The distribution of herbs and flowers is also surely, as Claudius admits, something of a 'document in madness' (IV.5.176). **Parodying** the Ghost, she awards Laertes rosemary and pansies, for remembrance and thoughts. Her words 'Pray you love, remember' (IV.5.174–5) are like an echo of the Ghost's commandment. Claudius recognises the suitability of these gifts: 'thoughts and remembrance fitted' (IV.5.176) and we can only assume the other plants are equally appropriate: fennel and columbines to the adulterous Queen, rue to the remorseful King. As explored in **Part Four: The second exposition**, Ophelia's madness can be seen as a parody of the Ghost's appeal to his son: 'Hadst thou thy wits, and didst persuade revenge/It could not move thus.' (IV.5.168–9) This appeal is given further weight by her **euphemistically** described suicide.

At her graveside, Ophelia becomes the focus for an unseemly fight between a second 'true love' and 'another one' (IV.5.23–4): Hamlet declares his love for Ophelia and angrily mocks the pretentious protests of her brother.

HORATIO

WHO IS HORATIO?

- Horatio is a poor Danish scholar, a fellow student of Hamlet's at the Protestant University of Wittenberg.
- With Marcellus and Barnardo, he remains loyal throughout the play to Prince Hamlet. He interacts very little with anyone else.
- Hamlet expresses unqualified love and admiration for him.
- Shakespeare uses him as a moral touchstone: someone whose values we respect and probably share.
- At the end of the play, he sums up the action and speaks Hamlet's **epitaph**.

A MORAL TOUCHSTONE

Horatio's role in *Hamlet* has something in common with Banquo's in *Macbeth* and Kent's in *King Lear*. In a play that deals with deception and betrayal, Shakespeare presents Horatio as someone whose integrity the audience can rely upon. He helps us to see other characters in perspective. In Act I Scene 2, Horatio confirms, when it seems only Hamlet believes it, that Gertrude's remarriage was indecently hasty: 'Indeed … it followed hard upon' (line 179).

CONTEXT **A03**

In *King Lear*, the Earl of Kent is a loyal friend to the King. He is a man who refuses to use flattery or tell lies even though he pays a heavy price for his honesty.

STUDY FOCUS: HORATIO AND THE GHOST **A02**

Horatio has a critical **dramatic function** because he establishes the reality and the nature of the Ghost. Sceptical, 'so fortified against our story' (I.1.32), and unexcitable by nature, Horatio's 'fear and wonder' (I.1.44) in Act I Scene 1 suspend the audience's disbelief in the terrifying Ghost. He acts as a **chorus** when he fills in the immediate historical and political context in which the Ghost appears and, like a scholar, compares it to similar supernatural omens which 'bode some strange eruption to [the] state' (I.1.69). His bold challenges to the Ghost, insisting that he will listen only to what will do 'good' and earn him 'grace' (I.1.131–2) introduce the spiritual dangers into which Hamlet may be tempted. Although Horatio confirms that the Ghost closely resembles Old Hamlet, he accuses it of 'usurping' that 'fair and warlike form' (I.1.46–7) and sees it as one of those 'extravagant and erring spirit[s]' (I.1.154) that are caused by a superior force. He is scrupulous in reporting to Hamlet what he saw, stressing its uncanny likeness to Old Hamlet but always referring to it as a 'thing' and an 'apparition' (I.2.210–11). Horatio spells out the risks involved for Hamlet and chorus-like paints a vivid picture of steep and rugged cliffs. In the midst of the confusion, he states his simple Christian faith: 'Heaven will direct it.' (I.4.91)

THE SCRUPULOUS SCEPTIC

Betrayed by everyone else, Hamlet expresses his admiration and love for Horatio in clear and unambiguous terms. He pictures him as a stoic (one who can endure hardship without complaint): 'A man that Fortune's buffets and rewards/Hast tane with equal thanks' who is not 'passion's slave' (III.2.57–62). Horatio makes no response but demonstrates his loyalty to the Prince throughout the play and, grief-stricken when Hamlet dies, acts with passion in attempting to take his own life. Hamlet is unable to share what the Ghost has said with the soldiers but we learn that he confides in Horatio afterwards and asks his friend to help him judge Claudius's response to *The Mousetrap*. Horatio's verdict is opaque but he makes an honest assessment of Hamlet's performance which he rates worth only 'half a share' (III.2.253).

In Act V, Hamlet no longer explores confused ideas in **soliloquy**; he is able to share his newly clear view of things with Horatio. Hamlet nominates his trustworthy friend to 'report [him and his] cause aright' (V.2.318). He presents a limited but succinct and honest summary of the whole action.

LACONIC HORATIO

Horatio is a man of very few words; unlike Rosencrantz and Guildenstern, fellow students from Wittenberg, he never engages in witty banter with Hamlet. Even in the graveyard scene (V.1) where there are no restrictions or pressures to inhibit their **dialogue**, Horatio plays second fiddle, content to allow Hamlet the limelight. His devotion to the Prince is absolute but he is respected by Hamlet because not only is he faithful but is frankly sceptical and uncompromisingly truthful, the opposite of a flatterer. His loyalty is always to Hamlet: unlike Laertes, he returned to Elsinore for Hamlet's father's funeral, not for Claudius's coronation. It is Horatio's idea to share knowledge of the Ghost with Hamlet rather than with the King. Seeing Gertrude sharing the stage with Horatio at the beginning of Act IV Scene 5, though necessary for giving information to the audience, also signals to the audience Gertrude's movement away from Claudius towards her son.

KEY QUOTATION: HORATIO A01

I do not know from what part of the world
I should be greeted, if not from Lord Hamlet. (IV.6.4–5)

- Horatio exists only as Hamlet's trustworthy friend.
- Although he tells Barnardo and Marcellus about Young Fortinbras's attack, he does not seem to be familiar with the Danish custom of heavy drinking, and doesn't know Laertes or Osric.
- We never learn his age or anything about his family.

YOUNG FORTINBRAS

WHO IS YOUNG FORTINBRAS?

- Young Fortinbras is the son of Fortinbras, sometime King of Norway whom Old Hamlet killed in mortal combat on the day Hamlet was born.

- He is nephew to the present King of Norway, described in the play as 'impotent and bed-rid' (I.2.29).

- He leads the attack on Denmark which results in the posting of sentries in Act I Scene 1. He leads an assault on an insignificant part of Poland which Hamlet comments upon in Act IV Scene 4.

- He is nominated by Hamlet to succeed to the throne of Denmark at the end of the play.

YOUNG FORTINBRAS AND YOUNG HAMLET

Although the opening scene suggests the play will explore parallels between Young Hamlet and Young Fortinbras (whose name means 'strong arm'), we learn almost nothing about the other Scandinavian prince. Sons of warrior kings, the princes have both somehow been supplanted by their uncles. Claudius mocks his opposite number, Norway, for being 'impotent and bed-rid' (I.2.29) but he restrains Young Fortinbras and diverts him to the Polish expedition. We briefly see his army setting off for Poland in Act IV Scene 4. His brief speeches there and at the end of the play are utterly impersonal: we learn little about his outlook or his values.

STUDY FOCUS: A 'DELICATE AND TENDER PRINCE' **A03**

Hamlet's idea of Young Fortinbras as a 'delicate and tender prince' (IV.4.48) in the final **soliloquy**, is read by most critics as a case of self-projection; Hamlet as the son of an epic warrior no doubt feels his father would have expected him to play such a role. The Polish campaign recalls the ambitions of Old Fortinbras. Just as his father was prepared to risk and lose all his lands in single combat, now his son hazards 'twenty thousand ducats' and the lives of 'two thousand' men in the pursuit of fame (IV.4.24). (See **Extended commentary: Scene 4, lines 33–66** in **Part Two: Act IV** on Hamlet's final soliloquy.) However, Horatio paints a picture of a son very different from his respected father. Old Fortinbras's challenge to Old Hamlet was 'Well ratified by law and heraldry' (I.1.87): a ceremonious and old-fashioned proceeding. Young Fortinbras, however, is an wild adventurer: 'of unimprovèd mettle hot and full' (I.1.96), leading a band of youths on a plundering expedition, hoping to take advantage of the supposed disorder in Elsinore following Old Hamlet's sudden death. He is happy to take advantage of the 'havoc' (V.2.343) of Act V Scene 2 to secure the Danish throne to which he accedes upon Hamlet's dying breath.

THE DIRECTOR'S CUT

Young Fortinbras and his manoeuvres are often cut when directors are searching for ways of shortening a very long play. In the late twentieth century, however, political readings of *Hamlet* sometimes developed the Fortinbras strand, stressing the significance of Denmark's falling into foreign hands as a mark of either Claudius's or Hamlet's failure as head of state.

CONTEXT **A04**

Whilst Shakespeare was writing *Hamlet*, the Earl of Essex was sent to Ireland to subdue the rebel Tyrone. Many of those who joined his expedition were similar to the men Horatio describes as Fortinbras's band of soldiers: 'a list of landless resolutes' who joined up just for 'food and diet' (I.1.98–9) expenses because they were excited by the prospect of a military adventure. The Earl of Essex was rash and impulsive, like Fortinbras, 'hot and full' (I.1.96).

ROSENCRANTZ AND GUILDENSTERN

WHO ARE ROSENCRANTZ AND GUILDENSTERN?

- These fellow students of Hamlet at the University of Wittenberg are summoned by Claudius to spy on their old friend.
- Hamlet realises what their game is and reveals nothing to them. As the play develops he makes increasing fun of their confusion.
- Sent with Hamlet on the mission to England during which Claudius planned for Hamlet to be executed, their plot is discovered and turned on them.

PLOTTERS SUBVERTED

Many readers suspect that Lewis Carroll's Tweedledum and Tweedledee (from *Through the Looking Glass*) owe something to Shakespeare's unconsciously comic double-act. Hamlet's disloyal schoolfellows sometimes share lines between them and it is impossible to distinguish one man from the other; they are one idea given two voices. It is a stage convention that Claudius can't remember which is which.

Just as Ophelia has no hesitation in acting as Claudius's decoy, so Hamlet's fellow students are perfectly happy to sell themselves for 'a king's remembrance' (II.2.26). They are not naturally vicious and when they meet Hamlet their 'modesties have not craft enough to colour' (II.2.265–6) what they are hiding from him. After this, Hamlet plays with them but reveals nothing of which Claudius can take advantage. Once the King's plans for Hamlet turn homicidal, Rosencrantz and Guildenstern find themselves out of their depth. Just as Polonius discovers 'to be too busy is some danger' (III.4.33) so this duo learns ''Tis dangerous when the baser nature comes/Between the pass and fell incensèd points/Of mighty opposites' (V.2.60–2). Hamlet feels no guilt in sending them not only to their deaths but to damnation: their execution warrant allows no 'shriving time' (V.2.45), i.e. time for confession. He answers Horatio's concerns by insisting: 'they did make love to this employment./They are not near my conscience.' (V.2.57–8)

CONTEXT **A04**

Although the action of *Hamlet* takes place in medieval Elsinore and Rosencrantz and Guildenstern have typical Danish names, Shakespeare presents events as if they were happening at a seventeenth-century English court.

CHECK THE FILM **A03**

The brilliant and witty *Rosencrantz and Guildenstern Are Dead* (directed by Tom Stoppard and based on his play) re-presents certain episodes from Shakespeare's *Hamlet* as they might have been perceived and interpreted by these two minor characters, caught up in and confused by a plot over which they have no control.

OSRIC

WHO IS OSRIC?

- Osric is a young and ridiculous courtier who appears in the last scene of the play

LINGUISTIC ABSURDITY

Osric is a perfect example of linguistic pomposity and insincerity. He arrives to provide comic relief at the tragic **denouement** and an even more ridiculous version of the verbal excesses we associate with Polonius. He is one of the many symptoms of Denmark's decline under Claudius, along with the fashion for child actors, public demand for the King's 'picture in little' (II.2.336) and 'pocky corses' (V.1.140). Hamlet describes him as 'spacious in the possession of dirt' (V.2.87), a fit courtier when 'a beast be lord of beasts' (V.2.85), the sort of showy, insincere and foolish courtier 'the drossy age dotes on' (V.2.166–7). Hamlet mercilessly **parodies** Osric's verbal extravagances: 'Sir … nothing more' (V.2.106–12): where a grand **rhetorical** pattern attempts to disguise the lack of substance. Even more absurdly than Polonius, Osric loves the sound of his own voice 'but blow them to their trial, the bubbles are out' (V.2.169–70). Osric is just froth.

CONTEXT A04

Shakespeare is parodying here an elaborately ornate style of writing known as euphuism. John Lyly's **prose** romances *Euphues: The Anatomy of Wit* (1578) and its sequel *Euphues and His England* (1580) were widely imitated.

KEY QUOTATION: OSRIC A01

Horatio says of Osric: 'His purse is empty already, all's golden words are spent.' (V.2.121)

- Horatio's succinct observation says more in ten words than Osric himself manages in a paragraph.
- Osric is recklessly extravagant with his words.

REVISION FOCUS: TASK 5

Consider the following statements:

- Denmark is a place in which characters' love for each other has been devalued.
- *Hamlet* is a play in which characters constantly betray each other.

Draft the opening paragraphs of essays based on the discussion points above.

THEMES

REVENGE

A QUESTION OF HONOUR

The ancient Roman code prized family honour above all things. The belief was that a man's reputation was what lived after him, so if he had been wronged, and the state failed to see that justice was done, it was a son's duty to take the law into his own hands and seek revenge. Although revenge was a criminal offence in England, bloody, Roman-style **Revenge Tragedies** were very popular in London in the 1590s. One of Shakespeare's most popular plays was the brutal Revenge Tragedy *Titus Andronicus*, written about six years before *Hamlet*.

STUDY FOCUS: REVENGE · A02

Revenge is the central theme of *Hamlet* and is also a common theme in modern cinema. Consider these questions:

- What do you understand by the term 'revenge'?
- How would you justify revenge?
- What makes the pursuit of revenge wrong?
- Is there a difference between the way we respond to revenge in a film and the way we respond to it in real life? See if you can explain why.

WILD JUSTICE

The seventeenth-century philosopher and statesman Francis Bacon condemned revenge as 'a kind of wild justice'. He argued 'it does ... offend the law [and] putteth the law out of office' ('Of Revenge', 1625). The Christian Church insisted that vengeance was God's business not man's. The Sixth Commandment is: Thou shalt not kill.

TWO IDEOLOGIES

In *Hamlet*, the incompatible value systems of the Roman and Christian codes of honour come into direct conflict to produce a far more complex Revenge Tragedy than had ever been seen on the London stage. For Laertes and Young Fortinbras, there is no moral problem: both believe in a simple code of honour which is rooted in family pride. Hamlet's case is far more complex. The Ghost talks like a Christian, telling his son there is judgement after death: he is suffering in Purgatory. But what he demands of Hamlet sounds Roman and, if obeyed, would send Hamlet to Hell. Torn between duty to a Ghost who might be his father and obedience to his God, it is no wonder Hamlet delays his revenge, is puzzled by the identity of the Ghost and wrestles endlessly with his conscience.

HAMLET: THE RELIGIOUS CONTEXT

When Gertrude says 'all that lives must die,/Passing through nature to eternity' (I.2.72–3), the circumstances make it sound shallow and conventional, but this is the **ideology** shared by all the major characters. The idea that bodies decay but souls are immortal has far-reaching implications for how people make the ethical choices which shape their lives. For those who believe that after death they will be judged on their conduct on Earth and be rewarded either with eternal pain or eternal bliss, all other considerations, including family honour, must seem trivial. According to this, to pursue revenge for the sake of restoring family honour but at the cost of suffering eternal torment would be a serious mistake. For further discussion of the theme of revenge, see **Hamlet** and **Laertes** in **Part Three: Characters**.

CHECK THE FILM · A04

Titus (1999) starring Anthony Hopkins is a powerful film adaptation of *Titus Andronicus*. The graphic, historically vague presentation of the play suggests interesting connections between Elizabethan and modern treatments of revenge. The film will give you a good idea of the moral attitudes and dramatic style of Shakespeare's play.

GRADE BOOSTER · A01

For the best grades, you need to be able to think beyond the obvious. For example, how far, and in what ways, does the pursuit of revenge corrupt the avengers, Hamlet and Laertes, in the play?

CRITICAL VIEWPOINT · A03

How far do you agree with the claim that in *Hamlet* the revenge plot deals out justice to all the characters?

MADNESS

STUDY FOCUS: A MINORITY OF ONE AO2

Madness can be defined as 'being in a minority of one'. Hamlet admires the one 'judicious' person in the audience whose 'censure … must … o'erweigh a whole theatre of others' (III.2.22–4) and if to be honest is to be 'one man picked out of ten thousand' (II.2.176), Hamlet is not afraid to be in a moral minority of one, as his black clothes in Act I Scene 2 demonstrate. Claudius tries to persuade Hamlet that his continued grieving for his father is 'to reason most absurd' (I.2.103) and since no one else in Elsinore seems to remember Old Hamlet, we could believe that Claudius was right in suggesting Hamlet's 'obstinate condolement' (I.2.93) was evidence of 'a mind impatient' (I.2.96). However, in this case, we have Horatio's confirmation of how recent Hamlet's father's death was (Act I Scene 2) and some weeks later comes Gertrude's frank admission to her husband that Hamlet's 'distemper' (II.2.55) is probably the result of 'His father's death, and [their] o'er hasty marriage' (II.2.57). If 'madness' is a label we attach to behaviour we find incomprehensible or completely unsympathetic, there is nothing 'mad' in Hamlet's distress in Act 1 Scene 2. We may find Claudius's and Gertrude's 'reasonableness' more disturbing than Hamlet's wildness.

CONTEXT AO2

Shakespeare uses a variety of terms for madness in this play, including 'distemper', 'ecstasy', 'distraction', 'lunacy', 'confusion' and 'wildness'.

PLAYING THE MADMAN

In Act I Scene 5, true to the conventions of **Revenge Tragedy**, Hamlet warns his friends that he may pretend he is mad, put on 'an antic disposition' (I.5.172), to help him carry out the Ghost's instructions without arousing suspicion. Whether Hamlet is subsequently mad, ever pretends to be mad or is considered mad by whom and at what times, is something over which critics of the play argue long and hard. No two performances will give the same impression of the state of Hamlet's mind in the episodes that follow his interview with the Ghost in Act I Scene 5.

CRITICAL VIEWPOINT AO3

'Hamlet does not play the madman; rather he plays the Fool, mocking and telling truths that no one wants to hear.' Do you agree?

Most, if not all, of the behaviour Ophelia describes in Act II Scene 1 sounds like play-acting. Hamlet appears to be doing what **Revenge Heroes** often do – trying to persuade his intended victim that he is a harmless madman so he will find it easier to carry out his task. He knows his eccentric behaviour will be reported to Polonius and then on to the King. But before he hears of this incident, Claudius tells us 'nor th'exterior nor the inward man' is like his former self (II.2.6–7). The person playing Hamlet, therefore, should probably be dressed oddly, not simply in black as he was in Act I Scene 2. And his behaviour must be more than bitterly melancholic as it was in that scene, if the audience is to understand the King's anxious description of Hamlet's behaviour as 'turbulent and dangerous lunacy' (III.1.4). Unless, of course, we believe Claudius's unease is excessive, almost paranoid, prompted by his own guilty conscience.

STUDY FOCUS: OPHELIA'S MADNESS AO2

We can see how Shakespeare presents 'genuine' madness in Ophelia's behaviour in Act IV Scene 5. Her 'pretty' (IV.5.41) nonsense can be acted as charming or disturbing but it is comprehensible and complete in itself: shock and bereavement make her 'incapable' (IV.7.178). One of the dramatic purposes in presenting Ophelia's state of mind in this stylised way is to help the audience to recognise Hamlet's more **realistic** madness.

REALLY MAD?

Making a judgement about Hamlet's madness would be much simpler if the Prince did not, in lines which are surely meant to sound sincere (V.2.198–216), tell Laertes that he really has been mad. For most of the play it has been clear to the audience that the Prince's madness has been an invention.

For example, often when Hamlet talks to Polonius, what sounds to the foolish old man like nonsense has a thread of bitter **satire** running through it. Hamlet's babble is not madness, but straightforward contempt, rudeness made possible in a court where no one speaks the truth. Similarly, when Hamlet taunts Rosencrantz and Guildenstern he uses, as they realise, 'crafty madness' (III.1.8) to mock them and lead them astray; his behaviour is fully under his own control. In Act III Scene 3 and Act IV Scene 1, Claudius asserts that his nephew is mad because he is convinced that he is not and he needs an excuse to get rid of the threat Hamlet poses. The Queen, in Act IV Scene 1, having watched Hamlet demonstrate his sanity, pretends her son is 'Mad as the sea and wind, when both contend/Which is the mightier' (IV.1.7–8) to excuse the murder of Polonius.

CHECK THE BOOK **A04**

For a new-historicist essay examining madness in *Hamlet* in relation to Essex's dangerous **subversion** of Queen Elizabeth's authority in the 1590s, see Karin S. Coddon's 'Suche strange desygns, Madness, Subjectivity and Treason in *Hamlet* and Elizabethan Culture', reprinted in Susan Zimmerman (ed.), *New Casebooks, Shakespeare's Tragedies* (1998).

Hamlet's passionate exchanges with Ophelia and his mother may be violent – he himself talks of 'words like daggers' (III.4.95) – but what he says is both understandable and purposeful: he believes he is being 'cruel only to be kind' (III.4.179). If he punishes Ophelia harshly for her betrayal of him, we may not like it but we can understand it.

WILD AND WHIRLING WORDS

It is at moments of intense excitement that Hamlet's behaviour is least comprehensible. His 'wild and whirling words' (I.5.133) following the Ghost's departure give way to the curious game he plays with 'this fellow in the cellarage' (I.5.151). In the confusion that follows the play-within-the-play (III.2.236–64), Hamlet is euphoric whilst Horatio is distinctly cool. It is in the major **soliloquies**, in Act II Scene 2 and Act IV Scene 4, that Hamlet's thinking is most confused. And, as we notice throughout the play, there is often a discrepancy between what Hamlet says he will do and his subsequent behaviour. But whether such episodes distance us from Hamlet as from a person whose 'wit's diseased' (III.2.291), or present sympathetically someone suffering extraordinary and sometimes bewildering stress is a matter for the audience to decide.

THE WOMEN IN *HAMLET*

SHAKESPEARE'S WOMEN

Shakespeare's major women characters are usually as Hamlet describes them in Act II Scene 2 lines 302–3: fearless and articulate. We are used to them speaking their minds robustly and virtuously. They challenge erring male authority figures, no matter how terrifying they are. Juliet, Portia, Hermia, Beatrice, Desdemona, Emelia, Cordelia, Perdita, Paulina and Miranda are all feisty, decisive, resourceful and outspoken women. Shortly before writing *Hamlet*, Shakespeare wrote *As You Like It* in which the major part is Rosalind's, with over a quarter of the play's lines. The Globe company possessed two outstanding boy actors who played women's parts and for them Shakespeare created strong, witty and fully realised characters including the indomitable Volumnia, Cleopatra and Lady Macbeth.

HAMLET'S PROBLEMATIC WOMEN

This makes Ophelia and Gertrude puzzling, exceptionally undeveloped creations and Hamlet's words to the Players sound peculiarly **ironic**. Ophelia, in the first three acts, is mostly silent and submissive to assertive male figures. Her role in the play is largely passive until her madness is used dramatically in Act IV and Act V Scene 1 to create **pathos**. Hamlet expresses his love for her most passionately when she is in her grave.

The adultery and incest of Gertrude are the focus of Hamlet's anger, the Ghost's affectionate dismay and Claudius's tenderness, but she is not presented as equal to the powerful feelings she arouses. If there is one moral principle which underpins all of Shakespeare's poetry and plays, it is his horror of sexual promiscuity. Chastity and faithfulness in marriage are continually endorsed; infidelity is presented as morally unacceptable. Desdemona and Hermione, groundlessly accused of adultery, are presented as heroic victims whilst Cressida is synonymous with betrayal. Much of Hamlet's fury at Gertrude and Ophelia can be explained by Shakespeare's own strong feelings about the supreme importance of loyalty and chastity.

STUDY FOCUS: THE CRITICAL DEBATE A03

Critics have long recognised that there is this problem with the way Shakespeare presents the women in *Hamlet*. T. S. Eliot famously complained that 'Shakespeare's *Hamlet* … is a play dealing with the effects of a mother's guilt upon her son' and judged the play 'an artistic failure' because 'Hamlet is dominated by an emotion which is … in excess of the facts as they appear' ('Hamlet' in *Selected Essays 1917–1932*, 1932); some **feminist critics** have talked about the 'silencing' of Gertrude and Ophelia. The major shortcoming of Eliot's essay is that it deals only with Gertrude. Because what is true of Hamlet's reaction to his mother's behaviour applies equally to his passionate fury with Ophelia. The striking similarities between two key scenes, the nunnery episode and the closet scene, illustrate the nature of the problem. In the latter episode, Gertrude is harangued for 80 per cent of the scene: there is little interplay between the characters; Hamlet has two-thirds of the lines in the nunnery episode. Shakespeare if not deliberately 'silencing' his women in this play, does not give them very much to say.

A PRACTICAL PROBLEM

A. C. Bradley in *Lectures on Shakespeare*, probably diagnosed the problem most usefully. Rather than putting it down to the original play that Shakespeare inherited (as Eliot speculated), a psychological issue about sex (as Eliot and Ernst Jones argued) or an anti-feminist agenda, Bradley observes that there was a practical difficulty. At over 4,000 lines, *Hamlet* is already 'too long' as Polonius cheekily observes (II.2.456); Shakespeare must have realised that he was testing both his actors and his audience to the limit. He never wrote as long a play again: the major **tragedies** *Othello* and *King Lear* are both about 500 lines (perhaps half an hour) shorter. In Claudius's **soliloquy**, we have the germs of the tragic **protagonist** who would eventually develop into Macbeth but in *Hamlet*, Shakespeare does not build upon the man he begins to explore so powerfully in the chapel scene, whilst Gertrude and Ophelia are given only the most sketchy of soliloquies. With so much attention on Hamlet's thoughts and behaviour, Shakespeare simply does not have the stage time to do more. Thus the women whom Hamlet feels have betrayed themselves as well as him exist only in outline and, principally, in Hamlet's reading of them. His responses are to much more developed characters than Shakespeare has given himself space to present.

APPEARANCE AND REALITY

The idea that what you see is not the truth, that appearances are deceptive, that there are 'tricks i'th'world' (IV.5.5) is a major theme running through Shakespeare's writing. In *Hamlet*, this theme has particular emphasis. Of course, the irony is that the play, which presents 'seeming' as cunning wickedness, is itself an elaborate imaginative construction, using all sorts of 'tricks' to suspend our disbelief and shape our response.

AS IF ...

Gertrude's ability to play-act, to dissimulate and to deceive shocked the Ghost and surprises her son. The Ghost calls Gertrude his '*seeming* virtuous queen' (author's italics, I.5.46). He contrasts his own straight-forward honesty: 'whose love was of that dignity/That it went hand in hand even with the vow/I made to her in marriage' (I.5.48–50) with Gertrude's disguised 'falling off' (I.5.47). In his first soliloquy, we hear how Hamlet is shocked to discover that his mother, the woman who used to 'hang on [her first husband]/*As if* increase of appetite had grown/By what it fed on' (author's italics, I.2.143-5) and wept so conspicuously and copiously at his funeral (I.2.148–9) was already her brother-in-law's mistress. This is why Hamlet explodes with fury when Gertrude accuses him of 'seeming', of acting his grief, (I.2.76–86). His sense of loss, he asserts, is genuine, not just 'actions that a man might play' (I.2.84).

Mad Ophelia's first song, addressed to Gertrude, draws attention to the insincerity of the Queen's 'true-love showers' at Old Hamlet's funeral (IV.5.40). But Gertrude's facade had already collapsed in the closet scene when she acknowledged the truth she had been concealing: 'Thou turn'st my eyes into my very soul,/And there I see such black and grainèd spots/As will not leave their tinct.' (III.4. 89–91)

In spite of this confession, we see Gertrude pretending again when she describes Ophelia's suicide. Her **lyrical** speech (IV.7.166–83) is designed to present Ophelia's death in a certain light, in order to minimise its impact on Ophelia's vengeful brother, Laertes, who is already incensed against Hamlet for the murder of Polonius – and shows how Gertrude manipulates appearances in the same way as her husband.

CHECK THE PLAY **A03**

The idea of people using cosmetics to disguise their true selves runs through the play and is perhaps best shown in Hamlet's words, aimed at Ophelia and women in general: 'I have heard of your paintings too, well enough. God hath given you one face and you make yourselves another' (III.1.137–8). This theme is also prominent in *Macbeth*. Lady Macbeth advises her husband to 'look like the innocent flower/But be the serpent under it' (I.5.63–4). He learns the lesson and concludes 'False face must hide what the false heart doth know' (I.7.82).

THE SMILING VILLAIN

Another practised 'seemer' is Claudius. When the Ghost reveals how he was murdered, we can hear that Hamlet has to work hard to believe that 'one may smile, and smile, and be a villain' (I.5.108); he has to write it down, he finds the idea that a rogue can look so innocent extraordinary. As another idealist, Othello says, 'Men should be what they seem' (*Othello*, III.3.132). Claudius reveals in an unexpected and shocking aside, that he knows he is a fraud: 'The harlot's cheek, beautied with plastering art,/Is not more ugly to the thing that helps it/Than is my deed to my most painted word.' (III.1.51–3)

But the King has no hesitation in cultivating an impression of himself which is anything but accurate. In Act I Scene 2 this passionate brother-killer presents himself as a reasonable man. In every crisis, he carefully glosses the truth with 'a double varnish' (IV.7.131) in order to massage public opinion. We see him pretending he believes Hamlet is mad in order to deflect enquiries into why the Prince should be after his blood. We hear him instructing Rosencrantz and Guildenstern to spin Hamlet's removal to England as a voyage undertaken for his health whereas he knows he is sending the Prince to his death. He pretends to be counselling Laertes in the process of manipulating him into murdering Hamlet. Everything Claudius reveals about the inmost working of his thoughts and feelings in his agonised **soliloquy** in Act III Scene 3, he spends the rest of the play disguising.

POLITICS AND POWER

The plot of *Hamlet* is set in motion by Claudius's murderous ambition to supplant his brother, the King. It ends with his replacement by Young Fortinbras, the Norwegian prince, as King. All political power in Denmark is concentrated on the throne. Although Denmark is an elective monarchy, in the play we see Claudius nominate his successor and Hamlet (who is technically, very briefly, the King) nominate his, without reference to anyone else. Referring to his questionable marriage to his sister-in-law, Claudius claims that the council has 'freely gone/With this affair along' (I.2.15–16) but Shakespeare nowhere shows anyone voicing this approval and the fact that when Laertes returns intent upon challenging the King's authority, he rapidly whips up overwhelming support, his supporters proclaiming: 'Choose we! Laertes shall be king.' (IV.5.106) suggests that Claudius was never a popular or very secure king. He laments that 'the distracted multitude' much prefer Hamlet (IV.3.4) and tells Laertes (IV.7.18) that 'the general gender' love Hamlet so much he dare not proceed against him in the law courts. Hamlet, who despises Claudius as an inferior type of creature from his father, tells Rosencrantz and Guildenstern that people mocked Claudius whilst Old Hamlet was alive (II.2.335) though now they queue up to buy 'his picture in little' (II.2.336).

For all these reasons, Claudius is a politician who is acutely aware of the need to manage public opinion (see **Claudius** in **Part Three: Characters and themes**). Old Hamlet, like his son, was an idealist, with a strong commitment to traditional notions of right and wrong. Claudius is a pragmatist: he acts as if he believes that the end justifies the means. He has no compunction about breaking the Ten Commandments by killing his brother and making men work on the Sabbath or defying convention and biblical authority by marrying his sister-in-law and failing to observe the appropriate period of mourning for a dead king. He intimidates Laertes by citing the Divine Right of Kings (IV.5.124–5) but apparently had no qualms about killing a king himself. However, his soliloquy explores the tensions between what he appears to believe and what his conscience tells him. Although Shakespeare does not devote much stage-time to the political dimension of his **tragedy**, many directors in the late twentieth century gave it emphasis through stage-business and, on film, by showing Fortinbras as a more complex and significant figure than the text alone suggests. (For a discussion of the role of Fortinbras, see **Fortinbras** in **Part Three: Characters and themes**.)

CONTEXT **A04**

The idea that kings are created by God and are answerable only to Him evolved in the Middle Ages. But it was James VI of Scotland, who became James I of England in 1603 (and was to become patron of Shakespeare's theatre company) who asserted the idea with great conviction in *The True Law of Free Monarchies* (1598) and *Basilikon Doron* (1599): the year in which Shakespeare was writing *Hamlet*. The books stress the duty of the King to respect biblical teaching: something which Claudius overlooks.

THE PROBLEM OF THE GHOST

A QUESTIONABLE SHAPE

Everyone who sees him finds the Ghost a terrifying and impressive figure: the sceptical Horatio is 'harrow[ed] … with fear and wonder' (I.1.44). Kozintsev's film, with the aid of Shostakovich's compelling score, conveys the awesome power of this supernatural visitor. Dressed in 'complete steel' (I.4.52) as Old Hamlet was when he 'smote the sledded Polack on the ice' (I.1.63), the Ghost looks every inch the god-like, warrior King. The scrupulous Horatio confirms that he looks exactly ('cap-a-pe', I.2.200) like Hamlet's famous father. And yet the men on watch continually refer to the Ghost as an 'illusion' (I.1.127), an 'apparition' (I.1.28), a 'thing' (I.1.21). And although at moments the Ghost appears 'majestical' (I.1.143) and moves 'with solemn march' (I.2.201) at other times it behaves very differently: it is 'offended' and 'stalks away' (I.1.50) when Horatio orders him 'By heaven' (I.1.49), to speak. When the cock crows, 'it start[s] like guilty thing/Upon a fearful summons' (I.1.147–8). We are meant to think about where that summons comes from. The mighty figure is literally diminished: 'it shrunk in haste away' (I.2.218). There is a more powerful force in the universe before whom the Ghost feels ashamed.

HOURS OF DARKNESS

Night time was much more daunting for the Elizabethans that it is for us with our televisions, street lighting and scepticism about the supernatural. It was the 'witching time of night,/When churchyards yawn, and hell itself breathes out/Contagion to this world' (III.2.349–51). We are given the sense that in the hours of darkness, wicked, hellish spirits have access to this world that is denied them during daylight. The idea that the Ghost, who appears to be the embodiment of the father Hamlet regarded as the perfect example of manhood and morally correct behaviour, could be a devil impersonating him is very potent. Elizabethans saw life as a battle between virtuous and vicious thoughts that would decide their fate in the afterlife, and being lead into temptation was something they prayed daily to avoid.

AN HONEST GHOST?

There is no reason to doubt the truth of anything the Ghost says; in that sense, Hamlet is quite right to describe him as 'honest' (I.5.138). But honesty is a matter of intention as much as the words spoken. The problem of the Ghost is this: are the information and instructions Hamlet is given likely to make his situation better or worse? What can a man do with 'thoughts beyond the reaches of our souls?' (I.4.56) As Hamlet puts it: 'What should we do?' (I.4.57). We saw how in Act I Scene 1 the watch continually distinguished between the 'apparition' and the person it resembled. In Act I Scene 5 and Act III Scene 4, Shakespeare complicates the picture by humanising the Ghost. Not only his appearance and his words, but his feelings and ideas seem to be those of Hamlet's father; as a character, a personality, The Ghost is much more fully developed than Gertrude. Hamlet's problem is not the simple alternative he poses in his Act II Scene 2 soliloquy: whether the Ghost is a devil; but whether he should regard the father he admires as, in some senses, 'a devil' (II.2.551) and his commandment as devilish.

CONFLICTING OBLIGATIONS

The better we know the play, we more we see that this idea is something Hamlet can never articulate in such stark terms. But throughout the play, Hamlet feels himself on the horns of a dilemma: loyalty to his father conflicts with his obedience to God: whose 'commandment' (I.5.102) should he obey? By moving to an understanding of how God works in Act V, Hamlet effectively frees himself from the Ghost. At the end of the play, the

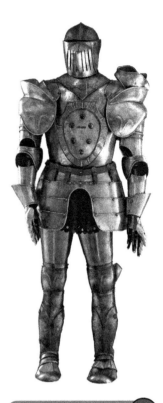

CONTEXT A04

In *Macbeth*, Shakespeare explores this idea on the night of Banquo's murder: 'Good things of day begin to droop and drowse/Whiles night's black agents to their preys do rouse' (*Macbeth*, III.2.52–3).

CONTEXT A04

'The devil can cite Scripture for his purpose,' (*The Merchant of Venice*, I.3.90) is an idea that Elizabethans were familiar with from the New Testament. In *The Merchant of Venice*, Antonio continues: 'An evil soul producing holy witness/Is like a villain with a smiling cheek'. Similar, false-face imagery can be found throughout Shakespeare and is dominant in *Hamlet*.

Ghost is no longer a problem because Hamlet forgets him. Instead of seeing himself as the Ghost's 'scourge and minister' (III.4.176), 'Hamlet the Dane' (V.1.225) takes on not only a king's identity but also accepts full moral responsibility for his actions, confident that Heaven will shape things for the best. His passive nature for which he criticised himself earlier in the play now becomes something positive: the humility of a Christian soul.

DOUBLE MESSAGES

There is no doubt that the messages the Ghost gives Hamlet are full of contradictions. He appeals to Hamlet's strongest feelings when he says: 'If thou didst ever thy dear father love – … Revenge his foul and most unnatural murder.' (I.5.23–5) Hamlet loved and admired his brave father. In the fallen world of Claudius's Denmark where 'things rank and gross in nature/Posses it merely' (I.2.136–7) Old Hamlet represents a simpler, nobler world of values and honesty where things were what they appeared to be. The Ghost reminds his son that his love 'went hand in hand even with the vow/I made to her in marriage' (I.5.49–50) at the very moment when Hamlet is devastated by his mother's adultery. Son and father have been shocked to discover that she was only a 'seeming virtuous Queen' (I.5.46): we recall Hamlet's indignation when Gertrude accuses *him* of 'seeming' (I.2.75–6). The Ghost's contempt for his incestuous, adulterate brother agrees with Hamlet's assessment of Claudius as a 'satyr' (I.2.140). But at the very heart of his sincere revelations, the Ghost uses a powerful **image**, one which Shakespeare uses repeatedly to dramatise the idea of temptation: 'virtue … never will be moved/Though lewdness court it in a shape of heaven' (I.5.53–4). The good man will be tempted. And temptation will be powerful because it arrives dressed in respectable clothes. The circumstances the Ghost describes are in fact true; the Ghost is who he appears to be. What is questionable is how his demands should be dealt with.

The Ghost's message is confusing; anyone would be thrown off balance at such shocking revelations and such confusing orders. Because the Ghost is not, as he implies, 'a radiant angel' (I.5.55), he tells Hamlet he suffers the agonies of 'sulphurous and tormenting flames' (I.5.3), that his 'prison house' (I.5.14) is a terrifying place, that he must 'fast in fires' for the 'foul crimes' (I.5.11–12) he committed. The Ghost simultaneously paints a terrifying picture of the afterlife and demands Hamlet commit a deed which will result in his going to Hell.

THE GHOST HUMANISED

The Ghost is humanly inconsistent. He tells Hamlet not to 'Taint' (I.5.85) his mind against his mother after telling him things which cannot fail to do that. The Ghost's love for the wife he condemns is one of his most touching, human attributes. But it makes Hamlet's dealings with her hopelessly complicated. Why should she be left 'to heaven' (I.5.86) whilst Claudius is dealt with on Earth? Hamlet's instincts work in precisely the opposite direction. He will do everything possible to save Gertrude's soul by encouraging her to repent; Claudius he will, effectively, leave to Heaven. He will feel guilty for failing to do what the Ghost commanded him to do but he would feel guiltier if he did it.

A FIGURE OF FUN

Shakespeare dramatises the duality of the Ghost's status – humanised and supernatural – by having him return at the end of Act I Scene 5 under the stage. The voice which had such dignity and poise when it revealed to us the circumstances of the murder now becomes a ludicrous figure as it scuttles about 'in the cellerage' (I.5.151), a voice without a body. Hamlet speaks to it using a totally different language: 'boy, sayst thou so? Art thou there truepenny?' (I.5.150). He is and is not talking to his dead father. He is 'this fellow in the cellerage' (I.5.151), 'old mole' (I.5.161), at best a 'perturbèd spirit' (I.5.183). No matter how much he respects his father, his father is dead: the living man has responsibilities that the dead have lost.

STRUCTURE

Hamlet is a play made up of two **Revenge Tragedies**. Acts I to Act IV Scene 4 present what may be called the **exposition** and development of the first Revenge Tragedy. Act IV Scenes 5 to 7 present the exposition and development of the second Revenge Tragedy. Act V sees these two Revenge Tragedies brought together and worked out to their tragic conclusion.

THE FIRST EXPOSITION: ACT I

The tragic **protagonist** Hamlet finds himself at odds with the King and the court and with public opinion in Denmark. Nobody shares his feelings of grief for the recently deceased king or his belief that Old Hamlet represented superior values to those of the people now in power. Alienated from all around him, Hamlet feels unable to voice his concerns since there is nobody with whom he can share his world view. However, a trio of minor characters is loyal to Hamlet, not the King. They share with him knowledge of the Ghost. The Ghost shares with him privileged knowledge about how the present state of affairs came about: through adultery, regicide and incest. The Ghost orders Hamlet to avenge his murder and put things right.

> **CRITICAL VIEWPOINT** **A03**
>
> 'The Ghost is the linchpin of *Hamlet*; remove it and the play falls to pieces.' John Dover Wilson, *What Happens in Hamlet* (1935) p. 52.

DEVELOPMENT: ACT II – ACT IV SCENE 4

The major part of the play explores Hamlet's response to the Ghost's 'commandment' (I.5.102). Reflection shows Hamlet that the Ghost's message is confused and confusing; simultaneously it orders him to pursue revenge and acknowledges that there is a supreme power in the universe which condemns revenge. This confusion is bewildering because the Ghost appears and claims to be the spirit of the father Hamlet admired. A strong sense of duty as a son clashes with Hamlet's religious instincts.

In Act II Scene 2 Hamlet articulates the idea that the Ghost may be a devil but it is his actions, or rather inactivity, which show that he has doubts about what he has been told to do. For much of the play, Hamlet is engaged in a vigorous but inconclusive exploration of what the correct response to the Ghost should be. It leads him to question the nature and value of thinking itself: 'for there is nothing either good or bad but thinking makes it so' (II.2.239–40). Whilst Hamlet delays, his powerful opponent, the King, disturbed by Hamlet's behaviour and realising when Polonius is killed that he is dangerous, takes steps to have him killed. Hamlet temporarily leaves the play.

THE SECOND EXPOSITION: ACT IV SCENE 5

The second Revenge Tragedy in which the protagonist is Laertes, is a highly concentrated, simplified version of the first. Prompted to revenge not by a ghost but by rumour and the madness of his sister, Laertes's response is uncomplicated by hesitation as to what is the right thing to do. Unthinkingly, he discounts the religious framework which shapes Hamlet's deliberations. Of all the major players in *Hamlet*, Laertes alone shows no fear of divine judgement: his behaviour is governed by an entirely secular concept of honour. Rash and impulsive, he is easily manipulated by the unscrupulous King into plotting the murder of Hamlet.

THE TRAGIC DENOUEMENT

In Act V, Shakespeare unites the two **Revenge Tragedies** in a thrilling way

Hamlet's off-stage experiences have transformed him. The man who returns to Denmark now believes the world is governed by God: on board ship his impulsive behaviour saved his life. He believes that God is looking after him. There is none of the agonised introspection of the earlier acts. He sees clearly that he has a moral duty: not to pursue revenge but to deliver justice and prevent Claudius doing further harm to the country. It is a significant revision of the Ghost's commandment. Hamlet recognises he has little time in which to act but puts together no definite plan.

Meanwhile the schemes of Claudius and Laertes shape the action. The King's plot brings about its own ruin: the Queen is accidentally poisoned and she identifies the cause. Laertes, similarly destroyed by the plot, publically accuses the King. Hamlet, with only minutes to live, kills Claudius in an act of retribution. The stage is littered with corpses, Denmark's throne passes to the Norwegian Young Fortinbras. It is left to Horatio and the audience to pass judgement on what has happened.

This double Revenge Tragedy is framed by another Revenge Story: we see young Fortinbras seeking to recover the lands lost by his father in a thoroughly lawful, ceremonial combat thirty years previously. We learn no more about Fortinbras's personality beyond what Horatio gives us in Act I Scene 1, there is little dramatic interaction between the Norwegian prince and the rest of the action and he achieves his goal by chance. But the **frame story** gives *Hamlet* a formal coherence which is both satisfying and problematic. Hamlet's dying endorsement means that Fortinbras's succession is lawful. It feels more like a healing than a further catastrophe for Denmark but the country has become subject to a foreign power. Claudius's murder of Old Hamlet has been a political disaster.

FORM

SHAKESPEAREAN TRAGEDY

Shakespeare radically developed the crude **Senecan** notion of tragedy which had been common on the English stage in the decades preceding *Hamlet*. Seneca's heroes have little inner self and their suffering is more likely to arouse feelings of horror than empathy. From *Titus Andronicus* (1592), through *Romeo and Juliet* (1595) to *Julius Caesar* (1599), we can see Shakespeare exploring what we understand by the word 'tragedy'. *Titus Andronicus* is a Senecan horror show, in which the **protagonist** is bloodily caught up in a savage world that bears little resemblance to that of Shakespeare and his contemporaries. The play **sensationalises** cruelty in ways which may remind a modern audience of the work of the film director Quentin Tarantino. We feel pity for Titus but few are likely to identify with him. In *Romeo and Juliet,* set in a recognisably Elizabethan world, the tragic protagonists are two irrationally warring families who pay for their foolishness by losing two essentially innocent children. *Julius Caesar* is different again, with the character of Brutus developed in powerful **soliloquies** in which we see a decent, just man struggling to do the right thing in the most challenging circumstances.

Hamlet (c.1600) is Shakespeare's most elaborate exploration of a single mind; the hero has some two hundred lines of soliloquy in which we see him wrestle with the burden imposed on him by the Ghost. Hamlet's inner life is the subject of the play: other characters pale into insignificance beside him. In his next **tragedy**, *Othello* (1604), Shakespeare produced a quite different kind of play, with the focus of dramatic attention divided between a flawed, egotistical hero and an engaging but ruthless villain. Shakespeare continued to explore and develop the idea of tragedy throughout his career. There is no such thing as a Shakespearean tragic formula.

CONTEXT **A04**

Seneca and Plautus were, respectively, the Roman masters of tragedy and comedy. Some of their plays were performed at Oxford and Cambridge universities in the 1580s and prompted the development of Elizabethan drama.

CRITICAL VIEWPOINT **A03**

'The figures in Seneca's *Oedipus* are Greek only by convention: by nature they are more primitive than aboriginals.' Ted Hughes, Introduction to his version of Seneca's *Oedpius* (1969).

STUDY FOCUS: REVENGE TRAGEDY A02

By the time Shakespeare came to rework the old play of *Hamlet*, Revenge Tragedy as a specific form had developed certain conventional ingredients. Sometimes there would be a Ghost (as in Kyd's *The Spanish Tragedy*), revealing how it had met its gruesome end through treachery. Ceremoniously, it might call upon the hero, for the sake of the family's honour, to settle accounts. Vengeance would always be delayed: what else could the play consist of? But these delays were commonly due to plotting and counter-plotting in which sometimes the hero would pretend to be mad to catch his intended victim unawares, not, as in *Hamlet*, through the protagonist's reluctance to do the wrong thing. But, as if to support Bacon's condemnation of such 'wild justice' ('Of Revenge', 1625), the price of revenge was usually the death of the person who carried it out. As the trailer for the 2002 film *Revengers Tragedy* puts it, 'He who seeks revenge should dig two graves.'

CONTEXT A04

The lost, early play, known as the *Ur-Hamlet* and possibly by Thomas Kyd, was very popular. Some idea of its style can be gained from reading Kyd's other popular Revenge Tragedy, *The Spanish Tragedy*.

LANGUAGE

We sense the virtuoso Shakespeare enjoying himself in this play, feeling his powers of invention reaching new heights and presenting a dazzling variety of language styles. The **colloquial** speech of the gravediggers in Act V does not sound like the grandiose language of the First Player in Act III, nor does the mannered style of Osric sound anything like Horatio's few well-chosen words. Claudius's clear-headed soliloquy could not be mistaken for one of Hamlet's emotional tangles and Ophelia's plaintive, broken songs are unlike anything else in the play. Gertrude's **lyrical** account of Ophelia's drowning is in a different register from Rosencrantz's **choric** description of a state's ruin and the Ghost's solemn and graphic description of his sufferings is very different from the muddled meanderings of Polonius. Exploring how Shakespeare creates so many different, distinct voices is one of the delights of studying the play. Hamlet is himself something of a chameleon, able to engage with and **parody** all types in their own language; he is a stern judge of the ways English can be misused. He pokes fun at both lawyer-talk and the language of diplomacy whilst Laertes is a case study in ranting **hyperbole**.

RHYMED AND UNRHYMED VERSE

The majority of *Hamlet* is written in **blank verse**. It is much more flexible than the verse of Shakespeare's early plays such as *The Merchant of Venice* where lines are regularly **end-stopped** and the expression feels stilted:

The devil can cite scripture for his purpose.
An evil soul producing holy witness
Is like a villain with a smiling cheek,
A goodly apple rotten at the heart.
O what a goodly outside falsehood hath! (*The Merchant of Venice*, I.3.96–100)

Compare the movement of Hamlet's final soliloquy:

How all occasions do inform against me,
And spur my dull revenge! What is a man
If his chief good and market of his time
Be but to sleep and feed? A beast, no more. (IV.4.32–5)

By writing flowing sentences which straddle the lines like this, Shakespeare makes the speech sound more natural, more suggestive of the way thoughts develop. The regular **pentameter** pulse holds the speech together whilst the rhythms of natural speech render it life-like and energetic.

The First Player's speech (II.2.410–22), which is an exuberant reworking of an episode in Book Two of Vergil's *The Aeneid*, is Shakespeare's parody of the **rhetorical** and ranting **melodramatic** style of Marlowe:

          Head to foot
Now is he total gules, horribly tricked
With blood of fathers, mothers, daughters, sons,
Baked and impasted. … Roasted in wrath and fire,
And thus o'er-sizèd with coagulate gore, (II.2.414–20)

But Shakespeare presents *The Mousetrap* in a very different theatrical style: quaint-sounding **rhyming couplets** with their trite classical **allusions** and old-fashioned **diction** create the impression of stylisation and 'otherness' appropriate to a play-within-a-play. The feebleness of some of the writing: 'For us and for our tragedy,/Here stooping to your clemency,/We beg your hearing patiently' (III.2.130–2) is deliberate: it helps sustain the illusion that whereas *The Mousetrap* is just a play, the rest of *Hamlet* is real life. Yet *The Mousetrap* is a witty and elaborate thing; it explores some of the play's major themes such as why we often fail to keep our promises and the rhyming couplets are handled with great flexibility. It merits careful critical attention.

Elsewhere, Shakespeare uses rhyming couplets to round off a scene with a flourish: 'It shall be so./Madness in great ones must not unwatched go' (III.1.181–2) or to suggest rehearsed insincerity as when Ophelia accuses Hamlet of neglecting her: 'for to the noble mind/Rich gifts wax poor when givers prove unkind' (III.1.100–1) and Gertrude tries to belittle Hamlet's grief with a bland-sounding cliché: 'Thou know'st 'tis common, all that lives must die,/Passing through nature to eternity.' (I.2.72–3)

IMAGERY

CHECK THE BOOK **A03**

For a survey of the pervasiveness of images of sickness and disease in *Hamlet*, see Caroline Spurgeon's ground-breaking study, *Shakespeare's Imagery* (1935).

Shakespeare's language is rich in **similes** and **metaphors**: he presents us with one memorable **image** after another. Critics have long noticed that in particular plays, there are clusters of certain kinds of image, where expression is coloured by two or three dominant ideas. In *Hamlet*, the majority of images concern disease, corruption and moral pollution, especially prostitution. Imagery like this does not give us information directly. It helps to create the mood, the colour of the play; it suggests the kind of world the characters inhabit.

THE GHOST'S BODY

The Ghost's stately and solemn verse is remarkable for its graphic imagery that draws us a picture: 'So lust, though to a radiant angel linked,/Will sate itself in a celestial bed,/And prey on garbage' (I.5.55–8). His vivid recollection of the workings of poison on his body (I.5.64–73) is rich in poetic effects, suggesting how lively movement: 'swift as quicksilver' gives way to paralysis: 'doth posset/And curd, like eager droppings into milk' and then hideous disfiguration: 'a most instant tetter barked about,/Most lazar-like, with vile and loathsome crust'. Where the **assonant** tripping **trisyllable** 'quicksilver' imitates rapid motion, the halting, congested sounds of 'posset … curd … barked about … lazar-like … loathsome crust' help to generate a disturbing picture of slowly advancing deformity.

DISEASE, POLLUTION AND PROSTITUTION

These powerful, literal images of bodily decay are part of the larger, more **figurative** presentation of corruption and disease which is found throughout the play. The idea is given its starkest expression by Marcellus: 'Something is rotten in the state of Denmark' (I.V.90). At the end of the play, Hamlet identifies Claudius, 'this canker [cancer] of our nature,' (V.2.69) as the source of this corruption. Everyone is shown to be infected in some way by the pollution oozing from the royal bed which has become 'a couch for luxury [lust] and damnèd incest' (I.5.83). Hamlet imagines his mother like a lusty horse '[posting]/With such dexterity to incestuous sheets' (I.2.156–7) … 'to live/In the rank sweat of an enseamèd bed,/Stewed in corruption, honeying and making love/Over the nasty sty' (III.4.91–4). He accuses her of polluting love itself; her sordid example: 'takes off the rose/From the fair forehead of an innocent love/And sets a blister there' (III.4.42–4).

The idea that honesty itself has been corrupted, so that 'reason panders will' (III.4.88) and a young girl has been turned into a whore deserving branding on the forehead, colours Hamlet's exchanges with Ophelia in the nunnery scene. Claudius also identifies himself with the whore, admitting 'The harlot's cheek, beautied with plastering art,/Is not more ugly to the things that helps it/Than is my deed to my most painted word' (III.1.51–3). Hamlet urges his mother to repent, to avoid further sin to prevent a tumour developing which: 'will ... skin and film the ulcerous place,/Whiles rank corruption, mining all within,/Infects unseen' (III.4.148–50).

'MANY POCKY CORSES'

We are given the feeling that Claudius's Denmark is a dangerously infectious place. Hamlet living amidst 'things rank and gross in nature' (I.2.136) describes his own flesh as 'sullied' (I.2.129, see **Glossary** in **Part Two: Act I Scene 1**) and Laertes although he trusts at her graveside that Ophelia's flesh remains 'unpolluted' (V.1.206), warns his sister about a world where 'canker galls the infants of the spring' (I.3.39) and 'contagious blastments are most imminent' (I.3.42). Hamlet describes how 'the dram of eale/Doth all the noble substance of a doubt' (I.4.36–7); bawd-like Polonius prostitutes his daughter, believing that 'love/In honourable fashion' (I.3.111) is a myth. In such a world, Ophelia can hope only to be 'a breeder of sinners' (III.1.119–20) unless she takes refuge in a nunnery.

In the second part of the play, Claudius recognises that he is infected. We learn that after *The Mousetrap*, the King is 'marvellous distempered' (III.2.273); Hamlet comments that his prayer is 'physic' and simply 'prolongs [his] sickly days' (III.3.96) and sees the King as 'a mildewed ear' (III.4.64). The King himself confesses that his sin is 'rank' (III.3.36). Meanwhile he sees Hamlet as a '[disease] desperate grown' (IV.3.9) which rages 'like the hectic in my blood' (IV.3.62). The people's thoughts are 'muddied' and 'unwholesome' (IV.5.80 and 81); the gravedigger tells us he has to handle 'many pocky [syphilitic] corses [corpses]' (V.1.140–1) nowadays. Even Fortinbras's army, crossing Denmark, is seen as catching the disease, the elaborate and shocking image of a tumour echoing the one Hamlet used in the closet scene:

This is th'impostume of much wealth and peace,
That inward breaks, and shows no cause without
Why the man dies. (IV.4.27–9)

DECADENCE

The related idea that Elsinore has become decadent is developed by news that the actors whose 'endeavour keeps in the wonted pace' are on the road, forced to make way for 'an eyrie of children' meaning that 'many wearing rapiers are afraid of "goose-quills"' (II.2.314–18). Those who once mocked Old Hamlet's younger brother now 'give ... a hundred ducats apiece for his picture in little' (II.2.336); the absurd Osric is the kind of courtier 'the drossy age dotes on' (V.2.166–7).

CONTEXT A04

Exquisite miniature portraits, 'picture[s] in little' (II.2.336), were highly prized in Elizabethan England. Nicholas Hilliard was the master of the craft. In many productions, Hamlet and Gertrude wear miniatures of Old Hamlet and Claudius in the closet scene.

HISTORICAL BACKGROUND

CRITICAL VIEWPOINT A03

'No one in this play "knows" or "understands" anyone else.' Linda Charnes, 'We were never early modern' in John J. Joughin (ed.), *Philosophical Shakespeares* (2000). How far do you agree with this point of view?

THE UNIVERSAL PLAYWRIGHT

It is difficult to put Shakespeare into perspective: there are no other English authors except Chaucer and arguably Dickens who have either his range of interests and human sympathies or his technical sophistication. Of his contemporaries, only Marlowe and Webster produced one or two plays which are regularly revived today whereas almost all of Shakespeare's thirty-eight continue to be performed regularly all over the world. Extraordinary creative genius is not simply a product of historical circumstances; Jonson was surely right when he recognised that Shakespeare 'was not of an age but for all time!'

A MIRROR OF ITS TIMES

If it is not limited by the conventions of its time or place, *Hamlet*, which enjoyed great success immediately, certainly reflects the age in which it was produced. At the beginning of the seventeenth century, London was a cauldron of competing ideas, fuelled by fundamental changes in the way people perceived the world. Just as the internet is transforming not only the way we communicate but the way countries relate to one another and the ways in which we think, so the fundamentals of society were being transformed in 1600. The discoveries of Copernicus and, later, Galileo displaced the world as the centre of the universe and called into question age-old certainties about man's place in the scheme of things. The world itself was changing in previously unimaginable ways: new lands and peoples were being discovered, Europe's economy and the relative political strength of fiercely competing trading nations was changing. Martin Luther's defiance of the authority of the Pope had led to the break up of the universal church and the questioning of all religious assumptions. England had swung from radical Protestantism back to repressive Catholicism and then back to a Protestantism somewhere in between within the previous half century.

For these reasons, we should think about Shakespeare's dramatisation of Hamlet's ethical dilemma not simply as an artistic creation but as a mirror revealing something about a particular moment in history when religious certainty had given way to almost unlimited questioning. Religious conflict was also joined by political uncertainty – after fifty years of stability, the reign of Elizabeth was coming to an end with no certainty about what would happen when she died. England was a small country at risk of invasion from Scotland, Ireland and Spain; Rumour was rife, and conspiracies (real or imaginary), government spies and informers were everywhere. We might read Polonius, the spymaster, as a comic take on a sinister and deadly government machine.

STUDY FOCUS: SPYING AND REPRESSION IN SHAKESPEARE'S ENGLAND A04

Three of Shakespeare's leading fellow-playwrights had been in trouble with the authorities. Kyd, falsely charged with libel and atheism and broken by torture, died at thirty-five having denounced his roommate, Marlowe, himself a government spy, who was summoned before the Privy Council and then murdered in mysterious circumstances. Ben Jonson, who narrowly escaped hanging for killing a man in a duel, had all his goods confiscated and was branded on the thumb. Every play was subject to government censorship. *The Isle of Dogs*, a **satirical** play judged to be inciting rebellion against the state landed Jonson in prison and temporarily closed the Swan Theatre. You may like to think about how the turbulent times in which Shakespeare was writing fed into *Hamlet*'s dark, uncertain atmosphere of intrigue and revenge.

NASTY, BRUTISH AND SHORT

Shakespeare's was a brutal, dangerous and, sometimes, terrifying world. Bear-baiting with dogs and the gruesome execution of traitors were popular spectacles. Poor sanitation and very limited medical expertise meant that plague and diseases such as smallpox, typhus and syphilis were widespread; both Jonson's and Shakespeare's sons died in childhood. Life expectancy in London was around thirty. No wonder *Othello*'s Iago thinks of himself as old and experienced at twenty-eight; Hamlet at thirty, like the actor, Burbage, who played him, is not a young man. This may contribute to the worldly-wise and at times weary tone of some of Hamlet's observations, a tone we might not expect from a thirty-year-old man today.

THE STATUS OF WOMEN

Without any way of controlling reproduction other than chastity, and primitive standards of hygiene and medicine, women in Shakespeare's day married young and spent most of their active years pregnant, managing the home and looking after children. Many of them died in childbirth: it was quite common for a man in his lifetime to have two or three wives. Very few women were academically educated, none were allowed to attend university, enter the professions or become priests and their rights in law were severely limited. The eldest male child usually inherited most of his father's property and on marriage any property a woman did possess became her husband's. Like most of the population, women had little say in the government of the country. But in a country ruled successfully by an exceptionally accomplished woman for forty-five years, women in literature, as in real life, certainly had a voice.

Although they are expected to defer to their fathers, brothers and husbands, Shakespeare's major women characters (played by boys) are usually bold, articulate and resourceful. Without being what we would understand as a **feminist**, Shakespeare did not usually 'silence' his major women characters, who generally have more self-confidence and are more fully developed and rounded personalities than women in Dickens, created two hundred and fifty years later. (See **The Women in Hamlet** in **Part Three: Themes**.)

Anne Bullen   Alte Hofdame   Damen am Hofe der Königin Katharina

SHIFTING POWER

It would take more than four centuries to give all English men and women the right to an education and the right to vote but within fifty years of *Hamlet's* first performance, the King would be executed and England declared a republic. Already in 1600, Parliament was testing the supremacy of the Crown, self-made men were challenging the power of inherited wealth. The very nature of power was changing. The land-owning aristocracy with its code of family honour was a shadow of its former self; the up-and-coming men were lawyers, financiers, self-made entrepreneurs. Shakespeare was such a man: in 1600, he was a prosperous and successful share holder in London's most popular theatre, and still not at the height of his powers. Shakespeare was ridiculed by Jonson for buying himself the respectability of a coat of arms but that a man from a modest background was able to retire to the best house in Stratford-upon-Avon was a sign of the rise of capitalism and England's increasing social mobility.

CRITICAL VIEWPOINT A04

'Shakespeare was always writing out of his own cultural moment.' James Shapiro, 1599: *A Year in the Life of William Shakespeare*, (p. 152).

LITERARY BACKGROUND

HAMLET AND ELIZABETHAN DRAMA

CHECK THE BOOK **A03**

Some impression of the power, range and limitations of **Senecan** tragedy can be gleaned from the modern English translations by David Slavitt: *Seneca: The Tragedies Volume One* (1992).

The development of English drama in the late sixteenth century was rapid and revolutionary. From modest beginnings in the universities and inns of court where Latin plays were performed, through the growth of companies under the patronage (support) of a handful of aristocrats in the 1580s and the creative genius of Marlowe and many lesser talents, Elizabethan drama developed quickly to be something completely different from the **morality and mystery plays** of the past. One of the dominant influences was that of Seneca, whose grand **rhetorical** patterns and recipe of merciless bloody revenge inspired English imitators such as Kyd. Another rhetorician, Lyly, offered a model of elegant **antithetical** elaboration which fed into the mix.

CHECK THE BOOK **A03**

Marlowe's *Tamburlaine, Parts One and Two*, represents the first flowering of powerful dramatic **blank verse** in England. Shakespeare **parodies** its rather stiff, pompous style in the Player's Hecuba speech.

Shakespeare's genius was to inject into these stiff rhetorical patterns and plodding **pentameter** lines the rhythms of natural English speech, whilst drawing upon a much wider range of **allusion**, **simile** and **metaphor** than is found in any other poet. He combined the benefits of a rigorous grammar school education in Latin literature and rhetoric with the advantages of a man who did not then proceed to university for more of the same but developed his craft in the working world.

HAMLET: A NEW KIND OF TRAGEDY

By the time he came to write *Hamlet*, Shakespeare had served a long apprenticeship, with at least twenty popular plays to his credit, most of which are still performed regularly today.

He was already widely recognised as the leading playwright of his generation and, established in the newly opened Globe, began to write the series of plays on which his reputation now largely rests. His company included the leading actors of his day and Shakespeare wrote with their strengths in mind. *Hamlet* was a new kind of **tragedy** in which spectacle was largely replaced by **word play**, the wit of the clown replaced by the wit of the intellectual. His hero was a man of reflection rather than a man of action; it was a movement towards naturalism and away from **sensationalism**. Hamlet's thinking is the heart of the play and his **soliloquies** are far more extensive than any seen before. A likely influence on these were the essays of Montaigne published in 1580. These humane, sceptical examinations of a man's thinking: 'it is my self I portray' were an attempt to hammer out honestly and frankly the nature of things. 'Every man beareth the whole stampe of human condition … I may cause men of understanding to thinke.' (Montaigne, 1580)

CONTEXT **A03**

Polonius's pedantic desire to pigeonhole types of drama parodies those critics who find Shakespeare's mixing of genres problematic. Hamlet could be described as 'tragical-comical-historical-pastoral' (II.2.365).

Within the framework of a double **Revenge Tragedy**, Shakespeare presents an educated man's **critique** of revenge. Not that Hamlet is detached from the action: he is caught up in it. The dramatic interest is in how a man of his intelligence copes with extraordinary pressures. The soliloquies are not so much private meditations as an appeal to the audience standing just a few feet from the actor. What would we do if we found ourselves in Hamlet's shoes? Rather than a hero like Othello, Macbeth or Coriolanus with their obvious tragic flaws, Hamlet is more like **Everyman**, 'bearing the whole stamp of the human condition' (Montaigne, 1580).

THE SOURCE OF HAMLET

Shakespeare's *Hamlet* was probably based upon an earlier play of the same name written by Thomas Kyd. Shakespeare would have performed in this version of *Hamlet* which was in

The Lord Chamberlain's Men's repertory (collection of plays performed) for many years. Though all copies have now disappeared, it was probably still being performed by travelling players who staged a performance of *Hamlet* in Germany in the 1620s. Older sources of the Hamlet story, Saxo Grammaticus's *Gesta Danorum* and Belleforest's French translation of it which describes Hamlet as melancholy may also have been known to Shakespeare. Based on the evidence of Kyd's popular Revenge Tragedy *The Spanish Tragedy* (in which Burbage starred as Hieronimo), the old play was probably rhetorical in the Senecan manner, included an importunate Ghost, a play-within-the-play, real and feigned madness and a morality which regards bloody revenge as an honourable response to a grievance. As well as transforming the character of the **protagonist** and firmly locating the play in a Christian context, Shakespeare almost certainly added Laertes and Young Fortinbras to the old story, presenting them as dramatic **foils** to Hamlet and developing the play as a critique of revenge rather than simply an illustration of it. *Hamlet*'s Ghost is quite different from Kyd's in *The Spanish Tragedy*. Rather than being restricted to a separate dramatic space where he comments upon the action, Shakespeare's Ghost interacts with the rest of the play and his behaviour is commented upon not only by Hamlet but by the soldiers on watch. His character is more strongly developed than in Kyd and his moral authority is debated.

THE TEXTS OF *HAMLET*

Three printed texts of *Hamlet*, known as Q1, Q2 (Quartos 1 and 2) and F (the Folio edition), were published between 1603 and 1623. Modern editions of the play are based upon all three, editors selecting the details they prefer. Q2 is the longest version of the play but as well as making some major cuts, F includes material not found in Q2. Q1 is a much shorter and, in places, muddled text.

There is much disagreement amongst scholars about the relative status of these three printed texts. Until recently it was difficult for students to compare them but the publication of the latest Arden edition (2006), in two volumes, conveniently presents all three texts in modernised spelling.

Some scholars believe Q1 is Shakespeare's first version of the play but most believe it was an acting version cobbled together by actors who had appeared in the Q2 version, relying upon their memories to reconstruct it. Since the scenes including Marcellus are most accurately recalled, it is thought the actor playing this minor part was responsible for the pirated text. For all its imperfections, Q1 offers *Hamlet* in a radically abridged and dramatically effective version and may well represent the play as it was acted on tour and in the universities, as the title page claims.

Q2 was almost certainly issued by The Lord Chamberlain's Men as a response to the pirating of their text as Q1. The title page claims it is 'enlarged to almost as much againe, according to the true and perfect copy' and this version of the play is the one most editors regard as closest to the play performed in 1600. F which was published with most of Shakespeare's other plays after his death, in 1623, is regarded by some scholars as a later version of the play, revised in the light of what worked on stage. It makes two major cuts: the speech about a tragic flaw (Act I Scene 4) and most of Act IV Scene 4, including Hamlet's final soliloquy. It includes the passage about the rival boys' companies, which is missing from Q2. There are many interesting minor textual variations. The importance of these printed versions is that they show that from very early on, people wanted to read *Hamlet*, not just watch it on stage. Although many critics argue that *Hamlet* is a text which comes alive only in performance, *Hamlet* has been read since the seventeenth century. Many more people read the play than see it performed.

WHERE NEXT? COMPARING *HAMLET* WITH OTHER TEXTS

Once you are thoroughly familiar with the text of *Hamlet*, you will find your understanding of its dramatic language and its approach to **characterisation** and **theme** are developed by comparing it with other texts. It is much easier to see what makes Shakespeare's

CONTEXT A04

'English Seneca read by candle-light yields many good sentences, as *Blood is a begger*, and so forth; and if you entreat him fair in a frosty morning, he will afford you whole *Hamlets*, I should say handfuls of tragical speeches.' Thomas Nash writing in 1589, more than ten years before the appearance of Shakespeare's *Hamlet*.

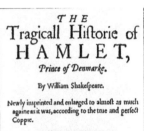

CONTEXT A04

In 1596 Thomas Lodge wrote about the well-known play in which the protagonist 'walks for the most part in black under the cover of gravity, and looks as pale as the vizard of the Ghost who cried so miserably at the Theatre like an oyster wife, "Hamlet, revenge!"'

presentation of women in *Hamlet* unusual and puzzling, for example, when you compare the way women are presented in his other **tragedie**s, such as *King Lear, Antony and Cleopatra* and *Macbeth*. The connotations of the phrase 'The fair Ophelia' (III.1.89) and *Hamlet's* thoughts about prostitution can be compared with the way Shakespeare dramatises the Fair Friend and the Dark Mistress in his *Sonnets*.

Shakespeare's ideas about dramatic art, as seen in Hamlet's advice to the players, link with his exploration of the way dramatic poetry works on the audience's 'imaginary forces' (I.18) in the **choruses** to *Henry V*, a play written shortly before *Hamlet*.

It is interesting to explore the ways Shakespeare's idea of tragedy develops from the 'star-crossed lovers' (Prologue, line 6) of *Romeo and Juliet*, through *Julius Caesar* and *Hamlet*, where the central protagonist is a moralist caught up in turbulent affairs, to later tragedies, such as *Othello* and *Coriolanus*, where the hero has the kind of tragic flaw Hamlet describes in Act I Scene 4. Your understanding of the Ghost and the moral challenges it presents to Horatio and Hamlet will be enhanced by comparing the way Banquo and Macbeth deal with the Witches. It is interesting to compare the crude way in which revenge and **characterisation** are presented in *Titus Andronicus* with the complex subtleties of *Hamlet*. *Measure for Measure* explores what happens when a self-righteous moralist is asked to reform a morally corrupt city: 'Hence we shall see/If power change purpose, what our seemers be' (I.3.54–5).

CHECK THE FILM A03

The cynical tone and depraved atmosphere of Middleton's play are captured in Alex Cox's witty and imaginative film adaptation *Revengers Tragedy* (2002), starring Christopher Ecclestone and Derek Jacobi.

STUDY FOCUS: *HAMLET* AND *THE REVENGER'S TRAGEDY* A03

Comparing *Hamlet* with a play by another Elizabethan or Jacobean playwright will emphasise the range and variety of Shakespeare's dramatic verse and show you how different dramatists present similar ideas using very different techniques and dramatic conventions. *The Revenger's Tragedy*, written by Thomas Middleton a few years after Shakespeare's *Hamlet*, and clearly influenced by it, presents a morally corrupt world in vivid language whose tone is more coarsely **satiric** than tragic. In 'this villainous dukedom vexed with sin' (V.2.5), the vicious prey upon the vicious and Vindice, the protagonist, bitterly criticises the moral corruption that surrounds him. There are many moments in the play which remind us of *Hamlet* but the darkly comic and brutal atmosphere is closer to the moral anarchy of Stanley Kubrick's *A Clockwork Orange*. In *The Revenger's Tragedy* there is striking use of a skull, not only as a **memento mori** but, poisoned, as a murder weapon. Where Hamlet 'speaks daggers' (III.2.357) to his adulterous mother, Vindice uses a real dagger to terrify his mother-turned-bawd back onto the path of righteousness.

THOMAS MIDDLETON
From the frontispiece to his Plays

The grim game played with the corpse of the murdered Duke is a cruder version of Hamlet's off-stage game of hide-and-seek with Polonius's body. This helps us to see the surprising humour in those scenes of *Hamlet* as a nod in the direction of a different set of theatrical conventions from tragedy. Working within its own peculiar style of 'tragic burlesque' (as Brian Gibbons calls it in the introduction to *Revenger's Tragedy*, 1967), *The Revenger's Tragedy's* chief protagonist is very different from *Hamlet*. Vindice has no interior life; we do not explore a developing character or see him struggling with conflicting morals. His identity is the product of his situation rather than a personality and his death is a **farcical** twist rather than a moment of tragic **pathos**. As Gibbons puts it, Vindice 'is not a character but a role'. The shifts in tone and register are quite different but possibly influenced by Shakespeare.

CRITICAL DEBATES

Hamlet has been more discussed than any other work of literature: an internet search will reveal a huge range of critical essays. The play is genuinely problematic for many different reasons and there is no prospect of the variety of responses diminishing. Below is a summary of the history of *Hamlet* criticism. It includes a handful of snippets from accessible and sometimes provocative views which we hope will encourage you to keep re-reading the play, check the evidence and develop your own insights into *Hamlet* more fully.

EARLY CRITICISM

Eye-witnesses suggest that *Hamlet* was an immediate popular success and few of the 'problems' which have concerned critics for the last three hundred years bothered Shakespeare's near-contemporaries. It was Thomas Hanmer in 1736 who drew attention to Hamlet's delay in carrying out his revenge, making the practical point that had the Prince carried out the Ghost's instructions straight away 'there would have been an End of our Play'. But this has not prevented later critics seeing Hamlet's delay as the central problem, to be investigated along psychological, **ideological** or **dramaturgical** lines.

NINETEENTH-CENTURY ROMANTICISM

During the **Romantic** period Hamlet attracted intense speculation: the agonies and insights of an individual alienated from society was a theme close to the Romantic way of thinking. Johann Wolfgang Goethe saw: 'A lovely, pure, noble and most moral nature ... [sink] beneath a burden which it cannot bear and must not cast away'.

Hamlet invited identification; his complex thoughts and ambiguous actions made him appear 'life-like', he could not easily be summed up. Samuel Taylor Coleridge saw in the Prince a man whose intellectual energy and alertness made action impossible; he sensed 'a smack of Hamlet' in himself. And as madness is another favourite theme in Romantic literature, Hamlet began to be talked about as if he were someone in real life, existing independently of the play. As people began to look at the text more closely, there developed a strong feeling that *Hamlet* was best enjoyed in the privacy of the study. William Hazlitt writing in 1817 lamented, 'There is no play that suffers so much in being transferred to the stage'.

LATER CRITICISM

A. C. BRADLEY

One of the most thoughtful, stimulating and influential readings of *Hamlet* appeared in 1904. Bradley saw Hamlet as a son distressed by his mother's sexual misbehaviour, who can respond to the Ghost's demand for action in words but not in deed. Bradley treats *Hamlet* as if it were a nineteenth-century novel rather than a seventeenth-century play but his careful attention to textual detail makes his one of the essays every student will find helpful. Bradley's insistence: 'The only way ... in which a conception of Hamlet's character could be proved true would be to show that it and it alone explains all the relevant facts presented by the text' is useful for any serious reading.

Here are a handful of Bradley's other remarks for you to discuss:

- 'In *Hamlet*, though we have a villain, he is a small one.' (Lecture III, p. 87)
- 'Surely it is clear that, whatever we ... may think about Hamlet's duty, we are meant in the play to assume that he ought to have obeyed the Ghost.' (Ib. p. 103)

CRITICAL VIEWPOINT A03

'No one is likely to accept another man's reading of *Hamlet* ... anyone who tries to throw light on one part of the play usually throws the rest into deeper shadow.' Maynard Mack, 'The World of Hamlet', 1952 in John Jump (ed.), *Shakespeare: Hamlet (Casebook series)* (1968), p. 87.

- '*Hamlet* deserves the title "tragedy of moral idealism" quite as much as the title "tragedy of reflection".' (Ib. p. 113)

- 'His chief desire is not … to ensure his mother's … acquiescence in his design of revenge; it is to save her soul. And while the rough work of vengeance is repugnant to him, he is at home in this higher work'. (Lecture IV, p. 134)

- 'The Queen was not a bad-hearted woman, not at all the woman to think little of murder. But she had a soft animal nature, and was very dull and very shallow.' (Ib. p. 159)

T. S. ELIOT

Eliot's brief, penetrating essay (1919) diagnosed that 'the problem' in *Hamlet* was the play itself: it was an artistic failure. Shakespeare was struggling to put into words a personal disgust he could not explain; Gertrude and her wrongdoings were out of proportion to the distress we see them cause her son:

- '[P]robably more people have thought *Hamlet* a work of art because they found it interesting, than have found it interesting because it is a work of art. It is the "Mona Lisa" of literature' (*Selected Essays*, p. 144)

- '[I]t … is a play dealing with the effects of a mother's guilt upon her son … Hamlet is dominated by an emotion which is inexpressible because it is in *excess* of the facts as they appear.' (Ib. pp. 143–5)

JOHN DOVER WILSON

The title of John Dover Wilson's *What Happens in Hamlet* (1935) may suggest that it provides all the answers. Dover Wilson considers the ambiguous nature of the Ghost and the impossibility of Hamlet's translating its instructions into a coherent plan of action. His book is readable, thorough and compelling; the few remarks quoted below cannot convey the rich impact of his carefully argued textual analysis.

- 'The usurpation is one of the main factors in the plot' (p. 34)

- 'Hamlet felt himself involved in his mother's lust; he was conscious of sharing her nature in all its rankness and grossness; the stock from which he sprang was rotten.' (p. 42)

- 'At the end of the first act Hamlet, together with Shakespeare's audience, is left in uncertainty about the "honesty" of the Ghost'. (p. 49)

- 'Most critics have completely misunderstood [the nunnery episode] because in their sympathy with Ophelia they have forgotten that it is not Hamlet who has "repelled" her but she him.' (p. 128).

ANTI-ROMANTICISM

For Wilson Knight (*The Wheel of Fire* 1930), Hamlet is not an heroic victim or a **Renaissance** scholar but a sinister presence in Denmark:

- 'Claudius, as he appears in the play, is not a criminal. He is … a good and gentle king, enmeshed by the chain of causality linking him with his crime …. Claudius can hardly be blamed for his later actions.' (p. 35)

- 'Hamlet is an inhuman – or superhuman – presence, whose consciousness – somewhat like Dostoyevsky's Stavrogin – is centred on death. Like Stavrogin, he is feared by those around him. They are always trying to find out what is wrong with him. They cannot understand him. He is a creature of another world.' (Ib.)

L. C. Knights (*An Approach to Hamlet*, 1960) also presented a reading of *Hamlet* that challenged **Romantic** ideas of the hero, seeing the Prince's judgements as brooding upon evil and pathologically unbalanced:

GRADE BOOSTER   **A03**

Try picking out a quotation from A. C. Bradley, T. S. Eliot or John Dover Wilson and using it to create your own essay title. Do you agree with his point of view, or not? Remember to root your discussion in close reading of the text.

CHECK THE BOOK   **A03**

In Dostoyevsky's novel *The Devils* (sometimes known as *The Possessed*) the charismatic central character, Stravrogin, is a murderous criminal who comes to acknowledge his guilt.

- 'The Ghost is tempting Hamlet to gaze with fascinated horror at an abyss of evil.' (*Some Shakespearean Themes and An Approach to Hamlet*, p. 188)
- 'Hamlet's intellectuality, the working of his mind, is largely at the service of attitudes of rejection and disgust that are indiscriminate in their working.' (Ib. p. 196)

HAMLET PSYCHOANALYSED

Ernest Jones's *Hamlet and Oedipus* (1949) takes the **psychoanalysis** of the characters in the play as if they were people in real life to an extreme position, suggesting that Hamlet has an Oedipus complex. How can he murder Claudius when his uncle has committed the deed he himself subconsciously wished to carry out?

- 'His uncle incorporates the deepest and most buried part of his own personality, so that he cannot kill him without also killing himself.' (in John Jump (ed.), *Shakespeare: Hamlet (Casebook series)* (1968), p. 59)

THE IMAGERY OF HAMLET

With Caroline Spurgeon (*Shakespeare's Imagery and What it Tells Us*, 1935) a new approach emerged. She explored the role of **imagery**. In certain plays, there are large numbers of particular kinds of images. She identified in *Hamlet*: 'the number of images of sickness, disease … the idea of an ulcer or tumour, as descriptive of the unwholesome condition of Denmark morally'. It is in this climate of disease that Hamlet inevitably succumbs.

In *The Development of Shakespeare's Imagery* (1951) Wolfgang Clemen comments: 'Hamlet's father describes … how the poison invades the body … this becomes the leitmotif of the imagery … The corruption of land and people … is understood as an imperceptible and *irresistible process of poisoning.*' (in John Jump (ed.), *Shakespeare: Hamlet (Casebook series)* (1968), p. 70) whilst Maynard Mack (*The World of Hamlet*, 1952) argued: 'The most pervasive … image pattern in this play … is the pattern evolved around the three words "show", "act", "play".' (Ib. p. 96)

> **CHECK THE BOOK** **A04**
>
> For a critical examination of psychoanalytic approaches to Shakespeare in general and to *Hamlet* in particular, see *Shakespeare in Psychoanalysis* by Philip Armstrong (2001).

RECENT DEVELOPMENTS IN HAMLET CRITICISM

More recently, radical critical theories have emerged which ask us to reconsider the way people read any literary text. This does not mean that the ways A. C. Bradley, for example, John Dover Wilson or Wolfgang Clemen examined *Hamlet* are no longer valid; many recent essays repackage the insights of earlier critics in the language of the moment. But awareness of different ways of thinking and writing about texts is not only sensible but also stimulating.

Many contemporary critics reject the idea that any work or any author can achieve the kind of universality and stability that generations of critics have claimed for *Hamlet* – the idea summarised by Ben Jonson in his tribute to Shakespeare that 'He was not of an age, but for all time' ('To the Memory of My Beloved the Author, Mr William Shakespeare and What He Hath Left Us' prefixed to the First Folio edition of Shakespeare's plays). Catherine Belsey talks of 'the myth of an unchanging human nature'. Such critics stress the way that any work of art mirrors the beliefs, assumptions and prejudices of the society in which it is produced and that any reading is similarly shaped by the intellectual climate in which it happens. Language itself is changeable: what we understand Shakespeare's words to mean and what they meant four hundred years ago demands critical attention.

> **CHECK THE BOOK** **A04**
>
> For an overview of late-twentieth-century approaches to *Hamlet*, see Michael Hattaway's *Hamlet: The Critics Debate* (1987).

STRUCTURALISM AND POST-STRUCTURALISM

Structuralist critics approach *Hamlet* as an interesting linguistic phenomenon. They explore the ways key words create force fields of associations and value systems and therefore mean more than is immediately apparent. In *New Essays on Hamlet*, first published in 1994, Mark Thornton Burnett talks of the unlimited range of meanings to be found in *Hamlet* and concludes that: 'Abundantly evident … is *Hamlet*'s refusal to fit into neat categorizations, its resistance to generic classifications and its unwillingness to affirm cherished ideals.' He shows that *Hamlet* revels in asking questions about identity and that the posing and answering of questions is one of the play's most striking features. *Hamlet*'s delight in doubling characters and situations contributes to the play's **subversion** of any straightforward reading, and helps 'to deny the closure that is only ever promised but never delivered'.

Taking this scepticism a stage further, post-structuralists insist upon the ambiguity of any work of art. They argue that a text has no primary or final meaning and that engaging with *Hamlet* is like a series of chess games in which there will be an almost infinite number of outcomes, none superior to any other.

FEMINIST CRITICISM

'For many feminist theorists, the madwoman is a heroine, a powerful figure who rebels against the family and the social order; and the hysteric who refuses to speak the language of the patriarchal order … is a sister.' (Elaine Showalter, 'Representing Ophelia: Women, Madness and the Responsibilities of Feminist Criticism' in Martin Coyle (ed.), *New Casebooks: Hamlet* (1992), p. 126)

Feminist criticism sets out to challenge and change assumptions about gender, showing us how sexual stereotyping and assumptions about sexual roles are frequently part of a text. They argue that the same is true of the way critics respond to a text and the way texts are re-presented in various media. Literature and the ways in which literature has been written about in the past are seen as having contributed to the marginalisation of women, denying them a voice.

CONTEXT **AO3**

The most celebrated paintings of Ophelia are those by Millais (1850) and Cabanel (1883). You can find these paintings online. How does the portrayal of Ophelia differ in these paintings, and from your own reading of her character?

In **The Women in *Hamlet*** in **Part Three: Themes** it is noted that neither Gertrude nor Ophelia is developed very fully; Shakespeare gives them far less stage time and far fewer lines than Hamlet's concern with them leads us to expect. Rather than see this as a compromise brought about by pragmatic considerations, feminist criticism looks at the 'silencing' of the women as part of the play's meaning. This then leads feminist critics to examine the ways different productions of *Hamlet*, on stage and screen, use non-verbal language to make statements about the place of women in the play. Such criticism reminds us that *Hamlet* is something not just to be read but also to be acted, and that in performance the words provide only part of what any audience responds to. Feminist criticism has also explored the ways in which readers, audiences and other artists have represented Gertrude and Ophelia, the latter having become, particularly through paintings, an icon of woman as victim. This leads into the interesting territory of how different societies have incorporated aspects or partial readings of *Hamlet* into wider use so that, in advertising for example, some of Shakespeare's words or the graveyard **tableau** have developed an existence independent of the play.

POLITICAL CRITICISM

'It is not the consciousness of men that determines their being but on the contrary, their social being that determines their consciousness.' Karl Marx, Preface to *A Contribution to the Critique of Political Economy* (1859)

Different kinds of political criticism have developed in the form of Marxist criticism and new historicism. Marxists believe that there can be no reading that is not 'political'. Critics such as Catherine Belsey look at the conflicting ideas of authority and power that give rise to so much of the dramatic interest in the play. Many nineteenth-century productions cut the Fortinbras strand entirely. Some modern critics argue that it is on the character of Fortinbras that the 'politics' of *Hamlet* hinge.

New historicists call attention to the fact that this play was written at a time when the absolute power of the monarchy was being tested by the rise of capitalism. Hamlet is at once a king's son, Claudius's heir and a voice that expresses dissatisfaction with those in power. The new historicists are concerned less with the words on the page than with the circumstances in which they were produced. Instead of looking closely at the work itself, such critics examine the **ideology** of the society in which the work was written. They also look at the ideology of the society in which the work is read. Rather than a powerful creative expression of Shakespeare's understanding of the universal and timeless human condition, the play is seen as a product of Elizabethan culture as it passed through a period of upheaval. Stephan Greenblatt's *Hamlet in Purgatory* (2001) attempts to 'understand what Shakespeare inherited and transformed' from medieval and sixteenth-century debates about the nature of Purgatory in his dramatisation of the theme in *Hamlet*: 'I believe nothing comes from nothing, even in Shakespeare. I wanted to know where he got the matter he was working with and what he did with that matter'.

Yet labels can be misleading. In its scrupulously text-centred argument, there is little in Victor Kiernan's 'Hamlet', in *Eight Tragedies of Shakespeare, A Marxist Study* (1996), which distinguishes it from the character analyst's approach. Although he takes account of the political aspects of Hamlet's situation, he sees them as no more important than Hamlet's thoughts and feelings which he identifies closely with Shakespeare's own: 'Hamlet himself can be thought of as probably like many Elizabethans, a mixture of Christian and pagan and sceptic'.

PERFORMANCE CRITICISM

'[T]he text of the play is only its starting point ... only in production is its potential realized and capable of being appreciated fully. Shakespeare is only one collaborator in the creation and infinite recreation of his play', J. S. Bratton and Julie Hankey, series editors, in Robert Hapgood (ed.), *Shakespeare in Production* (1999).

In comparison with much recent criticism, performance criticism can seem pleasingly approachable. Every performance is an interpretation and *Hamlet* has been performed, and continues to be performed, more than any other play. Some of the most penetrating criticism is to be found not in critical essays but in the increasingly large stock of performances available on the internet. Dozens of film versions can be compared with spectacular contemporary adaptations.

Robert Shaughnessy's collection of essays, *Shakespeare in Performance* (2000), examines the debates between theory and practice that have transformed our understanding of Shakespeare performance in recent years. Drawing upon textual theory, materialist cultural criticism, new historicism, feminism, post-colonialism, and psychoanalysis, the essays address Shakespeare's plays as texts in and for performance in a variety of contexts, from the **Renaissance** to the present.

CHECK THE BOOK **A04**

For a political reading of *Hamlet*, see Jan Kott's book *Shakespeare Our Contemporary* (1964).

CHECK THE BOOK **A04**

A thought-provoking study of how Shakespeare's *Hamlet* was first presented in the Elizabethan playhouses is provided in Andrew Gurr and Mariko Ichikawa's *Staging in Shakespeare's Theatres* (2000). Robert Hapgood's *Shakespeare in Production: Hamlet* (1999) contains a fine overview of *Hamlet* on stage and film from Burbage to Branagh.

CHECK THE BOOK **A04**

Stanley Wells's *Shakespeare in the Theatre, An Anthology of Criticism* (1997), includes vivid first-hand accounts of many performances, from the eighteenth to the late twentieth century.

PART SIX: GRADE BOOSTER

ASSESSMENT FOCUS

WHAT ARE YOU BEING ASKED TO FOCUS ON?

The questions or tasks you are set will be based around the four **Assessment Objectives**, **AO1** to **AO4**.

You may get more marks for certain **AOs** than others depending on which unit you're working on. Check with your teacher if you are unsure.

WHAT DO THESE AOs ACTUALLY MEAN?

ASSESSMENT OBJECTIVES	MEANING?
AO1 Articulate creative, informed and relevant responses to literary texts, using appropriate terminology and concepts, and coherent, accurate written expression.	You write about texts in accurate, clear and precise ways so that what you have to say is clear to the marker. You use literary terms (e.g. **protagonist**) or refer to concepts (e.g. **ideology**) in relevant places.
AO2 Demonstrate detailed critical understanding in analysing the ways in which structure, form and language shape meanings in literary texts.	You show that you understand the specific techniques and methods used by the writer(s) to create the text (e.g. **imagery, soliloquy**, etc.). You can explain clearly how these methods affect the meaning.
AO3 Explore connections and comparisons between different literary texts, informed by interpretations of other readers.	You are able to see relevant links between different texts. You are able to comment on how others (such as critics) view the text.
AO4 Demonstrate understanding of the significance and influence of the contexts in which literary texts are written and received.	You can explain how social, historical, political or personal backgrounds to the texts affected the writer and how the texts were read when they were first published and at different times since.

WHAT DOES THIS MEAN FOR YOUR STUDY OR REVISION?

Depending on the course you are following, you could be asked to:

- Respond to a general question about the text as a whole. For example:

Explore the ways in which Shakespeare portrays corruption in *Hamlet*.

- Write about an aspect of *Hamlet* which is also a feature of other texts you are studying. These questions may take the form of a challenging statement or quotation which you are invited to discuss. For example:

How far do you agree that Shakespeare's Romantic tragic heroes can be seen as individuals, alienated from society?

- Or you may have to focus on the particular similarities, links, contrasts and differences between this text and others. For example:

Compare the ways writers use comedy in *Hamlet* and the other text(s) you are studying.

EXAMINER'S TIP

Make sure you know how many marks are available for each AO in the task you are set. This can help to divide up your time or decide how much attention to give each aspect.

TARGETING A HIGH GRADE

It is very important to understand the progression from a lower grade to a high grade. In all cases, it is not enough simply to mention some key points and references – instead, you should explore them in depth, drawing out what is interesting and relevant to the question or issue.

TYPICAL C GRADE FEATURES

FEATURES	EXAMPLES
A01 You use critical vocabulary accurately, and your arguments make sense, are relevant and focus on the task. You show detailed knowledge of the text.	*Laertes's ranting hyperbole at Ophelia's graveside in Act V Scene 1 is contrasted with the simple sincerity of Hamlet's 'I loved Ophelia'. Hamlet mocks Laertes's exaggerations by parodying them: 'forty thousand brothers … with all their quantity of love'.*
A02 You can say how some specific aspects of form, structure and language shape meanings.	*Shakespeare suggests that Ophelia doesn't really feel what she says she feels through her use of the trite rhyming couplet: 'for to the noble mind/Rich gifts wax poor when givers prove unkind.'*
A03 You consider in detail the connections between texts, and also how interpretations of texts differ with some relevant supporting references.	*Actors have to decide whether to make Horatio's 'I did very well note him' sound sceptical, neutral or as agreeing with Hamlet's understanding of Claudius's reaction.* *In both "Hamlet" and "Macbeth", the supernatural characters are presented as tempters.*
A04 You can write about a range of contextual factors and make some specific and detailed links between these and the task or text.	*Gertrude's hasty marriage to the murderer of her husband would remind Shakespeare's audience of the case of Mary Queen of Scots.*

TYPICAL FEATURES OF AN A OR A* RESPONSE

FEATURES	EXAMPLES
A01 You use appropriate critical vocabulary and a technically fluent style. Your arguments are well structured, coherent and always relevant with a very sharp focus on task.	*Claudius's rhetoric in Act I Scene 2 is superficially fluent and cogent, suggesting he is a reasonable man, but his faulty arguments would alert those Hamlet refers to as 'the judicious' in the audience to Claudius's hypocrisy.*
A02 You explore and analyse key aspects of form, structure and language and evaluate perceptively how they shape meanings.	*In Act IV, Shakespeare deliberately parodies "Hamlet"'s revenge plot, showing Laertes responding not to a magisterial ghost but to rumour and his sister's madness. Laertes systematically rejects the ethical considerations which have troubled Hamlet's conscience.*
A03 You show a detailed and perceptive understanding of issues raised through connections between texts and can consider different interpretations with a sharp evaluation of their strengths and weaknesses. You have a range of excellent supportive references.	*"The Revenger's Tragedy" is clearly influenced by "Hamlet": some of Vindice's meditations on the skull recall Hamlet's reflections on Yorrick's skull. But although Vindice is entertaining, he has none of the intellectual sophistication of Hamlet: he pursues revenge with little self-examination or awareness of its moral challenges.*
A04 You show deep, detailed and relevant understanding of how contextual factors link to the text or task.	*Polonius may be a satirical portrait of Burghley, Elizabeth's chief minister, who provided his son with a list of precepts and spied on him when he was a student in Paris. Burghley's spymaster, Walsingham, was happy 'By indirections [to] find directions out'.*

HOW TO WRITE HIGH-QUALITY RESPONSES

The quality of your writing – how you express your ideas – is vital for getting a higher grade, and **AO1** and **AO2** are specifically about **how** you respond.

FIVE KEY AREAS

The quality of your responses can be broken down into **five** key areas.

1. THE STRUCTURE OF YOUR ANSWER/ESSAY

- First, get **straight to the point in your opening paragraph**. Use a sharp, direct first sentence that deals with a key aspect and then follow up with evidence or detailed reference.
- **Put forward an argument or point of view** (you won't **always** be able to challenge or take issue with the essay question, but generally, where you can, you are more likely to write in an interesting way).
- **Signpost your ideas** with connectives and references, which help the essay flow.
- **Don't repeat points already made**, not even in the conclusion, unless you have something new to say that adds a further dimension.

TARGETING A HIGH GRADE | AO1

Here's an example of an opening paragraph that gets straight to the point, addressing the question: **'*Hamlet* is not so much a Revenge Play as a critique of revenge.' How do you respond to this viewpoint?**

Although "Hamlet" is an exciting Revenge Drama, it is very different from other Revenge Plays. Shakespeare deliberately contrasts the behaviour of two Revenge Heroes, presenting on the one hand Laertes as a character untroubled by ethical considerations, perfectly happy 'to cut his throat in the church', and on the other Hamlet perplexed by that very situation. Shakespeare invites us to contrast these two young men who find themselves in similar circumstances and judge between them.

Immediate focus on task and key words and example from text

2. USE OF TITLES, NAMES, ETC.

This is a simple, but important, tip to stay on the right side of the examiners.

- Make sure that you spell correctly the titles of the texts, chapters, name of authors and so on. Present them correctly, too, with double quotation marks and capitals as appropriate. For example, '*In Act I of "Hamlet" …*'.
- Use the **full title**, unless there is a good reason not to (e.g. it's very long).
- Use the terms 'play' or 'text' rather than ' book' or 'story'. If you use the word 'story', the examiner may think you mean the plot/action rather than the 'text' as a whole.

3. EFFECTIVE QUOTATIONS

Do not 'bolt on' quotations to the points you make. You will get some marks for including them, but examiners will not find your writing very fluent.

EXAMINER'S TIP ✓

Answer the question set, not the question you'd like to have been asked. Examiners say that often students will be set a question on one character (for example, Claudius) but end up writing almost as much about another (such as Hamlet himself). Or, they write about one aspect from the question (for example, 'friendship betrayed') but ignore another (such as 'women as frail'). **Stick to the question**, and answer **all parts of it**.

The best quotations are:

- Relevant
- Not too long
- Integrated into your argument/sentence.

TARGETING A HIGH GRADE A01

Here is an example of a quotation successfully embedded in a sentence:

Claudius talks hypocritically about the 'divinity [that] doth hedge a king' in order to dupe Laertes. The audience is aware that Claudius had no scruples in murdering the king, his brother.

Remember – quotations can be a well-selected set of three or four single words or phrases. These can be easily embedded into a sentence to build a picture or explanation around your point. Or, they can be longer quotations that are explored and picked apart.

4. TECHNIQUES AND TERMINOLOGY

By all means mention literary terms, techniques, conventions or people (for example, '**paradox**' or '**parody**' or 'Montaigne') but make sure that you:

- Understand what they mean
- Are able to link them to what you're saying
- Spell them correctly.

5. GENERAL WRITING SKILLS

Try to write in a way that sounds professional and uses standard English. This does not mean that your writing will lack personality – just that it will be authoritative.

- Avoid **colloquial** or everyday expressions such as 'got', 'alright', 'OK' and so on.
- Use terms such as 'convey', 'suggest', 'imply', 'infer' to explain the writer's methods.
- Refer to 'we' when discussing the audience/reader.
- Avoid assertions and generalisations; don't just state a general point of view (*'Ophelia is a typical woman character'*), but analyse closely, with clear evidence and textual detail.

TARGETING A HIGH GRADE A01

Note the professional approach in this example:

At various times, it suits Polonius, Gertrude, Claudius, Ophelia and Hamlet himself to claim that he is mad. But even if we agree with Bradley that Hamlet is melancholy, Hamlet's state of mind is not presented as mental illness but, sympathetically, as a response to the grief and outrage occasioned by his situation in Act I Scene 2 and made worse by the Ghost's 'commandment' in Act I Scene 5. Hamlet's 'antic disposition' is most likely a satire of the Fool, e.g. when he calls Polonius a 'fishmonger', implying that the old man is behaving like a pander in using his daughter to win favour with the King.

GRADE BOOSTER A02

It is important to remember that *Hamlet* is a text created by Shakespeare – thinking about the way Shakespeare presents a variety of voices will alert you not only to his methods as a playwright, but also to his intentions, i.e. the effects he seeks to create.

QUESTIONS WITH STATEMENTS, QUOTATIONS OR VIEWPOINTS

One type of question you may come across may include a statement, quotation or viewpoint from another reader.

These questions ask you to respond to, or argue for/against, a specific point of view or critical interpretation.

For *Hamlet* these questions will typically be like this:

- **Discuss the view that the women in the play are of little dramatic interest.**
- **How far do you agree with the idea that Shakespeare presents Claudius as a clear-thinking and competent monarch?**
- **To what extent do you agree that Hamlet's greatest failing is 'thinking too precisely'?**

The key thing to remember is that you are being asked to **respond to a critical interpretation** of the text – in other words, to come up with **your own** 'take' on the idea or viewpoint in the task.

KEY SKILLS REQUIRED

The table below provides help and advice on answering this type of question:

SKILL	MEANS?	HOW DO I ACHIEVE THIS?
Consider different interpretations	There will be more than one way of looking at the given question. For example, critics might be divided about the extent to which Claudius will appear as capable or as vicious to a modern audience.	● Show you have considered these different interpretations in your answer. For example: *Although Claudius's authority is challenged by no one at court except Hamlet and he conducts foreign policy using modern diplomacy rather than by waging war as his brother did, many would argue his usurpation is a disaster for Denmark, paving the way for Fortinbras to assume power. A modern audience may not feel troubled by the incestuous marriage but they are unlikely to condone fratricide, especially as Claudius condemns it himself.*
Write with a clear, personal voice	Your own 'take' on the question is made obvious to the marker. You are not just repeating other people's ideas, but offering what **you** think.	● Although you may mention different perspectives on the task, you should settle on your own view. ● Use language that shows careful, but confident, consideration. For example: *Although it has been said that ... I feel that ...*
Construct a coherent argument	The examiner or marker can follow your train of thought so that your own viewpoint is clear to him or her.	● Write in clear paragraphs that deal logically with different aspects of the question. ● Support what you say with well-selected and relevant evidence. ● Use a range of connectives to help 'signpost' your argument. For example: *Although at first we may be impressed by Claudius, on reflection, we begin to ask questions. As the play unfolds, we see him behaving more and more unscrupulously, revealing himself as an unprincipled Machiavel. In the final scene, Shakespeare presents the King as the source of all corruption.*

ANSWERING A 'VIEWPOINT' QUESTION

Here is an example of a typical question on *Hamlet*:

Discuss the view that the women in the play are of little dramatic interest.

STAGE 1: DECODE THE QUESTION

Underline/highlight the **key words**, and make sure you understand what the statement, quotation or viewpoint is saying. In this case:

- **Key words** = *Discuss/women in the play/little dramatic interest*
- **The viewpoint/idea expressed is** = *the women in "Hamlet" are of very minor interest*

STAGE 2: DECIDE WHAT YOUR VIEWPOINT IS

Examiners have stated that they tend to reward a strong view which is clearly put. Think about the question – can you take issue with it? Disagreeing strongly can lead to higher marks, provided you have **genuine evidence** to support your point of view. Don't disagree just for the sake of it.

STAGE 3: DECIDE HOW TO STRUCTURE YOUR ANSWER

Pick out the key points you wish to make, and decide on the order in which you will present them. Keep this basic plan to hand while you write your response.

STAGE 4: WRITE YOUR RESPONSE

You could start by expanding on the statement or viewpoint expressed in the question.

- For example, in **Paragraph 1**:

  In order to examine the dramatic impact of women in the play, we can begin by looking at how much stage time they are given. Neither Gertrude nor Ophelia has a major soliloquy. We are not encouraged to explore their inner lives in the way we do Hamlet's and Claudius's.

This could help by setting up the various ideas you will choose to explore, argue for/against, and so on. But do not just repeat what the question says or just say what you are going to do. Get straight to the point. For example:

However, the women are of supreme interest to the play's protagonist; he is arguably more exercised by them than by his antagonist, Claudius. The Player Queen is presented entirely as a bait to Gertrude's conscience and two of the play's most emotionally charged scenes, the nunnery episode (III.1) and the closet scene (III.4), are central to our reading of Hamlet's character. The latter, where Hamlet confronts his mother, is the dramatic turning point of the play. In Act IV, Ophelia's madness is responsible for fuelling Laertes's passion for revenge …

Then, proceed to set out the different arguments or critical perspectives, including your own. This might be done by dealing with specific aspects or elements of the play, one by one. Consider giving 1–2 paragraphs to explore each aspect in turn. Discuss the strengths and weaknesses in each particular point of view. For example:

- **Paragraph 2:** first aspect:

  *To answer whether the critic's interpretation is valid, we need to **first of all** look at …*

  ***It is clear from this** that …/a **strength** of this argument is*

  ***However**, I believe this suggests that …/a **weakness** in this argument is*

- **Paragraph 3:** a new focus or aspect:

  ***Turning our attention to the critical idea that** … it could be said that …*

- **Paragraphs 4, 5, etc. onwards:** develop the argument, building a convincing set of points:

  ***Furthermore**, if we look at …*

- **Last paragraph:** end with a clear statement of your view, without simply listing all the points you have made:

  Thus although it is true that Shakespeare does not develop women in "Hamlet" as psychologically rich characters, their dramatic significance is considerable …

> **EXAMINER'S TIP** ✓
>
> You should comment concisely, professionally and thoughtfully and present a range of viewpoints. Try using modal verbs such as 'could', 'might', 'may' to clarify your own interpretation. For additional help on **Using critical interpretations and perspectives**, see pages 112–13.

> **EXAMINER'S TIP** ✓
>
> Note how the ideas are clearly signposted through a range of connectives and linking phrases, such as 'However' and 'Turning our attention to'.

COMPARING *HAMLET* WITH OTHER TEXTS

As part of your assessment, you may have to compare *Hamlet* with, or link it to, other texts that you have studied. These may be other plays, novels or even poetry. You may also have to link or draw in references from texts written by critics. For example:

> **Compare the dramatic presentation of the Ghost and its authority in** *Hamlet* **with the status of supernatural elements in other text(s) you have studied.**

THE TASK

Your task is likely to be on a method, issue, viewpoint or key aspect that is common to *Hamlet* and the other text(s), so you will need to:

> **Evaluate the issue** or statement and have an **open-minded approach**. The best answers suggest meanings and interpretations (plural):
>
> - What do you understand by the question? Is this theme or idea more important in one text than in another? Why? How?
> - What are the different ways that this question or aspect can be read or viewed?
> - Can you challenge the viewpoint, if there is one? If so, what evidence is there? How can you present it in a thoughtful, reflective way?

> Express **original or creative approaches** fluently:
>
> - This isn't about coming up with entirely new ideas, but you need to show that you're actively engaged with thinking about the question, not just reproducing random facts and information you have learned.
> - **Synthesise** your ideas – pull ideas and points together to create something fresh.
> - This is a linking/comparison response, so ensure that you guide your reader through your ideas logically, clearly and with professional language.

> **Know what to compare/contrast: form, structure** and **language** will **always** be central to your response, even where you also have to write about characters, contexts or culture.
>
> - Think about standard versus more conventional narration (for example, use of dramatic form, **characterisation**, stage business and **dramatic function** which lead to differentiation between the two texts).
> - Consider different characteristic use of language: lengths of lines, sentences, formal/informal style, dialect, accent, balance of dialogue and **soliloquy**; the difference between forms, if appropriate (for example **prose** treatment of an idea and a play) and the different ways two plays use the possibilities offered by drama.
> - Look at a variety of **symbols**, **images** and **motifs** (how they represent concerns of the author/time; what they are and how and where they appear; how they link to critical perspectives; their purposes, effects and impact on the play).
> - Consider aspects of genres (to what extent does Shakespeare and the author(s) of the other work(s) conform to/challenge/subvert particular genres or styles of writing?)

WRITING YOUR RESPONSE

The depth and extent of your answer will depend on how much you have to write, but the key will be to **explore in detail**, and **link between ideas and texts**. Let us use the same example:

> Compare the dramatic presentation of the Ghost and its authority in *Hamlet* with the status of supernatural elements in other text(s) you have studied.

INTRODUCTION TO YOUR RESPONSE

- Briefly discuss what 'authority' means, and how well this applies to your texts.
- Mention in support the importance of the Ghost's authority in *Hamlet* and the status of supernatural elements in other text(s).
- You could use a powerful quotation to launch into your response. For example:

'It is an honest Ghost, that let me tell you' says Hamlet immediately following his confrontation with the ambiguous and terrifying figure. And yet his subsequent behaviour suggests that it is exactly the Ghost's moral standing which puzzles him. In "The Spanish Tragedy", there can be no such questioning of the Ghost's authority. The Ghost is presented to the audience in a separate dramatic space from the other characters; there is no interaction. This invites us to question whether the two Ghosts are of similar standing and authority.

MAIN BODY OF YOUR RESPONSE

- **Point 1:** start with the dramatic presentation of the Ghost in *Hamlet* and what it tells us about the play's concerns. What is your view? Are the uses of the Ghost similar in the other text(s)? Are there any relevant critical viewpoints that you know about? Are there contextual or cultural factors to consider?
- **Point 2:** now cover a new treatment or aspect through comparison or contrast of this theme in your other text(s). How is this treatment or aspect presented **differently or similarly** by the writer(s) in the language, form, structures used? Why was this done in this way? How does it reflect the writers' interests? What do the critics say? Are there contextual or cultural factors to consider?
- **Points 3, 4, 5, etc.:** address a range of other factors and aspects, for example how the Ghost's authority is debated by other characters **either** within *Hamlet* **or** both in *Hamlet* and in another text. What different ways do you respond to these (with more empathy, greater criticism, less interest) – and why? For example:

The sceptical Horatio is important is establishing both the physical reality of the Ghost and its moral ambiguity. In "The Spanish Tragedy", the Ghost's existence and moral authority are a given; we are not provided with any terms in which to debate its moral standing. We can only question the moral stance of the play as a whole and its assumptions about revenge. In "Hamlet" we are expected to engage with such a debate: the play provides the necessary framework.

CONCLUSION TO YOUR RESPONSE

- Synthesise elements of what you have said into a final paragraph that fluently, succinctly and inventively leaves the reader/examiner with the sense that you have engaged with this task and the texts. For example:

Both Kyd and Shakespeare have created dramatic worlds in which revenge is demanded by a ghost. In each case, the audience is presented with a central character of great abilities who finds himself pursuing what he believes to be an ethically warranted course. But whereas Kyd does not invite us to question the morality of the Ghost's demand which operates independently of the protagonist, in "Hamlet", the Ghost's authority and implicitly the morality of revenge itself, is the central dramatic concern.

EXAMINER'S TIP ✓

Be creative with your conclusion! It's the last thing the examiner will read and your chance to make your mark. It's often effective to use a new, brief quotation to round off your essay with a flourish.

RESPONDING TO A GENERAL QUESTION ABOUT THE WHOLE TEXT

You may also be asked to write about a specific aspect of *Hamlet* – but as it relates to the **whole text**. For example:

> **Explore the way Shakespeare presents the relationships between parents and children in *Hamlet*.**

This means you should:

- **Focus on family relationships**; do not extend your enquiry into friendships.
- **Choose two or three key episodes from each text**, showing how they use different techniques. Use brief quotations to develop your comparisons, focusing on linguistic, dramatic and poetic details. Avoid simplistic generalisations.
- Look at aspects of the **whole text**, showing how the theme of parents and children relates to wider concerns in the text.

STRUCTURING YOUR RESPONSE

You need a clear, logical plan, as for all tasks that you do. It is impossible to write about every section or part of the text, so you will need to:

- Quickly note 5–6 key points or aspects to build your essay around:
  Point a: *Shakespeare is presenting children's duty of obedience to their parents critically, in both the main plot and the subplot.*
  Point b: *Hamlet is torn between his duty to his father and his duty to save his mother's soul.*
  Point c: *This conflict complicates the pursuit of revenge.*
  Point d: *Ophelia's unquestioning obedience to her father is radically different from the behaviour of the typical Shakespearean heroine. Laertes's concern with family honour motivates his revenge rather than strong feelings of respect for Polonius.*
  Point e: *"Hamlet" can be seen as a domestic drama.*
- Then decide the most effective or logical order. For example, **point e**, then **c, b, a, d**, etc.

You could begin with your key or main idea, with supporting evidence/references, followed by your further points (perhaps two paragraphs for each). For example:

Paragraph 1: first key point: *Although "Hamlet" is often thought of as a Revenge Play, it is equally concerned with the domestic theme of the relationship between parents and children.*

Paragraph 2: expand out, link into other areas: *Charged with avenging his virtuous father, Hamlet often appears more preoccupied with his sinful mother.*

Paragraph 3: change direction, introduce new aspect/point: *The subplot explores a related but very different family dynamic. Polonius, the authoritarian father who uses his daughter, is satirised by Hamlet as a pimp. Laertes, spied upon in Paris, is also subject to Polonius's disreputable control.*

And so on.

- For your **conclusion:** use a compelling way to finish, perhaps repeating some or all of the key words from the question. For example, either:

End with your final point, but **add a last clause** which makes it clear what you think is key to the question. For example: *The degree to which the commandment 'Honour thy father and mother' informs the moral choices made by children in "Hamlet" can hardly be overstated. The tensions inherent in such a moral imperative generate much of the play's dramatic interest.*

End with a **new quotation** or **an aspect that's slightly different from** your main point. For example: *Hamlet, chastising his errant mother, says he must be 'cruel only to be kind'. By challenging and reversing the parent–child relationship, he effects Gertrude's salvation. She dies affirming her loyalty not to her husband but to her son.*

Or, of course, you can combine these endings.

EXAMINER'S TIP ✔

You may be asked to discuss other texts you have studied as well as *Hamlet* as part of your response. Once you have completed your response on the play you could move on to discuss the same issues in your other text(s). Begin with a simple linking phrase or sentence to launch straight into your first point about your next text, such as: *In "Little Dorrit", the relationships between parents and children are shown to be not simply strained but dysfunctional. Mrs Clennam, in reality Arthur's stepmother, is a severe Calvinist moralist incapable of showing Arthur loving kindness. Her paralysis is a symbol …*

WRITING ABOUT CONTEXTS

Assessment Objective 4 asks you to 'demonstrate understanding of the significance and influence of the contexts in which literary texts are written and received'. This can mean:

- How the events, settings, politics and so on **of the time when the text was written** influenced the writer or help us to understand the play's themes or concerns. For example, to what extent Shakespeare's development of his **protagonist**'s inner life may have been influenced by French writer Montaigne's careful questioning of his own values and assumptions in the *Essais*. Or:

- How events, settings, politics and so on **of the time when the text is read or seen** influences how it is understood. For example, would audiences watching the play today see parallels between Hamlet's search for a difficult sincerity and Richard Dawkins's challenges to traditional religious belief?

THE CONTEXT FOR *HAMLET*

You might find the following table of suggested examples helpful for thinking about how particular aspects of the time contribute to our understanding of the play and its themes. These are just examples – can you think of any others?

POLITICAL	LITERARY	PHILOSOPHICAL
Elizabeth and Essex, Catholic plots, government surveillance	Developments in tragedy: Seneca, Kyd, Marlowe and Shakespeare's earlier plays	Humanism, Protestantism, **Machiavelli**, Montaigne

SCIENTIFIC	CULTURAL	SOCIAL
Discoveries in astronomy, geographic exploration	Renaissance idea of man as the measure of all things	Attitudes to the supernatural, courtly concept of honour

TARGETING A HIGH GRADE   A04

Remember that the extent to which you write about these contexts will be determined by the marks available. Some questions or tasks may have very few marks allocated for **AO4**, but where you do have to refer to context the key thing is **not** to 'bolt on' your comments, or write a long, separate chunk of text on context and then 'go back' to the play. For example, **don't** just write:

The late sixteenth century was a time of great religious ferment in England. Under the young King Edward VI, many Catholic rituals were abolished, only to be restored when Mary became Queen in 1553. During Mary's reign, almost 300 Protestants had been burnt at the stake for their beliefs; when her half-sister Elizabeth succeeded her in 1558, it was the turn of Catholics to be hounded and priests executed, especially when Mary's husband, Philip II of Spain, declared war on England in 1588. Hamlet was also influenced by Essex's rebellion.

Do write:

Shakespeare's first audiences would have found echoes of the religious controversies of their time throughout the play. Hamlet, like Marlowe's Doctor Faustus, was a student at Wittenberg, Martin Luther's own university, and, shows a similar concern with squaring behaviour with conscience. In the spirit of restless inquiry that is typical of the time, Hamlet challenges pagan revenge morality and rejects the courtly notion of honour, the religion of fame, represented in the play by Laertes. Although he asserts the contemporary notion of the divinity of kingship, Claudius is presented as almost Machiavellian in his pragmatism, albeit with a troubled Christian conscience. Gertrude's hasty marriage to her husband's brother would remind audiences of Henry VIII's break with Rome, which arose from his conviction he had been living in sin with his brother's widow.

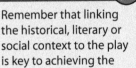

EXAMINER'S TIP ✓

Remember that linking the historical, literary or social context to the play is key to achieving the best marks for AO4.

USING CRITICAL INTERPRETATIONS AND PERSPECTIVES

THE 'MEANING' OF A TEXT

There are many viewpoints and perspectives on the 'meaning' of *Hamlet*, and examiners will be looking for evidence that you have considered a range of these. Broadly speaking, these different interpretations might relate to the following considerations:

1. CHARACTER

What **sort/type** of person Hamlet – or another character – is:

- Is Hamlet similar to later Shakespearean tragic heroes, a great man crippled by a tragic weakness of character, or is he more like Romeo, an innocent victim destroyed by the wickedness of others? What does he have in common with Hieronimo, Kyd's protagonist? Or is Hamlet unique amongst tragic **protagonists**?
- Does the character personify, symbolise or represent a specific idea or trope? (For example, the tendency to 'think too precisely' and get lost in subtle speculations?)
- Is the character modern, universal, of his/her time, historically representative? Can we see aspects of Hamlet's alienation from a corrupt society in heroic rebels in the contemporary world?

2. IDEAS AND ISSUES

What the play tells us about **particular ideas or issues** and how we can interpret these. For example:

- The importance of religious belief
- The dangers of temptation
- Definitions of madness
- Moral and social codes

3. LINKS AND CONTEXTS

To what extent the play **links with, follows or pre-echoes** other texts and/or ideas. For example:

- Its influence culturally, historically and socially (do we see echoes of the characters or genres in other texts?) How like Hamlet is Raskolnikov in Dostoyevsky's *Crime and Punishment*, and why? Does the play share features with **morality plays**?
- How its language links to other texts or modes, such as religious works, myth, legend, etc.

4. DRAMATIC STRUCTURE

How the play is **constructed** and how Shakespeare **makes** his **narrative**:

- Is its structure influenced by any particular dramatic conventions?
- What is the function of specific events, characters, theatrical devices and staging, in relation to narrative?
- What are the specific moments of tension, conflict, crisis and **denouement** – and do we agree on what they are?

CRITICAL VIEWPOINT A03

'The idea of Hamlet's confinement within a hospital-cum-prison is ever present, not just through alarm bells and security guards, but through the transformation of Polonius into a note-taking clinician. And Sheen's Hamlet is a classic Freudian case experiencing what the latest Arden edition, discussing the psychological approach to the play, neatly summarises as "fantasies concerning the need for masculine identity to free itself from the contaminated maternal body."' (Michael Billington, reviewing the 2011 performance at The Young Vic in the *Guardian*.)

5. AUDIENCE RESPONSE

How the play **works on an audience**, and whether this changes over time and in different contexts:

● Are we to empathise with, feel distance from, judge and/or evaluate the events and characters?

6. CRITICAL REACTION

And finally, how different audiences view the play: for example, different **critics over time**, or different **audiences** in **earlier or more recent years**.

WRITING ABOUT CRITICAL PERSPECTIVES

The important thing to remember is that **you** are a critic too. Your job is to evaluate what a critic or school of criticism has said about the elements above, and arrive at your own conclusions.

In essence, you need to: **consider** the views of others, **synthesise** them, then decide on **your perspective**. For example:

EXPLAIN THE VIEWPOINTS

Critical view A of Hamlet as hero:

> *Helen Gardner writes: '"Hamlet" towers above other plays of its kind through the heroism and nobility of its hero, his superior power of insight into, and reflection upon his situation, and his capacity to suffer the moral anguish which the moral responsibility brings.' Helen Gardner, "The Business of Criticism" (1960)*

Critical view B of *Hamlet* as hero:

> *Performance criticism might view Hamlet's delay as a consequence of a diseased wit, a pathological horror of sexual infidelity or an irrational hatred of women.*

THEN SYNTHESISE AND ADD YOUR PERSPECTIVE

Synthesise these views whilst adding your own:

> *The idea that Shakespeare is dramatising Hamlet's heroic struggle with conflicting notions of duty and morality as argued by Helen Gardner, could be considered persuasive. The sceptical Horatio's epitaph 'Good night, sweet Prince,/And flights of angels sing thee to thy rest', and Fortinbras's chorus-like tribute seem clear evidence for this. However, a performance in which extra textual business and theatrical effects were prominent might cause an audience to see Hamlet's behaviour differently – exaggerating his misogyny or his madness, for example, at the expense of his self-critical reflections.*
>
> *I feel that it is more satisfactory to view the play as a study of a protagonist who is troubled by very human doubts plunged into the hideous circumstances of a 'time ... out of joint' which would test anyone's resolve ....*

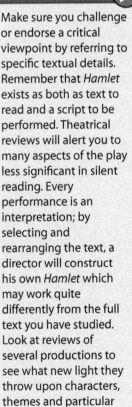

CRITICAL VIEWPOINT A03

'What struck me as strange is that in a play that deals so much in madness, either feigned or real, virtually everyone behaves throughout as if they have assumed an "antic disposition"' (Michael Billington on the 2012 production at Shakespeare's Globe in the *Guardian*.)

EXAMINER'S TIP ✓

Make sure you challenge or endorse a critical viewpoint by referring to specific textual details. Remember that *Hamlet* exists as both as text to read and a script to be performed. Theatrical reviews will alert you to many aspects of the play less significant in silent reading. Every performance is an interpretation; by selecting and rearranging the text, a director will construct his own *Hamlet* which may work quite differently from the full text you have studied. Look at reviews of several productions to see what new light they throw upon characters, themes and particular moments in the play.

ANNOTATED SAMPLE ANSWERS

Below are extracts from two sample answers to the same question at different grades. Bear in mind that these are examples only, covering all four Assessment Objectives – you will need to check the type of question and the weightings given for the four Assessment Objectives when writing your coursework essay or practising for your exam.

> Question: **How do tragic heroes respond to emotional stress in *Hamlet* and any other play you have studied?**

CANDIDATE 1

AO1 Secure focus on the question

AO2 Responds perceptively to textual detail; could also discuss the sounds of Hamlet's words here which emphasise his disgust

AO3 Shows awareness of different ways of reading Hamlet's behaviour, but references to critics could be more specific

AO1 Appropriate quotation worked into the argument

AO1 Well argued with close textual support; worth commenting upon the effect of the rhyming couplet here

AO4 Appropriate contextual detail worked into developing argument

In this essay I will look at "Hamlet" and "The Revenger's Tragedy" and contrast the way Hamlet and Vindice respond to being emotionally stressed. In Act 1 Scene 2, Hamlet is upset because his father has died suddenly but worse than that his mother has remarried very quickly to his uncle, the evil Claudius. Nobody seems to question things, we're told the court has 'freely gone/With this affair along' and this plunges Hamlet into despair because he wonders if he's mad. He's thinking about killing himself, 'self-slaughter'. We can tell he's disgusted because of the way he describes his mother 'post[ing]/With such dexterity to incestuous sheets'. This imagery makes her sound like a post horse in heat. Hamlet feels he has been made dirty by what she does, 'sullied' by it and that the world is full of corruption: 'unweeded garden' He is so stressed that he can't imagine doing anything to improve things until the Ghost's 'commandment' (1.5). What the Ghost says causes even more stress: 'O cursèd spite/That ever I was born to set it right'. The world Vindice finds himself in is also corrupt. The Duke poisoned Vindice's girlfriend because she refused to give in to his 'palsey-lust' and there is a general atmosphere of corruption. Vindice is like a vigilante, and his way to deal with emotional stress is to bypass the judges because they are corrupt under the 'royal lecher'. Bacon called revenge a 'kind of wild justice' and he was writing about the time the play was written. 'Wild justice' is what Vindice and Hamlet are after.

First I will examine Hamlet's situation. One critic said he was evil but another talked about his melancholy as perfectly understandable. I think the stress he is under is what makes him delay. Some people think he does this because he is the sort of person who can never make up his mind (like in Olivier's film). Other people argue that his delay is just a theatrical convention because if he acted immediately to kill Claudius, the play would be over. Most people think he delays because he is tackling such a difficult subject as revenge. Unlike Vindice, Hamlet is worried about whether revenge is the right thing to do.

AO1 Apt textual reference worked into argument

AO4 Contextual comment but not linked to argument

AO4 Appropriate contextual reference

AO1 Focused on the question, but rather underdeveloped conclusion

The other person in "Hamlet" who suffers emotional stress when his father dies is Laertes and if you compare the way he deals with it and Hamlet's you can see Hamlet's problem is in his conscience. Laertes says he'll 'dare damnation' and as far as he's concerned his conscience can go to 'the profoundest pit'. Hamlet though is worried about whether the Ghost is 'honest'. Laertes was spurred on by rumour, 'buzzers', and seeing mad Ophelia 'persuade' revenge. The Ghost commands Hamlet to revenge but tells him not to 'taint' his mind about his mother. Hamlet wants to save his mother more than he wants to kill Claudius because one is a positive thing but the other is negative and against the teaching of the Christian church. In those days everyone went to church every week. We know the Ghost is a confusing figure because it behaves inconsistently and Hamlet describes this with some antithesis: 'spirit of health, or goblin damned'. On the one hand he is like his father and stands for the qualities Hamlet admires, on the other he may 'be a devil' and be trying to tempt Hamlet to his destruction.

The main way Hamlet responds to emotional stress is in his soliloquies which show you how he thinks. Burbage would have shared these thoughts with the audience, not like a voice over as in Olivier's film. He tries to hammer out the truth but is so upset at times 'Fie on't' that his thinking is clouded. The verse doesn't flow smoothly, it keeps stopping and starting. This is called enjambment. In his last soliloquy, Hamlet tries to convince himself he should be like Fortinbras but he has just condemned what Fortinbras is doing, comparing it to an 'imposthume' so it's rather like his reaction to the actor: impressed at first but critical afterwards. He sounds most sincere when he tells Horatio why he loves him. Unlike all his other friends, Horatio can't be corrupted. That moment when he talks to Horatio is free of stress but most of the time people close to Hamlet cause him nothing but stress.

Interesting points but not tightly enough related to the question **AO1**

Incorrect use of literary term **AO2**

GRADE C

Comment

AO1 The essay is structured with a focused attention to the question though with unnecessary material. Quotations are well chosen if very brief and are worked appropriately into the argument.

AO2 There is some engagement with textual detail but also confusion over the technical term '**enjambment**' which detracts from the essay's progress.

AO3 The essay shows awareness of a variety of readings.

AO4 The essay makes some perceptive references to the play's historical context.

For a B grade

- A more varied way of referring to the question than simply repeating the words 'stress' and 'stressed' would help the essay to read more fluently. Words such as 'pressure', 'tension', 'distress', 'anxiety', 'grief' and 'frustration' might have been worked into a more sophisticated argument.

- This essay would be stronger if some close analysis of the language, especially the rhythms, of the **soliloquies** had been undertaken, together with more illustration of and commentary upon disease **imagery**.

- Consideration of one or two brief critical remarks might have given the student more to engage with as s/he developed a personal reading.

CANDIDATE 2

There are many ways of answering this question. The obvious one is the way that Hamlet responds to being plunged into emotional turmoil – he postpones doing anything until he can gather his thoughts. Many critics have argued that if Hamlet didn't delay, there wouldn't be a play: Shakespeare is deliberately posing a problem. **Why might a loyal son fail to do his noble but dead father's bidding?** In "The Revenger's Tragedy", Vindice's response to grief is much simpler. As his name suggests, his character is simply that of someone who responds to provocation by acting like a single-minded avenger. He delays for practical and dramatic but not for moral or psychological reasons. His distress is not complicated by conflicting emotions in the ways Hamlet's is. Both heroes are passionate men but Hamlet is much more of a thinker.

Excellent use of **rhetorical** *question* — **A01**

Whole introduction focuses on question and identifies useful ways of comparing texts — **A01**

Claudius suggests that we all fall short of what we promise to do. In testing Laertes's resolve to be a Revenge Hero, Claudius seems to be commenting upon Hamlet's 'dullness' as Hamlet and the Ghost call the Prince's lack of fire. Like Vindice, Laertes doesn't think twice about matters which we have seen making Hamlet pause and cogitate about in so many words: 'what would you undertake ... To show yourself in deed your father's son More than in words?' Laertes replies 'to cut his throat i'th'church'. Shakespeare is deliberately reminding us of the chapel scene in which Hamlet had the perfect opportunity to kill Claudius but chose not to. Vindice wouldn't understand the problem. Some critics think this delay was as Hamlet suggested: he wanted to achieve what he finally did achieve, killing Claudius only when he was 'about some act/That has no relish of salvation in't'. Dr Johnson, living at a time which shared the sixteenth century's views about punishment in the afterlife, believed Hamlet's explanation for sparing Claudius in the chapel and found it 'too horrible to read'.

Quotation would be useful here — **A02**

Well-chosen quotations and textual reference worked into argument linking both texts — **A01**

Intelligent use of critical view to explore play's historical context — **A04**

But many other critics argue that this is too complicated. Hamlet simply couldn't kill a man at prayer because he felt it was wrong. The cause of Hamlet's delay is thus most likely a basic conflict in Hamlet's mind between his duty to Old Hamlet his father and his belief in God and this causes him huge distress in the play. Hamlet's mother has morally declined from the woman she appeared to be with Old Hamlet in a 'celestial bed' to a creature that 'prey[s] on garbage'. This polarised imagery shows how Hamlet tends to think in extremes. Hamlet idealises his father in a series of classical allusions, making him sound like a god: Hyperion's curls, Jove's forehead, Mars's eye, Mercury's bearing and so on: 'a man, take him for all in all' i.e. the embodiment of perfection. His immediate response to the Ghost is to promise to be dedicated to revenge: 'I'll wipe away ...' He will replace God's sixth commandment with the Ghost's single 'commandment' (1.5.102). But the situation is even more difficult for a Christian: the fifth commandment, coming even before 'Thou shalt not kill', is to honour one's father and mother. Hamlet is being

Clearly articulated analysis of central dilemma — **A01**

Well argued, begins to explore language — **A02**

Close reading of significant detail; appropriate technical term — **A02**

Contextualises Hamlet's inner conflict — **A04**

A04 Contextualises Claudius's villainy

pulled in different, emotionally confusing, directions. Everyone in the play, except perhaps Laertes, speaks as if s/he believes in God, the afterlife and the reality of damnation. Even Claudius who is Machiavellian in many respects, has a conscience and a terror of divine judgement.

A01 Keeps question in focus

Another possible explanation (put forward by Bradley) for Hamlet's delay is that he is melancholic as a result not only of his father's death but because of his mother's sinful adultery and incest. He feels contaminated, 'sullied' by her example. This is added to when Ophelia rejects him for no good reason and joins forces with those Hamlet sees as his enemies. His two school friends betray Hamlet too. Such emotional stress might make anyone depressed and lethargic.

A03 Shows awareness of a different point of view

A01 Keeps answer rooted in the question, but could be further developed

Act V shows Hamlet having a new certainty that Claudius deserves to die: not so much for his past crimes (including his attempt on Hamlet's own life) but because of what he might do. He now sees this as his princely duty ('This is I, Hamlet the Dane') and believes it would be damnable to let Claudius live and 'come/In further evil'. None the less, he still does not act 'With fiery quickness' as Claudius, feeling threatened, does. We could say that his emotional stress has been lessened by his sense of what is right, and the play itself takes over from here. When he kills Claudius, it is more like a public execution in response to the accusations of the Queen and Laertes, than an act of private vengeance carried out to satisfy the demands of a confused and confusing Ghost. When we consider Vindice's responses to an unjust and corrupt society, we see a very different pattern and a very different emotional mix.

A01 Well-chosen quotations used to develop argument

A01 Lucid conclusion articulating informed personal response

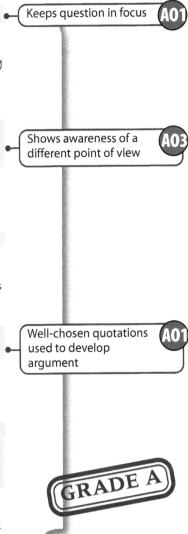

GRADE A

Comment

A01 The developing argument is cogently structured with a focused attention to the question and no extraneous material. Quotations are well chosen and are worked effectively into a convincing personal reading.

A02 There is engagement with textual detail and awareness of the role of disease **imagery** in the play.

A03 The essay explores a number of points over which there is a range of critical opinion, citing Bradley to good effect.

A04 The essay makes several perceptive references to the religious context in which the play is rooted and makes appropriate reference to **Machiavelli**.

For an A* grade

- Quotations should identify distinctive features of the play's rich poetic language rather than simply its **prose** sense, using appropriate technical terminology. A fuller discussion of the imagery of disease might have been worked into the reading of Hamlet's emotional state.

- A discussion of the variety of Hamlet's own language styles might have been used to illustrate the complexity of his response, for example the **satiric** wit in his dealings with Polonius and the stylistic differences between the **soliloquies**.

- It would have been appropriate to illustrate Vindice's frame of mind by briefly contrasting his language (not simply his behaviour) with Hamlet's.

- The complete essay would need a strong conclusion, drawing together insights into both texts.

WORKING THROUGH A TASK

Now it's your turn to work through a task on *Hamlet*. The key is to:

- Read/decode the task/question.
- Plan your points – then expand and link them.
- Draft your answer.

TASK TITLE

How far do you agree that Shakespeare presents Claudius as a capable and efficient ruler rather than as a contemptible villain?

DECODE THE QUESTION: KEY WORDS

How far do you agree ...?	= what are **my** views?
Shakespeare presents	= a reminder that this is a literary creation
capable and efficient ruler	= a man with admirable qualities
a contemptible villain	= a thoroughly wicked character

PLAN AND EXPAND

- Key aspect: evidence of Claudius being a capable and efficient ruler

POINT	POINT EXPANDED	EVIDENCE
Point a Nobody but Hamlet (and Horatio in Act V) criticises Claudius.	The court have endorsed Claudius's judgements. Polonius praises his diplomacy. He acts decisively in a crisis.	'freely gone with this affair along' 'This business is well ended.' Deals with Laertes's challenge in Act IV. Controls Hamlet's behaviour. Plots Hamlet's death.
Point b Claudius's skills in persuasive public speaking	Different aspects of this point expanded *You fill in*	Quotations 1–2 *You fill in*

- Key aspect: evidence of Claudius being a 'contemptible villain'

POINT	POINT EXPANDED	EVIDENCE
Point a *You fill in*	Different aspects of this point expanded *You fill in*	Quotations 1–2 *You fill in*
Point b *You fill in*	Different aspects of this point expanded *You fill in*	Quotations 1–2 *You fill in*
Point c *You fill in*	Different aspects of this point expanded *You fill in*	Quotations 1–2 *You fill in*

CONCLUSION

POINT	POINT EXPANDED	EVIDENCE
Key final point or overall view *You fill in*	Draw together and perhaps add a final further point to support your view *You fill in*	Final quotation to support your view *You fill in*

DEVELOP FURTHER AND DRAFT

Now look back over your draft points and:

● Add further links or connections between the points to develop them further or synthesise what has been said, for example:

> *Wilson Knight famously praised Claudius as showing 'every sign of being an excellent diplomatist and king'. He is certainly shown as being quick-thinking, resourceful and decisive, untroubled by morality. But his usurpation results ultimately in Denmark's falling into foreign hands and his confident exterior conceals a troubled mind, conscious of its criminality. His acute sense of sin rescues him from being a simple Machiavel and has tragic potential. In many ways he is a forebear of Shakespeare's tragic hero Macbeth.*

● Decide an order for your points/paragraphs – some may now be linked/connected and therefore **not** in the order of the table above.

> *The Ghost describes Claudius's 'wicked wit and gifts'. Although there is a touch of jealousy in his words, they confirm the impression we are given of this charming villain in Act I Scene 2. Claudius is bright, articulate and clear-thinking. But beneath his persona as a reasonable and sophisticated man of the world, lurks a darker, ruthlessly ambitious self. Shakespeare is fascinated by this smiling villain. In Claudius's major soliloquy (III.3) we have a glimpse of how he might have developed the King into a complex, tragic figure.*

● Now draft your essay.

Once you've written your essay, turn to page 128 for a mark scheme on this question to see how well you've done.

FURTHER QUESTIONS

1) 'Laertes represents a courtly notion of honourable behaviour which the play invites us to criticise.' How far do you agree with this statement?

2) 'Polonius is essentially a figure of fun, the straight man to Hamlet's witty observations about him and the values of a corrupt court.' How far do you agree with this idea? Is there any more to Polonius than a 'figure of fun'?

3) 'Ophelia, although presented as powerless in the first half of the play, has considerable dramatic power after the death of her father.' Discuss the ways Shakespeare presents Ophelia in the play as a whole. Do you agree that she is more powerful mad than when she is sane?

4) Examine the ways in which Shakespeare uses Horatio, Rosencrantz and Guildenstern to explore the theme of loyalty and betrayal in *Hamlet*.

5) Write an essay exploring the importance of disease imagery in *Hamlet*. How does the idea that 'something is rotten in the state of Denmark' colour the play's language?

ESSENTIAL STUDY TOOLS

FURTHER READING

Once you are thoroughly familiar with the text of *Hamlet*, you may like to broaden your understanding of its relationship to the times in which it was written, see how it resembles and differs from other plays of the period and explore some of the rich critical literature which the play has occasioned.

SENECA

Some idea of the power, dramatic style and tone of Seneca's tragedies can be gained from these modern English versions:

Ted Hughes (adapted by), *Seneca's Oedipus*, Faber and Faber, London, 1969

David R. Slavitt Johns (ed. and trans.), *Seneca: The Tragedies Volume One*, Hopkins University Press, Baltimore, 1992

T. S. Eliot, *Shakespeare and the Stoicism of Seneca*, 1927
Seneca in Elizabethan Translation, 1927
Two useful surveys of the influence of Seneca on Elizabethan drama

ELIZABETHAN AND JACOBEAN TRAGEDY

(Dates all approximate)

Christopher Marlowe, *Tamburlaine*, 1587–8

Christopher Marlowe, *The Jew of Malta*, 1589

Christopher Marlowe, *Dr Faustus*, 1589–93

Thomas Kyd, *The Spanish Tragedy*, 1582–92

Thomas Middleton (attrib.), *The Revenger's Tragedy*, 1606

William Shakespeare, *Titus Andronicus*, 1592

William Shakespeare, *Romeo and Juliet*, 1595

William Shakespeare, *Julius Caesar*, 1599

William Shakespeare, *Macbeth*, 1606

All of these plays offer fascinating contrasts with *Hamlet*, from the heavily **rhetorical** *Tamburlaine* whose language *Hamlet* at times **parodies**, to the poetic sophistication of *Macbeth*, with its very different notion of **tragedy** and its strong women characters.

Andrew Gurr, *The Shakespearean Stage 1574–1642*, Cambridge University Press, Cambridge, 1992
An excellent account of the circumstances in which Shakespeare worked

Andrew Gurr and Mariko Ichikawa, *Staging in Shakespeare's Theatres*, Oxford University Press, Oxford, 2000
Includes a chapter exploring how *Hamlet* might have been presented at the Globe in 1601

HISTORICAL CONTEXT

John Guy, *The Tudors: A Very Short Introduction*, Oxford University Press, Oxford, 2000
A brief, authoritative survey of Tudor history

James Shapiro, *1599: A Year in the Life of William Shakespeare*, HarperCollins, New York, 2005
A lively account of the circumstances in which *Hamlet* was written

SHAKESPEARE'S LANGUAGE

Caroline Spurgeon, *Shakespeare's Imagery and What it Tells Us*, Cambridge University Press, Cambridge, 1935

Wolfgang Clemen, *The Development of Shakespeare's Imagery*, Methuen, London, 1951, 1977
Groundbreaking studies of image clusters in Shakespeare's plays, particularly the disease imagery in *Hamlet*

Frank Kermode, *Shakespeare's Language*, Penguin, London, 2000
A penetrating and lively study of the rich variety of Shakespeare's language with a very useful chapter on *Hamlet*

SHAKESPEARE IN THE THEATRE AND ON THE SCREEN

John Russell Brown, *Hamlet*, Palgrave Macmillan, Basingstoke, 2006
An excellent scene-by-scene analysis of how the play works in performance

Anthony B. Dawson, *Shakespeare in Performance: Hamlet*, Manchester University Press, Manchester, 1997
An account of many productions, from the eighteenth century to modern film versions

Robert Hapgood (ed.), *Shakespeare in Production: Hamlet*, Cambridge University Press, Cambridge, 1999
Examines the way *Hamlet* has been performed, from Burbage to Branagh

Russell Jackson (ed.), *The Cambridge Companion to Shakespeare on Film*, Cambridge University Press, Cambridge, 2000
Discusses many film versions of *Hamlet*

AN INTRODUCTION TO *HAMLET* CRITICISM

A. C. Bradley, *Shakespearean Tragedy: Lectures on Hamlet, Othello, King Lear and Macbeth*, Macmillan, London, 1904
The most influential study of Hamlet's character

Martin Coyle (ed.), *New Casebooks: Hamlet*, Macmillan, Basingstoke, 1992
Very useful anthologies of *Hamlet* criticism from the eighteenth to the twentieth century, exploring many different critical methodologies, from character analysis to close reading, feminist and new historicist approaches

John Dover Wilson, *What Happens in Hamlet*, Cambridge University Press, Cambridge, 1935
A scholarly and stimulating close reading of *Hamlet*

T. S. Eliot, *'Hamlet' in Selected Essays 1917–1932*, 2nd edn., Faber and Faber, London, 1934
A provocative essay arguing that the insubstantial presentation of Gertrude fatally flaws the play

Samuel Johnson, *Preface to Shakespeare; Notes on Hamlet*, London, 1765
Fascinating insights from one of the first editors of Shakespeare

John Jump (ed.), Shakespeare: *Hamlet (Casebook series)*, Macmillan, Basingstoke, 1968
See note on Casebook series under Martin Coyle

Eleanor Prosser, *Hamlet and Revenge*, Stanford University Press, 1967
Controversial, historically focused close reading of *Hamlet*

EDITIONS OF *HAMLET*

Harold Jenkins (ed.), *The Arden Shakespeare: Hamlet*, Methuen, London, 1982

Philip Edwards (ed.), *The New Cambridge Shakespeare: Hamlet*, Cambridge University Press, Cambridge, 2003
Authoritative critical editions with excellent introductory essays

Ann Thompson and Neil Taylor (ed.), *The Arden Shakespeare: Hamlet*, Methuen, London, 2006
Two volumes presenting the three texts of *Hamlet* (Q1, Q2, F) in a convenient form

BACKGROUND READING

John Adler (ed.), *Responses to Shakespeare*, Routledge/Thoemmes Press, 1997

Philip Armstrong, *Shakespeare in Psychoanalysis*, Routledge, London, 2001

Anna Brownell Jameson, *Characteristics of Shakespeare's Women*, 1832

Maurice Charney, *Hamlet's Fictions*, Routledge, 1998

Janette Dillon, *The Cambridge Introduction to Shakespeare's Tragedies*, Cambridge University Press, Cambridge, 2007

Fyodor Dostoyevsky, *The Devils*, 1872

Terry Eagleton, *William Shakespeare*, Wiley-Blackwell, 1986

T. S. Eliot, *On Poetry and Poets*, Faber and Faber, London, 1957

David Farley-Hills, *Critical Responses to Hamlet 1600–1900* v.4, AMS Press, 2004

Marilyn French, *Shakespeare's Division of Experience*, Summit. Books, New York, 1981

Stephan Greenblatt, *Hamlet in Purgatory*, Princeton University Press, 2001

Robert Hapgood (ed.), *Shakespeare in Production*, Cambridge University Press, Cambridge, 1999

Michael Hattaway, Hamlet: *The Critics Debate*, Palgrave Macmillan, 1987

Howard and Shershow, *Marxist Shakespeares*, Routledge, London, 2001

Lisa Jardine, *Reading Shakespeare Historically*, Routledge, London, 1996

Samuel Johnson, *Notes on the Plays*, 1765

Samuel Johnson, *Preface to Shakespeare; Notes on Hamlet*, 1765

John J. Joughin (ed.), *Philosophical Shakespeares*, Routledge London, 2000

James Joyce, Ulysses, *Shakespeare and Company*, Paris, 1922

Victor Kiernan, *Eight Tragedies of Shakespeare, A Marxist Study*, Verso, London, 1996

Walter N. King, *Hamlet's Search for Meaning*, University of Georgia Press, 1982

Wilson Knight, 'The Embassy of Death' in *The Wheel of Fire*, Oxford University Press, 1930, 1949

L. C. Knights, *Some Shakespearean Themes and an Approach to Hamlet*, Chatto, London, 1960

Jan Kott, *Shakespeare Our Contemporary*, Panstwowe Wydawnictwo Naukowe, Warsaw, 1964

Charles Lamb, *The Tragedies of Shakespeare*, 1818

Peter Mercer, *Hamlet and the Acting of Revenge*, University of Iowa Press, Iowa City, 1987

Michael Pennington, *Hamlet, A User's Guide*, Nick Hern, London, 1996

William Richardson, *Some of Shakespeare's Remarkable Characters*, 1783

Robert Shaughnessy (ed.), *New Casebooks: Shakespeare on Film*, Palgrave Macmillan, Basingstoke, 1998

Mark Thornton Burnett and John Manning (eds.), *New Essays on Hamlet*, AMS, New York, 1994

Herman Ulrici, *Shakespeare's Dramatic Art*, 1839

Stanley Wells, *Shakespeare in the Theatre, An Anthology of Criticism*, Oxford University Press, Oxford, 1997

John Willett (tr.), *Brecht on Theatre*, Methuen, London, 1964

Susan Zimmerman (ed.), *New Casebooks, Shakespeare's Tragedies*, Palgrave Macmillan, 1998

LITERARY TERMS

Alliteration an intensifying effect where a consonant sound is repeated, usually on a stressed syllable: 'drains his draughts of Rhenish down' (I.4.10)

Allusion (v. allude) a reference, e.g. to other works of art or events. There are allusions to Shakespeare's earlier tragedy *Julius Caesar* in *Hamlet* I.1.113–125 and III.2.91

Antagonist the principal opponent of the the **protagonist**

Anthology a collection of poems and/or prose extracts, bringing together the best examples of various styles of writing. Gertrude's description of Ophelia's drowning (IV.7.166–183) is a natural 'anthology piece', enjoyed by many people who do not know the rest of *Hamlet*

Antithesis setting one idea in a logical, balanced way against another:

with mirth in funeral and with dirge in marriage (I.2.12)

Aside a common dramatic convention in which a character speaks in such a way that some of the characters on stage do not hear what is said, while others do. It may also be a direct address to the audience, revealing the character's views, thoughts, motives and intentions

Assonance intensification achieved by repeating vowel sounds:

There is a willow grows aslant a brook
That shows his hoar leaves in the glassy stream. (IV.7.167–8)

Blank verse verse written in lines of unrhymed iambic pentameter. An unstressed syllable followed by a stressed syllable make up one iamb; five iambs in a line make iambic pentameter:

When **he** is **drunk** as**leep**, or **in** his **rage** (III.3.90)

Rigid iambic pentameter has stresses falling regularly on the even syllables, each line of verse consisting of a sentence or a self -contained clause: 'Take **thy** fair **hour Laertes**, **time** be **thine**,/And **thy** best **gra**ces **spend** it **at** thy **will**.' (I.2.62–3)

But in *Hamlet* Shakespeare's verse is becoming increasingly flexible; the underlying pentameter pulse is always felt but the words sound more like spontaneous speech. Stresses are not invariably regular; there are pauses within a line (**caesurae**) and ideas spill over from one line into the next (**enjambment**):

is't not perfect conscience
To quit him with this arm? And is't not to be damned
To let this canker of our nature come
In further evil? (V.2.67–70)

Cadence (adj. **cadential**) a sense of closure (see **interrupted cadence**). Often Shakespeare will bring a scene crisply to an end with a rhyming couplet

Caesura A pause in the middle of a line of verse, usually where a sentence ends:

Yet here Laertes? Aboard, aboard for shame! (I.3.55)

Characterisation the art of creating sharply differentiated personalities. Shakespeare's major characters have distinctive ways of thinking and speaking. They cannot be mistaken for one another

Chorus (choric utterance) a chorus voices impersonal, general observations, which are usually reliable and objective. At times, characters in *Hamlet* adopt a choric dramatic function as when Marcellus says: 'Something is rotten in the state of Denmark' (I.4.90).

Colloquial speech everyday, informal chat such as the gravediggers use in Act V Scene1

Couplet a pair of consecutive lines of poetry which rhyme:

The time is out of joint: O cursèd spite,
That ever I was born to set it right. – (I.5.189–90)

Critique A rigorous appraisal of a work of literature, a literary convention, a political idea or a state of affairs, etc

Denouement the climax of a story, the moment when the whole plot is finally revealed (from the French for 'untying a knot')

Dialogue conversation between characters in a play

Diction the sorts of words a writer uses in particular situations. In *Hamlet*, Shakespeare gives Osric and the gravediggers, for example, very different vocabularies

Dramatic function the role a character performs in a play. Horatio's dramatic function is to provide a touchstone of what the audience/reader should believe. Horatio establishes the 'reality' of the Ghost and provides reliable descriptions of its appearance and behaviour. He does not confirm that Claudius revealed his guilt whilst watching *The Mousetrap*

Dramatic irony this occurs when what a character says means much more than he or she realises. Often the audience has information the speaker lacks. The effect is usually to make the speaker seem foolish and/or vulnerable. Polonius talking about being killed when he played Julius Caesar (III.2.91–2) anticipates his murder a few minutes later. The moment is doubly ironic since the same actor in Shakespeare's company played Caesar and Polonius

Dramaturgical another word for 'dramatic' when talking about plays

Dumbshow a mime prefiguring the action of the play

End-stopped an end-stopped line of verse is one in which the end of the line coincides with the conclusion of a sentence, or the strongly marked end of a phrase, signalled by punctuation (see **blank verse**)

Enjambment where a sentence 'runs on' into a second or even a third line of verse (see **blank verse**)

Epic originally a long poem featuring larger than life, godlike characters. Epic **imagery** suggests things happening on a huge scale. When Horatio tells us Old Hamlet 'smote the sledded Polacks on the ice' (I.1.63) the epic image conjures up the picture of a mighty warrior destroying a fearsome army with a single blow

Epitaph verse or prose suitable for inscribing on a person's tomb: 'Good night, sweet prince,/And flights of angels sing thee to thy rest.' (V.2.338–9)

Euphemism dressing up something unpleasant or overtly sexual in an evasive commonplace. Describing sexual intercourse as 'sleeping together' or a lavatory as 'the bathroom' are examples of euphemism

Everyman a character in drama (or a novel) who represents mankind as a whole, a sympathetic figure who displays the characteristic strengths and weaknesses of humanity. The name derives from the protagonist in the mediaeval **morality play**, *Everyman*

Exposition the opening part of a play in which the main characters and their situation are introduced

Farce comic action pushed to ludicrous extremes

Feminist criticism critical approaches which focus upon how women are represented in literature and other arts

Figurative the imaginative, as opposed to the literal use of language. Claudius is literally a murderer, figuratively a cancer blighting Denmark (see **metaphor**)

Foil a contrast achieved by putting an inferior example alongside a more impressive one. Hamlet tells Laertes his own poor swordsmanship will show everybody how accomplished Laertes is: 'I'll be your foil Laertes.' (V.2.227). But in the play as a whole, Laertes acts as a foil to Hamlet. His unthinking pursuit of revenge emphasises how complex Hamlet's thinking about the matter is

Frame story coming (mostly) at the very beginning and at the very end of *Hamlet*, the story of Young Fortinbras's successful avenging of his father's defeat by Old Hamlet provides an satisfying framework to the tragedy and serves as a parallel to Hamlet's story

Freudian a way of reading human behaviour which is influenced by the psychoanalytical theories of Sigmund Freud. Freud stressed the role of subconscious sexual feelings in shaping the way people think, feel and act. Freud's disciple, Ernst Jones, suggested Hamlet had an Oedipus complex, that subconsciously he was sexually attracted to his mother and regarded his father as a hateful sexual rival. He couldn't kill Claudius because he'd done what Hamlet himself had longed to do

Hyperbole exaggeration. Laertes's hyperbole in V.1.214–21 makes him sound ridiculous, theatrical and insincere. Hamlet **parodies** his excesses

Ideology the values and beliefs which shape the way we think

Imagery pictures in words. Clusters of related images often develop a theme. *Hamlet* is pervaded by disease images such as when Hamlet describes Claudius as 'a mildewed ear' (III.4.64)

In media res when Act IV Scene 7 begins, it's as if Claudius and Laertes have been talking for some time. The scene starts 'in the middle of things'

Interlude an episode which momentarily lowers the dramatic tension, lightens the mood and serves to make the resumption of the tragedy proper feel all the more intense. In Act V Scene 2, lines 80–170, Shakespeare deliberately introduces a scene of high comedy with Osric so that the tragic **denouement** which follows makes more impact

Interrupted cadence where a scene appears to be coming to an end but is unexpectedly extended as in Act III Scene 4 (178)

Irony when what a person says is not necessarily what he or she means. Meaning is as much a matter of tone of voice as the literal sense of words. Irony can be sarcastic and funny, as when Hamlet describes Claudius and his mother as 'the good king and queen' (II.2.266) or scathing and bitter as when Hamlet tests his mother's resolution: 'Let the bloat king tempt you again to bed' (III.4.183)

Juxtaposition setting side by side contrasting characters, episodes or ideas

Lyrical song-like, melodious

Machiavellian ruthlessly pragmatic: the belief that the end justifies the means. Niccolo Machiavelli (1469–1527) was the author of *The Prince*, a hugely influential tract which recommended princes gain and maintain power by all necessary means, including the use of deceit and brute force. In Jacobean drama, the term 'Machiavel' simply meant 'cunning villain'

Melodrama a play in which people behave in an intensely emotional way which we feel to be excessive, sensational and unconvincing. Characters are sharply polarised, they are either good or bad, psychologically two-dimensional and without a rich inner life; surprising things happen in order to generate excitement rather than arising convincingly from the situation presented. Tabloid journalism often presents news in a melodramatic fashion

Memento mori the phrase means 'remember you are mortal'. In Shakespeare's time, many people hung memento mori in their homes to remind them of the brevity of human life. Paintings of skulls, wasting candles and decaying fruit remind us that human life is a brief moment compared with eternity. Act V Scene 1 is a powerful memento mori, putting Hamlet's concerns into the context of the whole of human history and emphasising that man's primary concern should be to prepare for what awaits him in 'The undiscovered country from whose bourn/No traveller returns' (III.1.79–80)

Metaphor a figurative way of comparing something to something else, for example when Hamlet describes Claudius simply as 'a paddock [toad], … a bat, a gib [cat]' (III.4.191) he is using metaphors. See **simile**

Mimetic rhythm where the movement of the verse imitates the movement being described: 'heavy-headed revel' (I.4.17) suggests swaggering, clumsy dancing

Monosyllables words consisting of single syllables: 'Now might I do it pat' (III.3.73)

Morality play in the fourteenth and fifteenth centuries, many plays were composed and performed which presented the struggle between good and evil, in Christian terms. The play's central character represented humankind whilst other characters represented aspects of temptation and encouragement in the human struggle to achieve salvation

Mystery play a dramatisation of a story from the Old or New Testament. Mystery plays evolved steadily from about the tenth century onwards. The verse tends to be rough and vigorous, but the later plays show a strong sense of character and inner-life. Mystery plays were still being performed in Shakespeare's lifetime. They were called mystery plays because each play in a cycle was performed by practitioners of a particular craft ('mystery'): carpenters usually performed the Crucifixion play

Narrative telling a story

Narrator the voice telling the story

Paradox a statement which although true appears to contradict itself: 'O limèd soul that struggling to be free/Art more engaged!' (III.3.68–9)

Parody an imitation, sometimes comic, of a dramatic or poetic style. The Pyrrhus speech (II.2.426–55) is a parody of the declamatory style of Marlowe

Pastiche writing in the style of another author. Whereas parody often makes fun of someone else's way of writing, pastiche is more like a tribute

Pastoral writing which idealises and celebrates the virtues of living in the country, free of the vices of the town. The description of Ophelia's suicide is highly decorative and stylised, its descriptions of flowers lend it a pastoral flavour; it is not a realistic account of such a death

Pathos (adj. **pathetic**) feelings of sadness, pity and compassion aroused for example by Ophelia's madness in Act IV Scene 5

Pentameter a line with five stressed syllables (see **blank verse**)

Platitude a trite, commonplace idea, a cliché: 'all that lives must die,/Passing through nature to eternity' (I.2.72–3) trivialises a profound idea by presenting it in a glib rhyming couplet

ESSENTIAL STUDY TOOLS

Prose the way we usually write and speak: in language which, unlike verse, is not rhythmically organised

Protagonist the main character, the hero of a tragedy

Psychodrama a battle for the soul between good and evil forces. Act III Scene 4 can be seen as a psychodrama in which Hamlet fights to save Gertrude from damnation by forcing her to admit her sins and repent

Pun simple wordplay, exploiting two different meanings of a word. When Hamlet says he is 'too much i'th'sun' (I.2.67), his primary meaning is that far from being in the shade, as Claudius suggests he is, he has had more than enough sunlight: he wishes he were in his grave. But 'son' and 'sun' sound the same. Hamlet is also saying that he finds Claudius's calling him his 'son' offensive. And Hamlet feels that he is 'too much' his heroic father's son to submit to Claudius

Realism writing which attempts to present the world as it is, with all its blemishes, rather than in a stylised, idealised or sentimentalised way. It may include painstaking descriptions of people and things as well as a deliberate attempt to avoid romanticising or simplifying the way the world works

Renaissance in the period during which Shakespeare was writing, education, politics and the creative arts were flourishing, steeped in the Humanism which had 'rediscovered' the sublime classical writings of Ancient Rome and to a lesser extent, Ancient Greece. Humanism celebrates the creative and intellectual potential of the individual mind: 'What a piece of work is a man! How noble in reason, how infinite in faculties' (II.2.286–7) It is a reaction to the narrow piety and pedantry of much mediaeval thinking

Revenge Tragedy see **Study focus: Revenge Tragedy** in **Part Four: Form**

Rhetoric patterned, persuasive speech, often using figures such as **antithesis** and **anaphora**

Rhyming couplet see **Couplet**

Romantic the nineteenth-century artistic movement in which the emphasis upon the imagination, fantasy and the cult of the passionate individual represented a reaction against the eighteenth century's preference for restraint and 'reasonableness'. Romantic art is distinguished by its refusal to follow conventional forms and its exploration of the interior lives of individuals. Instead of being at the centre of a community of civilised like-minded companions, Hamlet is like many Romantic heroes: an outsider, alienated from a hostile, wicked and uncomprehending world

Satire making fun of moral, social or political abuses by exaggerating or ridiculing them. Hamlet mocks Rosencrantz by calling him a 'sponge' (IV.2.12) soaking up the King's bribery. He calls Polonius a 'fishmonger' (pimp, II.2.172) for abusing his daughter

Senecan influenced by the tragedies of the Roman poet Seneca (c. 4 BC–AD 65) or in the style of the English sixteenth-century dramatists who adopted aspects of Seneca's rhetorical and bloody Revenge Tragedies

Sensationalism generating excitement by exaggerating violent, disturbing or surprising incidents whilst suppressing necessary truths such as the human cost of violence or the political agendas of those involved

Set piece a self-contained episode which demonstrates the playwright's skill. Hamlet contains a large number of magnificent set pieces, including the Ghost's account of his sufferings (Act I Scene 5), Polonius's advice to his son (Act I Scene 3), the First Player's Pyrrhus speech (Act II Scene 2) and the soliloquies of Hamlet and Claudius

Sibilants hissing syllables: 'speed … dexterity … incestuous sheets' (I.2.156–7)

Simile a figurative way of comparing something to something else using 'like' or 'as', for example 'like a man to double business bound' (III.3.41). See **metaphor**

Soliloquy a speech in which, alone on stage, a character explores his or her innermost thoughts and feelings. At the Globe, such deliberations would be shared with the audience standing on three sides of the actor and close to him. Modern productions often present soliloquies like cinematic voice overs

Specious reasoning false reasoning, usually designed to deceive

Staccato usually rapid, crisply enunciated, clipped speech: 'a little more than kin, and less than kind' (I.2.65)

Stichomythia a passage of verse in which two characters speak alternate lines, usually rapidly and generating excitement:

Hamlet	Hamlet, thou hast thy father much offended.
Gertrude	Mother, you have my father much offended.
Hamlet	Come, come, you answer with an idle tongue.
Gertrude	Go, go, you answer with a wicked tongue. (III.4.9–12)

Subversion undermining the authority of a character, an idea or a convention, for example, by making it seem inadequate, absurd or meaningless

Tableau the positioning of characters on stage, involving, sometimes, the use of props, to create a picture which makes an immediate impact upon the audience. Seeing Hamlet holding the skull of Yorrick is as important a part of the theatrical effect as what he says

Tautology saying the same thing twice, unnecessarily, tediously: 'Thus it remains, and the remainder thus.' (II.2.104). The pompous Polonius tries to create the impression that what he is saying is important by repeating it

Tragedy whereas a comedy ends happily, often in marriage(s), a tragedy ends badly, usually with the death of the hero and often of other people too. At the end of a tragedy we feel a sense of sadness and waste. Shakespeare's early tragedy *Romeo and Juliet* presents the young lovers as innocent victims fatally caught up in the struggle between their families. In *Macbeth*, one of Shakespeare's much later tragedies, the hero's military prowess is compromised by his 'vaulting ambition': the hero is clearly to blame for his downfall. In *Julius Caesar* and *Hamlet*, the central protagonist is less obviously to blame. The circumstances in which he finds himself make it almost impossible for him to succeed. He is more like an innocent victim than a fatally flawed character

Trisyllable a word of three syllables, e.g. tormenting, distracted, remember

Word play Shakespeare loves exploring the ambiguity of words and phrases. For example, Hamlet and the gravedigger have fun with puns

TIMELINE

WORLD EVENTS	SHAKESPEARE'S LIFE (DATES FOR PLAYS ARE APPROXIMATE)	LITERATURE AND THE ARTS
1492 Columbus sails to America		**c.1215** Saxo Grammaticus, *Gesta Danorum*
1517 Luther's *95 Theses* posted at Wittenburg		
1530 Universities declare it to be against divine law for a man to marry his brother's widow		**1557** Surry's translation of *Æneid* into blank verse
1534 Henry VIII breaks with Rome and declares himself head of the Church of England	**1564** Birth of Shakespeare	**1559 onwards** Senecan plays performed in universities and Inns of Court
		1564 Birth of Marlowe
1543 Copernicus argues that the Sun, not the Earth, is the centre of the universe		**1566–83** Belleforest, *Histoires tragiques*
		1580 Montaigne, *Essais*
1558 Elizabeth's accession to the throne		**c.1585** Leicester's Men perform at Elsinore
1570 Pope excommunicates Elizabeth		**1587** Marlowe's *Tamburlaine the Great* performed by The Admiral's Men
1577–80 Drake's circumnavigation of the world		**c.1588** Kyd, *The Spanish Tragedy*
1587 Mary Queen of Scots implicated in plot against Elizabeth and executed	**c.1590–2** Writes for Pembroke's Men Plays include *Titus Andronicus*	**c.1588** Early *Hamlet* play, probably by Kyd
1588 Defeat of the Spanish Armada	**1593** Writes *Lucrece, Venus & Adonis*	**1592** Marlowe, *Dr Faustus*
1593 Plague temporarily closes theatres	**1593–1603** Writes the *Sonnets*	**1593** Marlowe murdered, aged twenty-nine
		1594 Formation of The Lord Chamberlain's Men, including Kempe, Burbage and Shakespeare as shareholders performing at The Theatre Kyd dies, aged thirty-five
	1595 *Romeo and Juliet*	**1596** The Lord Chamberlain's Men touring
	1596 Shakespeare's son, Hamnet, dies, aged eleven	
1597 *The Isle of Dogs* scandal at the Rose Theatre		**1597** The Lord Chamberlain's Men move to The Curtain
		1598 The Lord Chamberlain's Men perform Jonson's *Every Man In His Humour*
1599 Earl of Essex leaves for Irish expedition	**1599** *Henry V, Julius Caesar, As You Like It*	**1599** Kempe (clown) leaves The Lord Chamberlain's Men Globe Theatre, owned by The Lord Chamberlain's Men, opens on Bankside
1601 Essex's rebellion and execution	**1600** Shakespeare's *Hamlet* probably first performed	**1600** Children's companies active at St Paul's and Blackfriars
1603 Death of Elizabeth, accession of James I	**1603** Publication of Q1 text of *Hamlet*	**1603** Kempe dies in poverty Publication of Florio's translation of Montaigne's *Essais*
	1604 *Othello*	**1604** The Lord Chamberlain's Men become The King's Men
1605 Guy Fawkes's plot to blow up parliament	**1605** *King Lear* Publication of Q2 text of *Hamlet*	
	1606 *Macbeth*	**1606** *attrib.* Middleton, *The Revenger's Tragedy*
	1608 *Coriolanus*	**1609** The Lord Chamberlain's Men develop Blackfriars Theatre for winter performances
1611 Publication of *King James's Bible*		**1614** Globe rebuilt following disastrous fire
	1616 Dies, aged fifty-two	**1623** Publication of the First Folio

REVISION FOCUS TASK ANSWERS

TASK 1

Polonius is a shrewd and caring father to his children.

- Polonius has commercial instincts; he sees his children as investments to be shrewdly managed and controlled. The business language he uses shows this.
- He shows little loving care for them; he expects obedience, does little to earn their respect. He is happy to spy on them and use them, ignoring their feelings.
- Polonius has a cynical view of love and low expectations of his children.
- Polonius sees his duty to the King overriding any family considerations.
- Polonius's children do not question or defy his authority; when he dies, they are devastated.

Hamlet's mind is perplexed by his circumstances.

- Grief for his father's sudden death is complicated by his negative reaction to his mother's marriage and instinctive hatred of the hypocritical Claudius.
- His situation is complicated by the Ghost's commandment. The moral ambiguity of the call to revenge perplexes Hamlet throughout the play.
- A further complication is Ophelia's perplexing rejection of him.
- Nevertheless, Hamlet decides to feign madness in order to give himself time to clarify his thinking.
- His wit, rather than 'diseased', remains razor-sharp.

TASK 2

Claudius's self-awareness makes him more like a tragic hero than a villain.

- In his **aside** (III.1.50–4) and his agonised soliloquy (III.3) we see a more complex character than is revealed elsewhere: a man struggling with his sense of guilt.
- However, these moments of insight do not control his behaviour; he is unscrupulous in plotting Hamlet's death; he warns but does not save the Queen.
- Although he is much more than a simple villain, apart from this moment of self-knowledge, there is nothing heroic about him. He dies without arousing feelings of pity in the audience

Gertrude is not developed as a dynamic character.

- Gertrude is given little stage time in which to develop. She has no major soliloquy so we judge her mostly by her behaviour.
- The closet scene unsettles her complacency. She admits her guilt and, shocked by discovering Old Hamlet was murdered, switches her loyalty from Claudius to Hamlet.
- She dies a victim of Claudius's treachery; at the end of the play we feel a pity for her which we did not feel at the beginning.

TASK 4

Claudius is at his best in an emergency.

- Isolated, with nothing but his wits and Gertrude's support to save him from Laertes's insurrection, Claudius acts with customary guile and hypocrisy.
- He cites the divinity of Kingship before which 'treason can but peep ... Acts little of his will' (IV.5.125–6) as all the protection he needs even though he himself murdered the King, his brother.
- In **Machiavellian** terms, Claudius excels; as a human being, he is morally corrupt.

Laertes is no match for the sophisticated and cunning King.

- Although Laertes insists on how important his honour is and that he'll not be 'juggled with' (IV.5.130), the King has no difficulty recruiting him as Hamlet's assassin.
- Laertes boldly discounts the scruples which we saw restrain Hamlet's revenge: 'Conscience and grace to the profoundest pit!/I dare damnation .../... both the worlds I give to negligence, /Let come what comes, only I'll be revenged/Most thoroughly for my father.' (IV.5.132–6). But rather than make him sound decisive and fearless, his words reveal him as rash and unsophisticated.
- Even Claudius is taken aback by Laertes being prepared to 'cut [Hamlet's] throat i'th'church' (IV.7 125). He sees Laertes as a poseur, wittily discounting his rebellion as 'giant-like' (IV.5.122).

TASK 4

The Hamlet Shakespeare presents in Act V is in many ways a different man from the Hamlet we saw earlier in the play.

- Hamlet has no soliloquies in Act V; he is able to share his most intimate thoughts with Horatio.
- He is no longer confused by the the Ghost's 'commandment' (I.5.102); he sees it as his duty, 'perfect conscience' (V.2.67), to kill Claudius, and damnable to let him live and further infect the country.
- There is a new philosophic strength and simplicity in Hamlet's expression; his faith in God is now a positive support rather than something which plunges him into moral confusion.
- He is still witty and intellectually curious: the exchanges with Horatio, the gravedigger and Osric recall the Hamlet of earlier episodes with Rosencrantz and Guildenstern and Polonius.
- At the end of the play, it is no longer Hamlet but Claudius who is isolated; the dying words of Laertes and the Queen distance them from the wicked King.

Hamlet is a play in which Shakespeare satirises the misuse of language.

- The play presents the abuse of language as characteristic of dishonesty.
- In the graveyard, Hamlet is taken to task for not using language precisely enough. This is a humorous comment upon his own demand that language be used responsibly.
- Claudius, Gertrude, Ophelia, Polonius, Laertes and Osric all misuse English in different ways in order to deceive. Hamlet parodies many of their deceptions. Horatio's honesty serves as a dramatic contrast to their ornate dishonesty.

TASK 5

Denmark is a place where love has been devalued.

- The love between Hamlet and Horatio and the affection Old Hamlet feels for his disloyal wife represent positive loving relationships which contrast with most others in the play.
- Gertrude's adultery and incest give rise to the stream of disease **imagery** which colours the play. Hamlet feels the world is populated by things 'rank and gross in nature' (I.2.136). Love has been replaced by lust.
- Hamlet's love for Ophelia is not returned; she betrays him to his enemies.

- Rosencrantz and Guildenstern, Hamlet's old friends, also sell themselves to the King.
- Polonius sees his children as valuable property to be preserved for investment. He shows little fatherly love for them beyond giving Laertes a list of sensible rules to follow. Hamlet sees Polonius as a bawd prostituting his daughter.
- The play ends not with casual slaughter but with Horatio's loving farewell to his friend. It sounds a positive note in a world of devalued love.

Hamlet is a play in which characters constantly betray each other.

- Horatio's loyalty to Hamlet is contrasted throughout the play with the treachery of others.
- Claudius murders his own brother; Gertrude commits adultery, betraying the husband who loves her even after his gruesome death.
- Despite Hamlet's evident sincerity, Ophelia rejects his love in obedience to her father, something very unusual in Shakespearean daughters. She allows herself to be used in spying on Hamlet.
- Rosencrantz and Guildenstern sell their old friend to the King.
- Laertes is corrupted by Claudius into deceit against the man he murders in 'a brother's wager' (V.2.225).

MARK SCHEME

Use this page to assess your answer to the Worked task, provided on pages 118–19.

Aiming for an A grade? Fulfil all the criteria below and your answer should hit the mark.*

> **How far do you agree that Shakespeare presents Claudius as a capable and efficient ruler rather than as a contemptible villain?**

ASSESSMENT OBJECTIVES	MEANING
AO1 Articulate creative, informed and relevant responses to literary texts, using appropriate terminology and concepts, and coherent, accurate written expression.	• You make a range of clear, relevant points about Claudius and how he is presented by Shakespeare. • You write a balanced essay covering both positions, i.e. that he can be seen as capable and efficient but also as a contemptible villain. • You use a range of literary terms correctly, e.g. **antagonist**, **antithesis**, **Machiavellian**, **soliloquy**. • You write a clear introduction, outlining your thesis, and provide a clear conclusion. • You signpost and link your ideas.
AO2 Demonstrate detailed critical understanding in analysing the ways in which structure, form and language shape meanings in literary texts.	• You explain the techniques Shakespeare uses to present the character of Claudius at different moments and link them to main themes of the play. • You may discuss, for example, the way that Claudius ingratiates himself with the Court in Act I Scene 2 by examining features of his **rhetoric** (see extended commentary on pages 17–18) and manages public opinion after *The Mousetrap*. You may like to explore the way he corrupts Laertes in Act IV Scene 7. • You explain in detail how your examples affect meaning, e.g. you may wish to examine how the notion of himself as a 'reasonable' man which Claudius projects in Act 1 Scene 2 conflicts with what the audience learns about his character as revealed in his soliloquy in Act III Scene 3. • You may like to explore how Claudius's aside in Act III Scene 1 (lines 49–54) undermines the impression which has been built up of his complacency.
AO3 Explore connections and comparisons between different literary texts, informed by interpretations of other readers.	• You might look at the very different ways, for example, L. C. Knights and G. Wilson Knight 'read' Claudius's character. • You may like to compare the presentation of Claudius in *Hamlet* with Shakespeare's presentation of Macbeth, especially the idea of 'vaulting ambition' as a tragic flaw. • You assert your own independent reading clearly, supported by brief textual references.
AO4 Demonstrate understanding of the significance and influence of the contexts in which literary texts are written and received.	You explain how relevant aspects of social, literary and historical contexts of *Hamlet* are significant when interpreting the character of Claudius. For example, you may discuss: • Literary context: comment upon the ways Claudius's pragmatism recalls the teaching of Machiavelli in *The Prince*, e.g. by ignoring the Ten Commandments. • Historical context: Claudius's political skills belong to a modern, very different world from his brother's medieval concept of chivalry. • Social context: corruption at Claudius's court could be seen as symptomatic of a more general decline in manners in Shakespeare's day.

* This mark scheme gives you a broad indication of attainment, but check the specific mark scheme for your paper/task to ensure you know what to focus on.